IMAGES
*of Rail*

# Caltrain and the Peninsula Commute Service

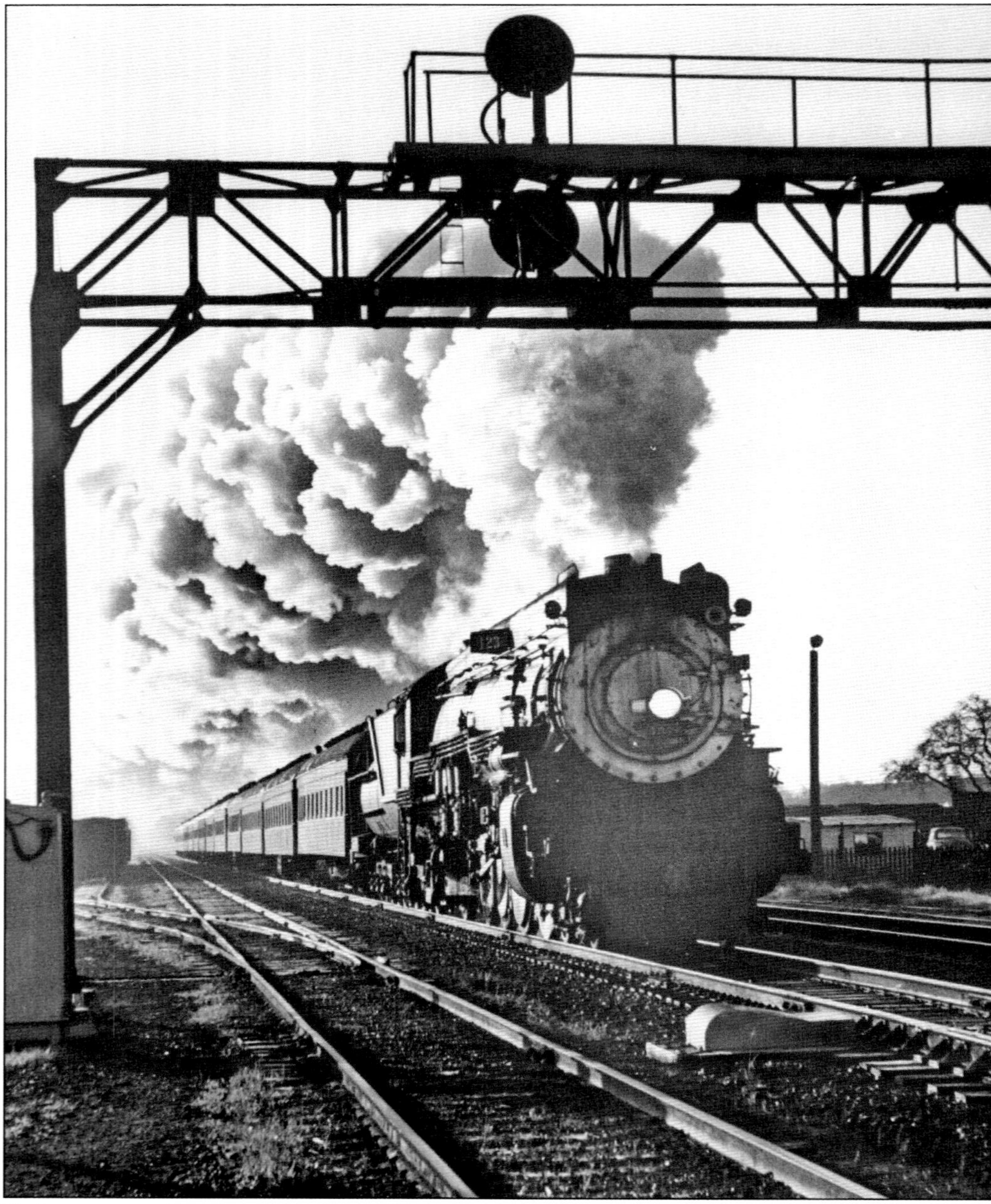

Early-morning Southern Pacific commute train No. 123, pulling 12 cars, speeds toward San Francisco with its exhaust dramatically etched against the cold sky. Taken south of Redwood City near the interlocking tower, this March 22, 1954, photograph showcases a 4300 series 4-8-4 locomotive on the head end. (Reg McGovern.)

**On the Cover:** Over decades of rail service, this October 19, 1953, scene has been repeated as generations of passengers board the railroad, known first as the San Francisco & San Jose Railroad, then the Southern Pacific, and finally, Caltrain. These commuters are boarding a steam train in Redwood City to San Francisco. (Reg McGovern.)

IMAGES
*of Rail*

# CALTRAIN AND THE PENINSULA COMMUTE SERVICE

Janet McGovern

ARCADIA
PUBLISHING

ISBN 978-0-7385-7622-0

Published by Arcadia Publishing
Charleston, South Carolina

Printed in the United States of America

Library of Congress Control Number: 2011927874

For all general information, please contact Arcadia Publishing:
Telephone 843-853-2070
Fax 843-853-0044
E-mail sales@arcadiapublishing.com
For customer service and orders:
Toll-Free 1-888-313-2665

Visit us on the Internet at www.arcadiapublishing.com

*To my husband, Reg McGovern, who patiently took me on countless train rides before I learned to love trains, too; and to Bruce Shelton and Arthur Lloyd, for generously opening doors and their knowledge of Caltrain history for this book*

# Contents

# Acknowledgments

I wish to thank the many contributors identified in this book who shared photographs, collections, memories, and insights about this railroad. In addition, I am particularly grateful for the generous editorial assistance of Henry E. Bender Jr., whose second railroad book—about Southern Pacific depots—is to be published soon; and to Arthur Lloyd, Steve Miller, Eric Schatmeier, Bruce Shelton, and Greg Welker for sharing their knowledge and expertise. I would also like to thank the following individuals and organizations: Brian Adams, Ed Adams, John Bromley, Vern Bruce and the Millbrae Train Museum, Caltrain, Bob Castiglione, Don Douglas, Rita Haskin, Kevin Hecteman, Bill Kepner, Anna Massolo and the Millbrae Historical Society, Doug Gross and Joe Hoffman of the South Bay Historical Railroad Society, John Poultney, Cara Randall, John R. Signor, Mark Simon, Dave Stanley, Al Sturken, Stu Swiedler, and Nick and Betty Veronico. Readers who wish to delve deeper into the history of Caltrain and its predecessors are encouraged to read Mark Duncan's excellent history and extensive bibliography at www.askmar.com/Railroad/rail.html, where links to other histories are available as well.

Henry Bender, Dana Dillard, Tom Gray, Reg McGovern, and Greg Welker contributed both photographs they took, as well as items from their collections, which are differentiated accordingly in the photograph credits.

Photograph credit key:
Peninsula Corridor Joint Powers Board: Caltrain
San Mateo County Transit District: SamTrans
South Bay Historical Railroad Society, Inc.: SBHRS

# Introduction

Not long after California became a state in 1850, the first attempt was made to initiate a railroad between San Francisco and San Jose, which was briefly the state capital. Steamboats required five hours to get from San Francisco to Alviso, where travelers had to board stages for the last leg of the trip. Proponents argued that a railroad down the Peninsula would increase population and land values, reduce spoilage and freight costs for farm products, and provide a potential link to the coming transcontinental railroad. After three unsuccessful attempts by prior companies and entrepreneurs, on August 18, 1860, the San Francisco & San Jose Railroad (SF&SJ) was incorporated. To overcome some of the financial problems encountered with earlier companies, the state legislature allowed the three counties through which the railroad was to pass to vote on stock subscription bonds. In a partnership that was to be repeated more than a century later, citizens of San Francisco, San Mateo and Santa Clara Counties got behind the venture. The counties voted to buy $600,000 of the $2 million in stock available for purchase.

Ground-breaking took place at San Francisquito Creek near the landmark El Palo Alto coast redwood, and construction began on July 15, 1861, with more than 300 men laboring at five work camps. When the first section of the line opened between San Francisco and Menlo Park on October 17, 1863, an inaugural train ran from the terminal at about Eighteenth and Valencia Streets to Mayfield (now Palo Alto), turning back for a sumptuous picnic at Menlo Park. The second part of the nearly 50-mile line to San Jose was finished on January 16, 1864. When 2,000 people wanted to ride to San Jose for the celebration, they had to pile into cattle cars and boxcars when there were not enough passenger cars. A 36-gun salute greeted the arrival of not one but two trains, with a combined total of 29 cars jammed with excited passengers as they pulled into the new depot on San Pedro Street. This 19th-century version of the "Baby Bullet" cut an eight-hour steamboat and stagecoach trip down to 3.5 hours by rail and the fare from $30 to less than $3. No wonder the celebration lasted for days.

Meanwhile, construction of a transcontinental railroad authorized by Congress was under way, and the San Francisco-to-San Jose segment was seen as a possible western link, reaching all the way to the Missouri. In 1869, the fledgling Southern Pacific Railroad extended the line from San Jose to Gilroy, and in 1870, the SF&SJ was absorbed into the Southern Pacific Railroad of California. In the early years, passenger rail service enabled wealthy San Franciscans to establish splendid estates in the pastoral Peninsula setting for weekend and summer retreats. Farmers could transport goods such as hay, fruit, barley, and potatoes by rail as well, from freight sheds at many stations.

When the rail line opened, many of the pioneer stations were merely "flag stops" with or without shelters, but depots were soon put up at San Mateo, Belmont, Menlo Park, Mayfield, and San Jose. In San Francisco, meanwhile, tracks were soon extended from Twenty-fifth and Valencia Streets, along Harrison Street and then, curving eastward, to Fourth and Brannan Streets, where a new passenger and freight station was established. The SF&SJ had also purchased land at Fourth and Townsend Streets for a terminal, but the property was underwater and awaited bay reclamation before it could be developed for use. Engineers had foreseen that the original San Francisco alignment, through the Mission District and on to San Bruno Mountain, would be problematic, and early operations on the steep single-track line vindicated this assessment. Helper engines were required to get longer trains over the grade of the Bernal Cut and on to the Ocean View summit.

It was not until December 1907, when the 9.81-mile Bayshore Cutoff opened for service, bringing the rail line closer to the Bay, that the tortuous uphill climb was eliminated. One of the most expensive railroad projects to that time, the cutoff required the construction of five tunnels and a double-track line. It cost almost $1 million a mile and is the alignment that remains in use today. That the three-year project was completed was in large part owing to SP president E.H. Harriman, whose task was vastly complicated by the San Francisco earthquake in 1906. *Southern Pacific Bulletin's* April 1956 issue is both a riveting and remarkable account of corporate responsibility at a time when the city was under martial law, and the railroad itself was reeling. The quake and fire destroyed SP's record storage building at Fourth and Townsend Streets and came perilously close to the rail station and freight sheds in the China Basin area. From his office in New York, Harriman telegraphed instructions to put the railroad at the service of Gen. Frederick Funston, and then steamed across country by special train to personally assist. Staggered by the advancing fire and devastation, homeless San Franciscans camped in Golden Gate Park or on the streets. SP's response was heroic. Freight sheds had been saved, and stored food was distributed to a hungry city. In addition to evacuating an estimated 224,000 passengers by train and ferry boat at no charge, SP donated $200,000 for the relief effort.

The completion of the Bayshore Cutoff the following year cut travel time on the rail line by 17 minutes and vastly improved efficiency. Later, with a reduction in fares and the subdivision of large estates, working people could afford homes on the Peninsula and to take the train to work. Early real estate developers promoted what today is called "transit-oriented development," advertising the ease and convenience of the train. For the SP, it was a time of expansion. A Mission-style "temporary" terminal was built at Third and Townsend Streets for the 1915 Panama-Pacific International Exhibition, and the SP's general office building on Market Street became the largest office building in the West when it opened in 1917. Train frequency gradually increased and by 1925, all of 34 trains were running daily, and stations and rolling stock were upgraded. Freight traffic centered at the Bayshore Yard was booming too.

Until the 1930s, the Bayshore Highway consisted of two lanes of traffic with a middle lane for passing and was not completed to Santa Clara. San Mateo County residents had additional transit options in the Market Street Railway, while the Peninsular Railway connected Santa Clara County communities. At the San Francisco terminal, travelers could board the glamorous *Del Monte* and the *Lark* to far-flung destinations. For decades, the *Suntan Specials* carried weekenders to Santa Cruz. Its corporate headquarters in San Francisco, the railroad was an important Bay Area employer, and workers got together after-hours for social, sports, theatrical and community clubs, and organizations. World War II's impact on the SP was profound. Skilled employees departed for the front, and women filled vacant jobs. SP transported members of the military along the Peninsula corridor and ran extra trains to Camp Roberts and Fort Ord. After the war, veterans returned as commuters, and ridership remained robust through the 1950s. In the postwar period, businessmen piled onto suburban coaches to get to work, reading the newspaper, playing cards, or smoking. They even formed a commuters' club to socialize, with SP employees among the members. But the postwar construction and expansion of freeways proved a formidable competitor to the Peninsula Commute Service (PCS). With declining ridership, SP began to argue that passenger service was a money-loser and that the company should not be compelled to operate it. Critics contended ridership erosion was the result of inadequate investment and lack of commitment to the service. By the 1970s, SP petitioned state and federal authorities to be allowed to discontinue passenger service. A 1976 SP offer to set up a vanpool program for the remaining weekday riders, with up to 1,000 vans to get it started, was greeted with derision from local officials, passengers, and rail fans.

In 1978, facing the prospect of an end to passenger rail service, the San Mateo and Santa Clara County transit agencies decided to purchase bulk tickets and resell them to riders at a 30-percent discount. The plan worked at shoring up ridership. The State Legislature authorized the Department of Transportation to negotiate with SP to continue the service. In June 1980, CalTrans signed a 10-year "purchase of service" agreement with SP that allowed for a first public subsidy. SP crews and management remained in place, but overall responsibility for the railroad shifted to CalTrans. Appropriately, the railroad had a new name—*CalTrain*. The CalTrans era, which lasted 12 years, ushered in a period of station improvements, restoration of historic properties, new schedules to serve the growing "reverse commute" market, and new rail equipment with the CalTrain "brand."

Later legislation called for CalTrans to assign the operating agreement to a local entity by July 1, 1992. The three partner agencies in the Peninsula Corridor Joint Powers Board—the San Francisco Municipal Railway, the San Mateo County Transit District, and the Santa Clara County Transit Agency—were waiting in the wings for the handoff. The three-county alliance had effectively come full circle from those formative days. With $124 million in Proposition 116 funds, the JPB assembled the $220 million to purchase the right-of-way. On July 1, 1992, Amtrak became the new contractor, and for the first time in well over 100 years, SP neither owned nor operated PCS trains. In an inaugural reminiscent of that first ride in 1864, excited crowds turned out from San Francisco to the new southernmost station in Gilroy to celebrate the dawn of a new day.

Building upon the foundation of Caltrans's capital improvements and vision for a new Caltrain, a railroading renaissance ensued over the next two decades, with millions of dollars invested in tracks, signal systems, station and parking upgrades, and equipment. If an image as a lumbering relic had hobbled Caltrain, it was swept aside by the introduction of sleek new Baby Bullet express trains. Light rail connections in three cities and sports facilities in walking distance of the San Francisco and San Jose stations opened new vistas. Ridership broke records year after year. Long-term goals, including electrification and the extension of the rail line to downtown San Francisco, and service across the old Dumbarton rail bridge, gained traction. The California High Speed Rail Project proposed the Caltrain corridor as a key link.

The euphoria over the "new Caltrain" may have obscured but has never erased the problem that SP had identified: how to cover the cost of operating service. Caltrain lacks its own dedicated funding source and relies on contributions from the three partner transit agencies. The annual struggle to cobble together the local subsidy came to a crisis in 2011, when draconian service cuts and station closures were proposed—and held at bay. The railroad known today as Caltrain has rolled up a remarkable history of accomplishment, surviving from the 19th century through to the 21st, transitioning from steam to diesel to the Baby Bullets, connecting communities, and preserving its unique historic depots. Today's generation has inherited in Caltrain an enduring transportation resource—albeit with major challenges to resolve.

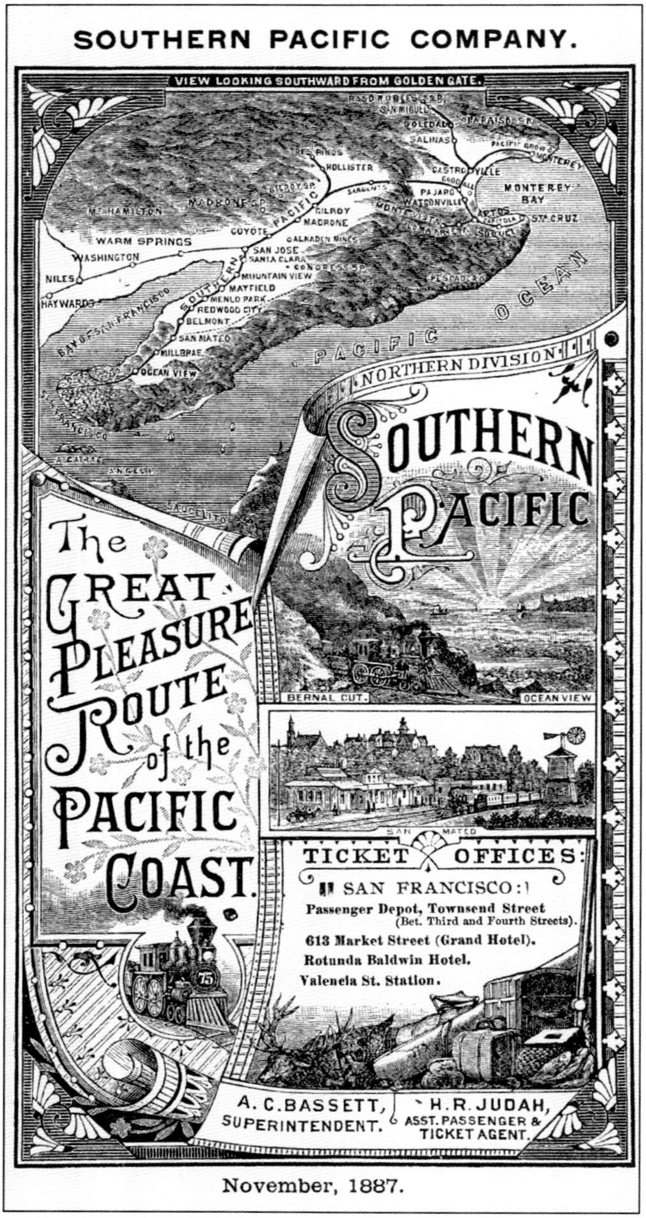


This 1887 Southern Pacific (SP) timetable about Coast Line attractions enticed tourists to the "Great Pleasure Route of the Pacific Coast," promoting winter and summer resorts one could reach by train, among them Menlo Park, San Jose, and Santa Cruz. After leaving the Third and Townsend Streets depot, trains might stop at Valencia Street or Ocean View before continuing south toward the Colma and Cemetery Stations and on toward San Bruno. After that, trains made stops along the Peninsula before heading south to Gilroy, Castroville, and Monterey. On the Peninsula, there were stations with names unchanged to this day, including San Mateo, Belmont, Santa Clara, and San Jose. There are also stations later renamed, such as Fair Oaks (now Atherton), Mayfield (now California Avenue), and Murphy's (now Sunnyvale). A train left daily from Townsend Street at 8:30 a.m., arriving in San Jose at 10:28 a.m. (Greg Welker collection.)

# *One*

# Two Cities are Connected

When the San Francisco & San Jose Railroad took some San Francisco officials down the Peninsula as far as Belmont in September 1863, it was a thrill ride for the crowd aboard. In the words of a news reporter, "the engine was put upon her speed, and well she acquitted herself, making the remarkable speed of 15 miles in 15 minutes. Hats had to be held onto with tightened grasp, while cigars fell from the mouths because the speed was so great that the smokers could not compress their lips about their Havanas!" A month later, California governor Leland Stanford was among the 400 passengers aboard for an inaugural trip as far Mayfield (now part of Palo Alto), three months before the line was finally completed to San Jose. By 1870, the railroad had been merged into the Southern Pacific Railroad of California, of which Stanford was a director. The earliest Peninsula steam trains featured wood-burning locomotives pulling wooden cars with open platforms. Later, coal- and then oil-burners succeeded them, hauling all-steel Harriman cars. The Peninsula in those days consisted of vast countryside punctuated with settlements and gestating cities. Communities lobbied to get train stations, and depots often were one of the first buildings in a town; manned by an agent, they served functions as diverse as ticket sales and mail delivery. Transporting agricultural goods was the primary business of the railroad for some 50 years. SP's maintenance yards in San Francisco and San Jose kept the passenger and freight fleets on the move. When the rail line opened, trains traveled through San Francisco's Mission District, but a new waterfront alignment, which opened in 1907, cut travel time by 17 minutes and helped make the railroad a viable travel mode for the growing population. Over the years, train frequency and patronage gradually increased as cities expanded, and depots in several cities had to be moved or rebuilt. Another important change for the railroad occurred in 1935 in San Jose, when the original station on Market Street moved to Cahill Street on a new alignment.

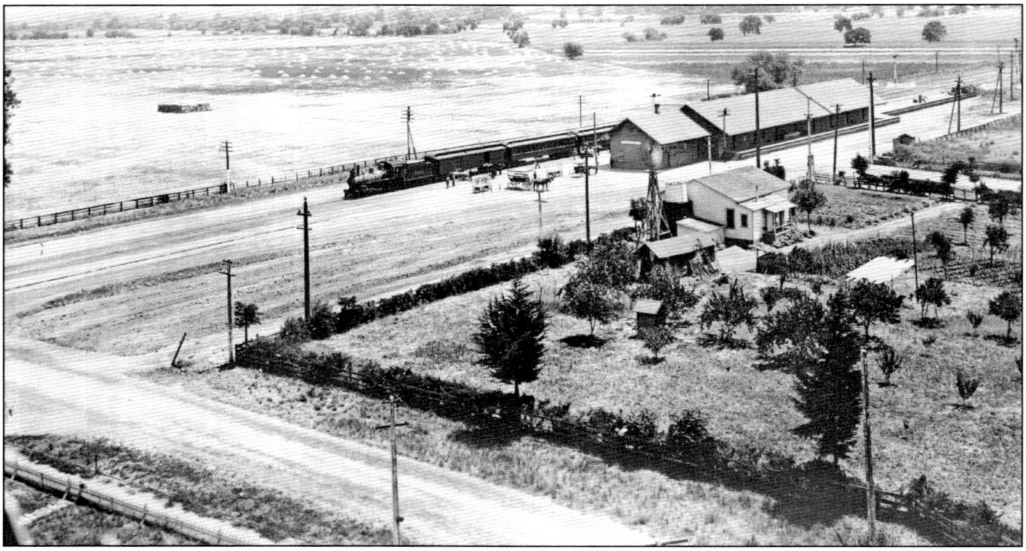

This c. 1900 photograph shows a train stopped at the Santa Clara depot, where horse-drawn carts and wagons stand by. The passenger depot opened in December 1863, a month before service on the San Francisco & San Jose Railroad (SF&SJ) was extended to San Jose. Although the rural surroundings are a distant memory, the one-story frame structure survives remarkably intact. (Courtesy Sourisseau Academy for State and Local History, San Jose State University.)

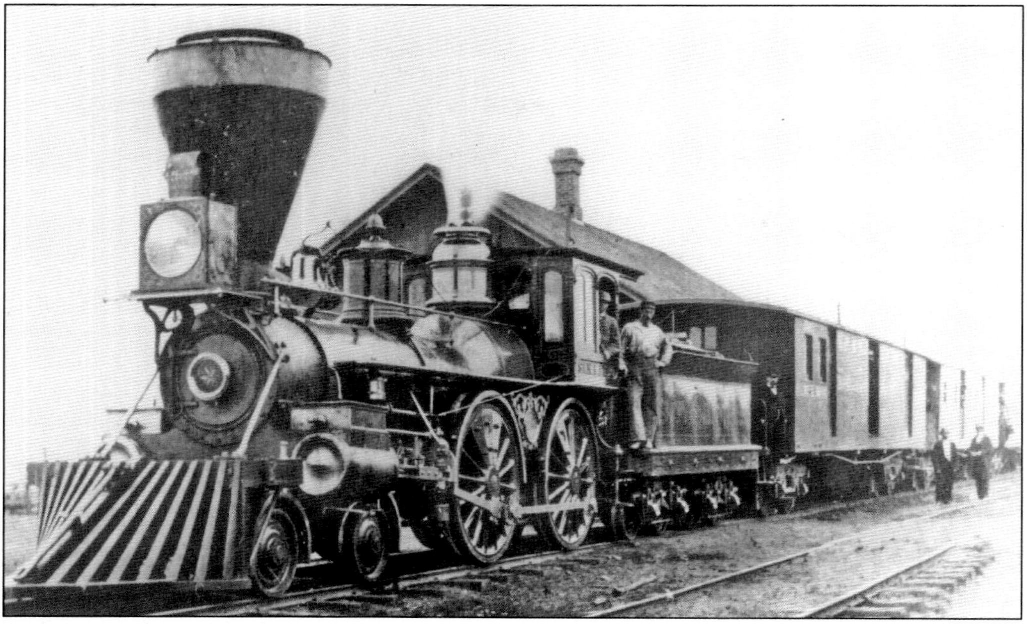

Built in 1864 by Danforth, Cooke, and Company, the locomotive *San Mateo* is shown in Belmont about 1866, two years after the railroad opened. The ornate wood burner had lots of brass and an elaborate builder's plate. The *San Mateo* later became SP Nos. 5 and 1112 and was a San Jose yard switch engine before being scrapped. (Tom Gray collection.)

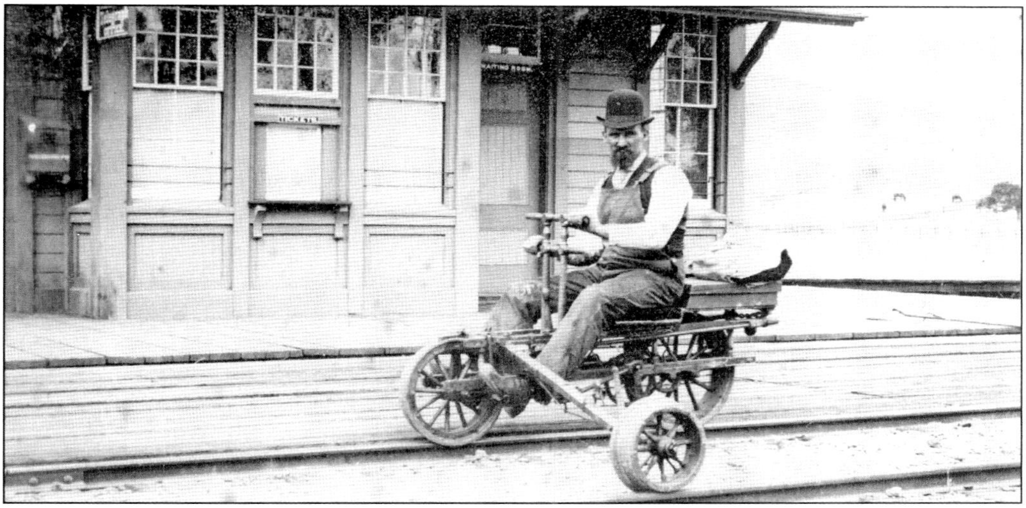

An early-day worker for the SP pauses in front of the depot at Hillsdale, located about five miles south of San Jose at the New Almaden Branch junction. Henry Bender, the noted authority on Southern Pacific depots, believes this one probably was moved around 1893 to Morgan Hill, or "Morganhill," as SP spelled it. SP renamed Hillsdale "Lick" in 1914. (Arthur Lloyd collection.)

SAN FRANCISCO AND SAN JOSE RAILROAD.

**TIME TABLE**

For the government and information of employes only. It is not intended for the information of the public, the Company reserving the right to vary therefrom as circumstances may require.

TAKES EFFECT AUGUST 1ST, 1866.

| NORTHWARD TRAINS. Sundays. Eve. | Sundays. Eve. | Sundays. Mor. | Week Days. Frt. | Week Days. Eve. | Week Days. Mor. | Week Days. Mor. | Distance from San Jose. | NAMES OF STATIONS AND PASSING PLACES. | Distance from San Francisco. | SOUTHWARD TRAINS. Week Days. Mor. | Week Days. Eve. | Week Days. Eve. | Week Days. Frt. | Sundays. Mor. | Sundays. Mor. | Sundays. Eve. |
|---|---|---|---|---|---|---|---|---|---|---|---|---|---|---|---|---|
| 9.50 | 6.10 | 10.30 | 11.30 | 6.10 | 9.30 | 8.30 | 49¾ | Ar. San Francisco,......Dep. | | 8.20 | 4.30 | 5.30 | 12.30 | 8.30 | 9.50 | 4.10 |
| 9.45 | 6.05 | 10.25 | | 6.05 | 9.25 | **8.25** | 46½ | " * Mission.............. " | 3¼ | **8.25** | 4.35 | 5.35 | | 8.35 | 9.55 | 4.15 |
| 9.40 | 6.00 | 10.20 | | 6.00 | 9.20 | 8.20 | 45½ | " * Bernal, .............. " | 4¼ | 8.30 | 4.40 | 5.40 | | 8.40 | 10.00 | 4.20 |
| 9.30 | 5.50 | **10.10** | 10.50 | **5.50** | 9.10 | 8.10 | 43½ | " * San Miguel,......... " | 6¼ | 8.40 | 4.50 | **5.50** | | 8.50 | **10.10** | 4.30 |
| 9.23 | 5.43 | 10.03 | | 5.43 | 9.03 | 8.03 | 40¾ | " * School House. ...... " | 9 | 8.47 | 4.57 | 5.57 | | 8.57 | 10.17 | 4.37 |
| 9.16 | 5.36 | 9.56 | | 5.36 | **8.56** | 7.56 | 38¼ | " * 12 Mile Farm,...... " | 11½ | **8.56** | 5.06 | 6.06 | | 9.06 | 10.26 | 4.46 |
| 9.09 | 5.29 | 9.49 | | 5.29 | 8.49 | 7.49 | 35½ | " * San Bruno,.......... " | 14¼ | 9.01 | 5.11 | 6.11 | | 9.11 | 10.31 | 4.51 |
| 9.00 | 5.20 | 9.40 | | **5.20** | 8.40 | 7.40 | 33. | " Millbrae, ............ " | 16¾ | 9.10 | **5.20** | 6.20 | 2.00 | 9.20 | 10.40 | 5.00 |
| 8.50 | **5.10** | **9.30** | 9.25 | 5.10 | 8.30 | 7.30 | 29 | " San Mateo,........... " | 20¾ | 9.20 | 5.30 | 6.30 | 2.20 | **9.30** | 10.50 | **5.10** |
| 8.37 | 4.57 | 9.17 | 9.10 | 4.57 | 8.17 | 7.17 | 24¾ | " Belmont,....... .... " | 25 | 9.33 | 5.43 | 6.43 | 2.35 | 9.43 | 11.03 | 5.23 |
| 8.30 | 4.50 | 9.10 | 8.50 | 4.50 | 8.10 | 7.10 | 21½ | " Redwood City,...... " | 28¼ | 9.40 | 5.50 | 6.50 | 2.50 | 9.50 | 11.10 | 5.30 |
| 8.20 | 4.40 | 9.00 | 8.20 | 4.40 | 8.00 | 6.55 | 17¼ | " Menlo Park,.......... ' | 32½ | 9.50 | 6.00 | 7.00 | 3.15 | 10.00 | 11.20 | 5.40 |
| 8.13 | 4.33 | 8.53 | 8.10 | 4.33 | 7.53 | 6.50 | 15¼ | " Mayfield,..... ....... " | 34½ | 9.57 | 6.07 | 7.10 | 3.30 | 10.07 | 11.27 | 5.47 |
| 8.02 | 4.22 | 8.42 | 7.45 | 4.22 | 7.42 | | 9¾ | " Mountain View,.... " | 40 | 10.08 | 6.18 | | 4.00 | 10.18 | 11.38 | 5.58 |
| 7.48 | 4.08 | 8.28 | 7.27 | 4.08 | 7.28 | | 6 | " Lawrence's,.......... " | 43¾ | 10.22 | 6.32 | | 4.20 | 10.32 | 11.52 | 6.12 |
| 7.40 | 4.00 | 8.20 | 7.15 | 4.00 | 7.20 | | 3¼ | " Santa Clara,......... " | 46½ | 10.30 | 6.40 | | 4.35 | 10.40 | 12.00 | 6.20 |
| 7.30 | 3.50 | 8.10 | 7.00 | 3.50 | 7.10 | | | Dep. San Jose,............. Ar. | 49¾ | 10.40 | 6.50 | | 5.00 | 10.50 | 12.10 | 6.30 |

☞ * Indicates Flag Stations.

☞ 1. The figures set against San Francisco Northward, and San Jose Sonthward, are the times to REACH those Stations The other figures represent the times of LEAVING the Stations against which they are placed.

☞ 2. The figures in large black type designate the meeting places of trains, and the time of passing.

☞ 3. In case freight train is not at passing place on time, passenger train will proceed with caution until such train is passed

☞ 4. Freight train must keep clear of all regular passenger trains at least ten minutes.

☞ 5. All irregular trains must keep clear of regular trains at least fifteen minutes.

☞ 6. Freight train leaving San Jose at 7.00, P. M., will wait the arrival of the 4.30, P. M., train from San Francisco.

☞ 7. The 7.00, P. M., freight from San Jose must not pass Mayfield until the 5.30, P. M., train from San Francisco arrives.

☞ 8. Should freight train leaving San Francisco at 12.30, A. M., be delayed it must keep clear of trains leaving Mayfield at 6.50, A. M., and San Jose at 7.10, A. M.

☞ 9. **All Regular Passenger Trains will wait twenty (20) minutes at passing places designated in the Time Table, and then proceed, always keeping twenty (20) minutes behind Card time until the expected train is passed. When both trains lose the twenty (20) minutes, they will proceed with flag in advance, and run with caution until trains pass.** See General Rules, No. 24.

☞ 10. **San Francisco and San Jose are terminal stations. All regular passenger trains will leave terminal stations on time, notwithstanding trains may be due. A train loses its right of road which does not reach the terminus before the starting time of a regular train. No excuse will be received for neglect of any of these rules.**

CHAS. B. GOULD, Acting Superintendent.

Oct. 31. st. 1923

When the SF&SJ Railroad opened, its depots were in San Francisco, San Mateo, Santa Clara, and San Jose, with 15 stations between the two terminals. In the early years, some stations, such as Redwood City and Menlo Park, had separate freight and passenger depots, but at some others (Millbrae and Santa Clara are examples), they were combined. Fair Oaks (later Atherton) and Castro were flag stops. (SBHRS.)

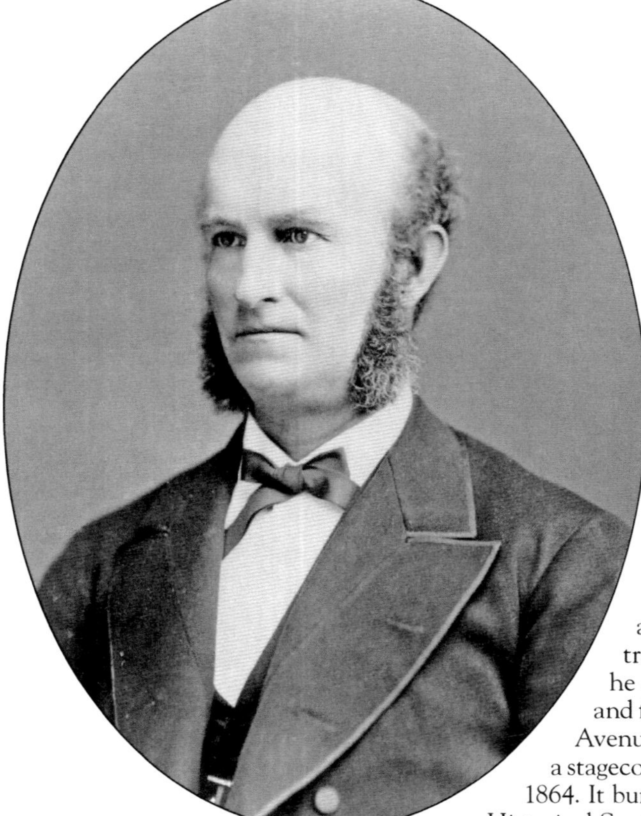

The development of the Peninsula is inextricably connected with the railroad, and Millbrae is a notable example. Banker Darius Ogden Mills and his brother-in-law, Ansel Easton, each bought acreage in what is now Millbrae and Burlingame. Mills, who cofounded the Bank of California in 1864, bought part of the Spanish Rancho Buri Buri, where he built a magnificent estate. He wanted a train station so guests could visit, so he deeded the land for the right-of-way and for Millbrae's first depot, on Millbrae Avenue. Initially named 17 Mile House for a stagecoach stop, the depot was completed in 1864. It burned down in 1890. (Both, Millbrae Historical Society.)

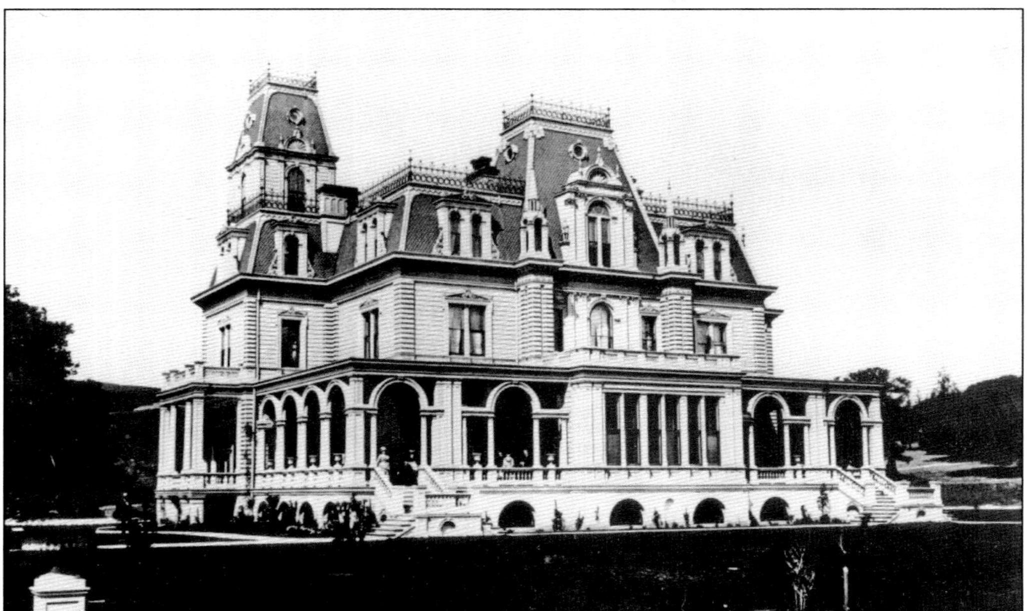

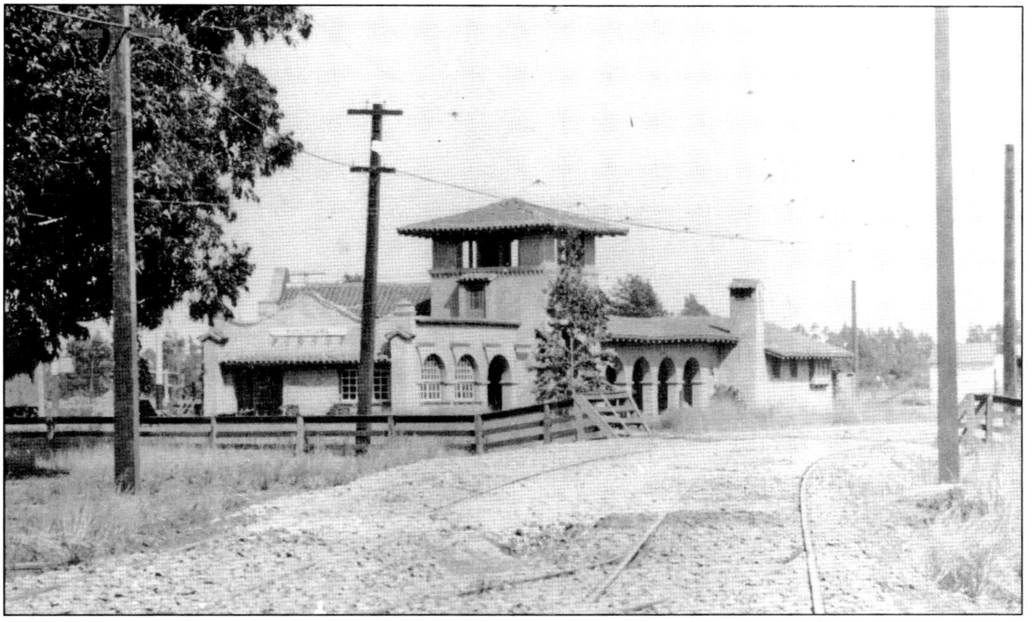

When the Burlingame Country Club opened in 1893, members chipped in $3,000 to cover the cost beyond that of a standard depot. The first commercial building in Burlingame, the depot was completed the next year at the end of Burlingame Avenue, a dirt road leading to the country club. In 1895, stationmaster, telegraph operator, and Wells Fargo agent George Gates and his bride moved into their quarters. (Tom Gray collection.)

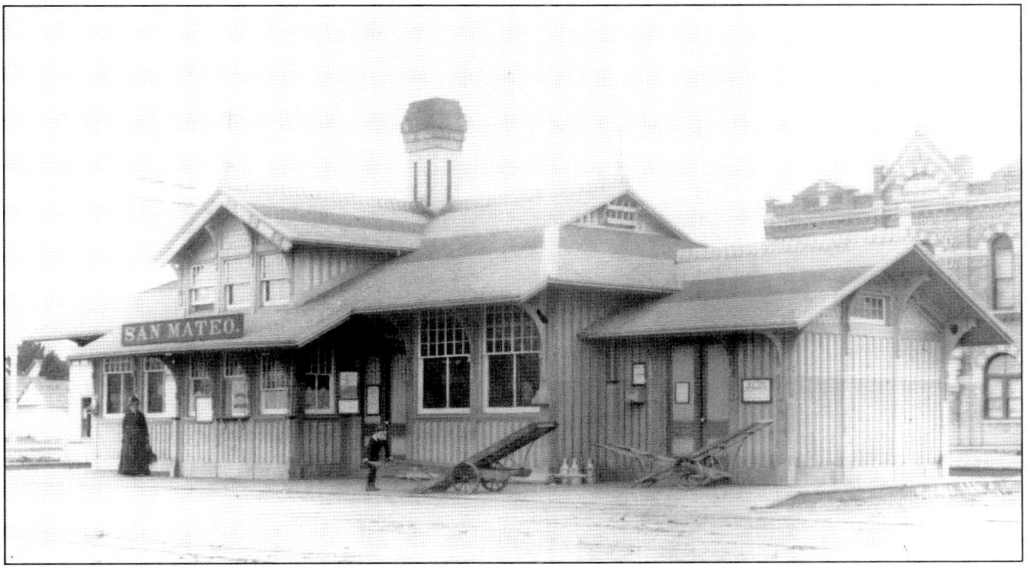


This is the second of five San Mateo depots. More elaborate than the original one, this building had gingerbread trim, a Queen Anne-style gable, and a long umbrella shed, which was added around 1900. A woman is shown in the photograph, taken around 1910. The depot was replaced in 1925, at Third and B Streets. (Henry Bender collection.)

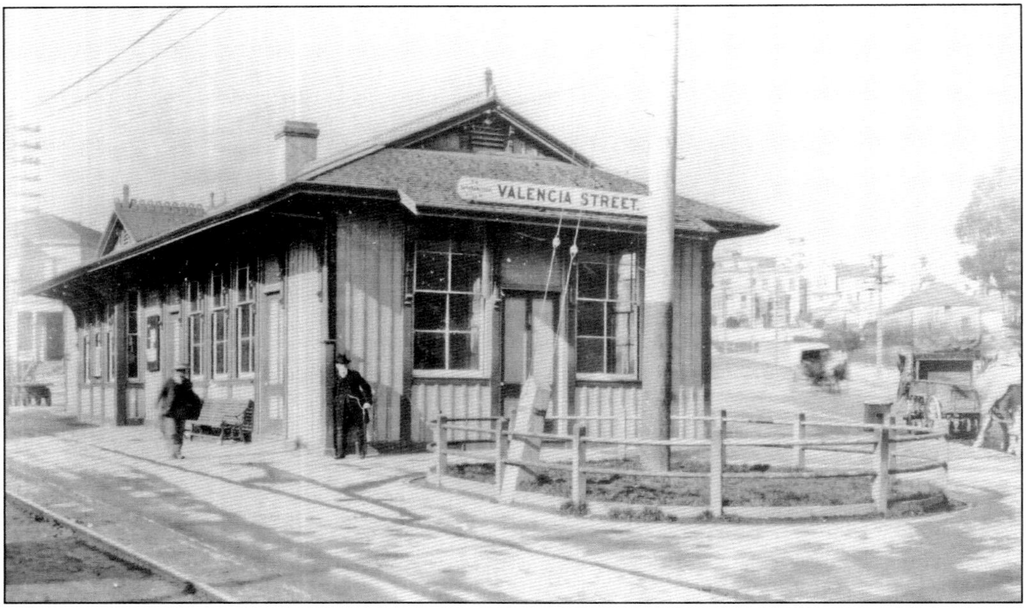


Pictured in about 1912, the Valencia Street station was on the original alignment of the SF & SJ, which went through the hills of San Francisco. Passenger, as well as freight trains, operated on narrow, twisting city streets. As time went on and the population grew, the need for a new southern approach to the city had become apparent well before the Bayshore Cutoff project was undertaken. (Tom Gray collection.)

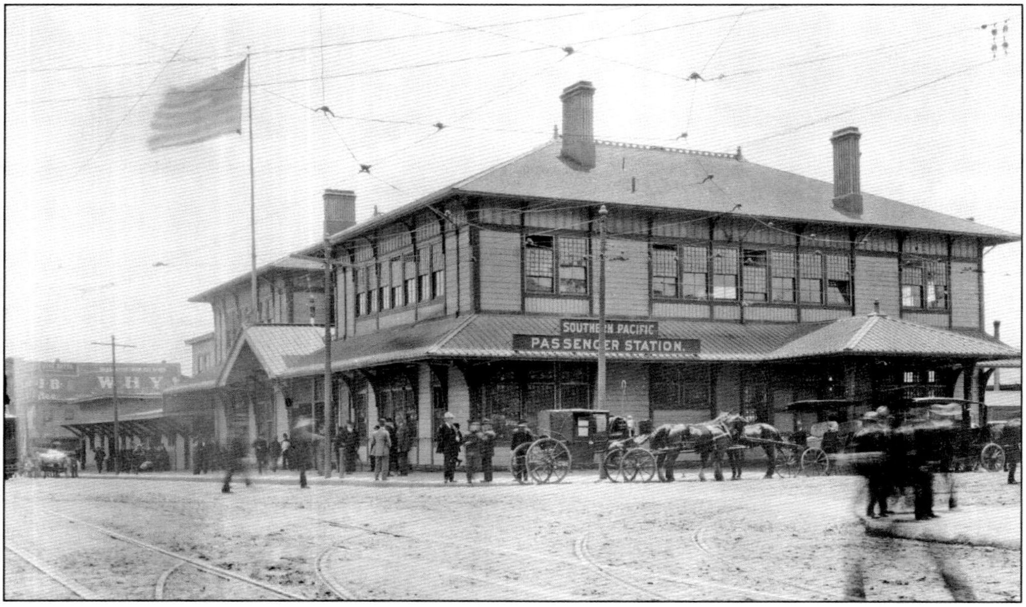

This is the SP passenger terminal at Third and Townsend Streets in 1896. The wood-frame structure, which opened in 1889, replaced a smaller one that had stood near the bay since 1874. The new terminal had two two-story sections with a roofed passageway in between. Known as the "Old Depot Building" after 1915, it was relocated in 1914 because of the construction of a new terminal. (Henry Bender collection.)

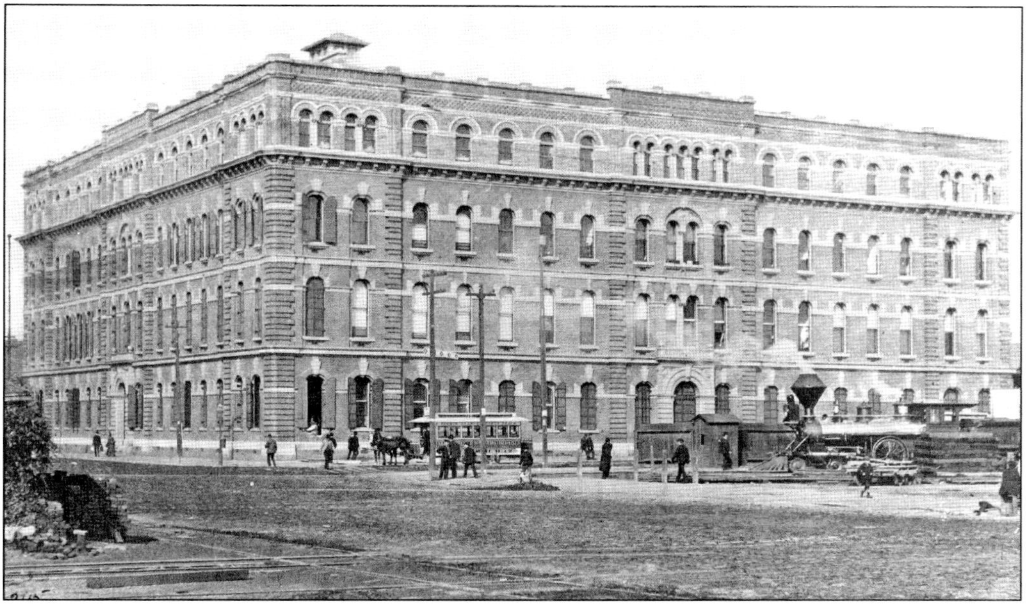

The Southern Pacific's 1873 general office building was at Fourth and Townsend Streets. This pair of photographs shows the building after the fourth story was added in 1888 and after the great earthquake of 1906, which sent shock waves through the sleeping city that April 18 morning. Although the quake rocked foundations, it was the ensuing fires that broke out that triggered widespread devastation as the inferno swept from one neighborhood to the next. As the conflagration spread toward the rail facilities on Fourth Street, fire crews battled to save the freight sheds where food and other provisions vital to the relief effort were stored. Fortunately, the freight sheds survived. (Above, courtesy California State Railroad Museum; below, Henry Bender collection.)

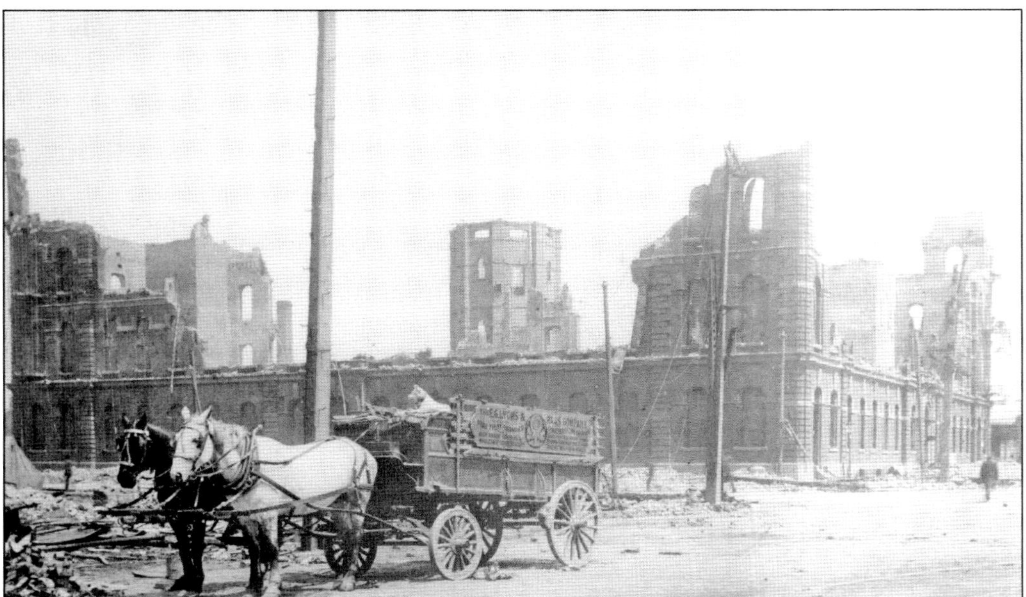

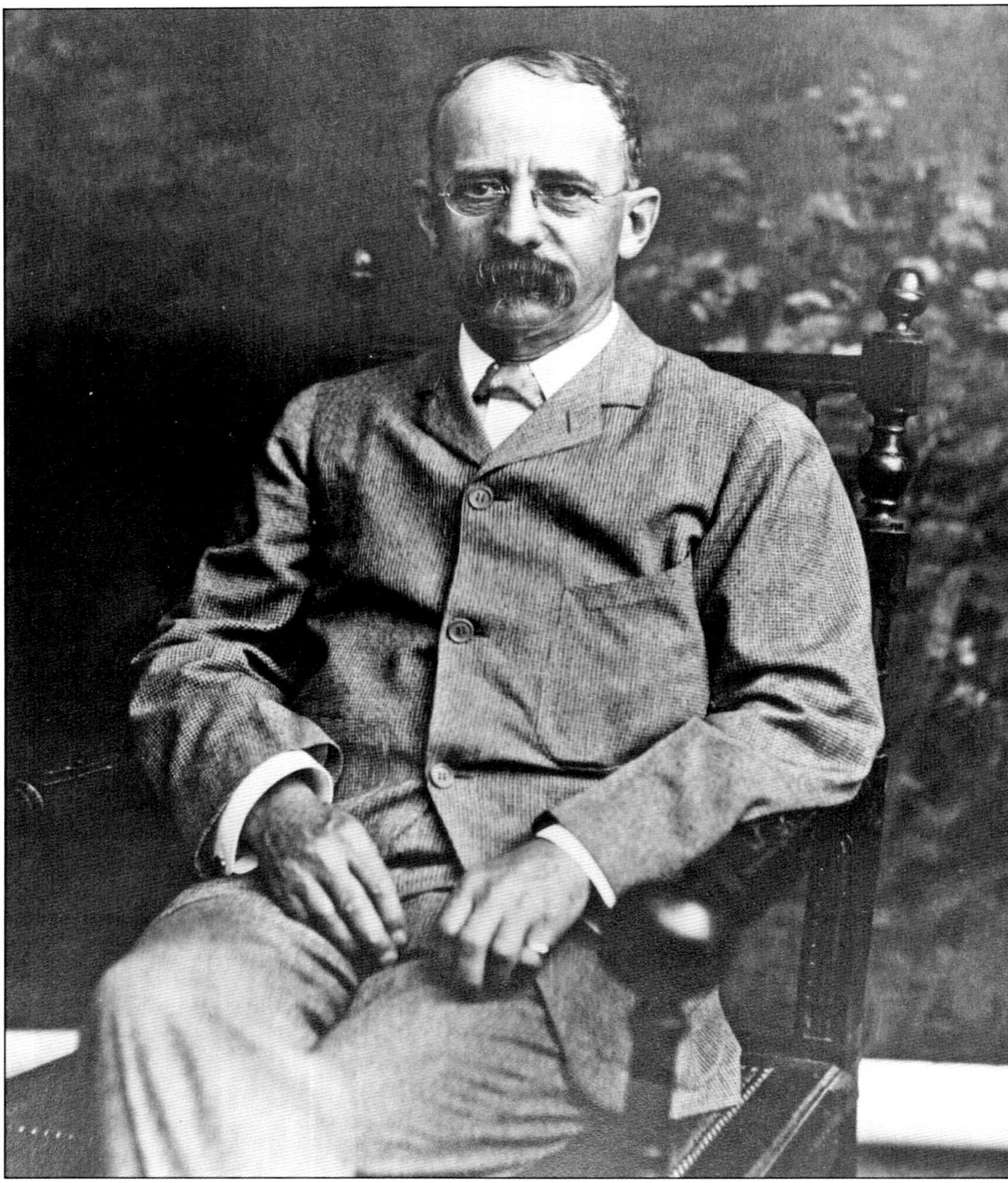

Edward Henry Harriman was president of the Southern Pacific at the time of the San Francisco earthquake in 1906. Born with a natural proclivity for business, he was a member of the New York Stock Exchange at the age of 23 and headed a thriving Wall Street brokerage firm. When he was 50, Harriman embarked on a phenomenal drive acquiring and rebuilding railroads and became president of both the Union Pacific and SP. Harriman's characteristic decisiveness kicked in when the earthquake struck San Francisco: he immediately rushed from New York on a special train so he could direct SP's relief efforts. In a *Southern Pacific Bulletin* story about the accomplishments of the Harriman era, author John R. Signor noted that, despite the railroad magnate's death in 1909 at 61, "leaving much that he had wanted to do undone, [Harriman's] bold management ideas dominated SP policies for two more decades." His most famous offspring was New York governor and ambassador W. Averell Harriman. (Courtesy Union Pacific Museum.)

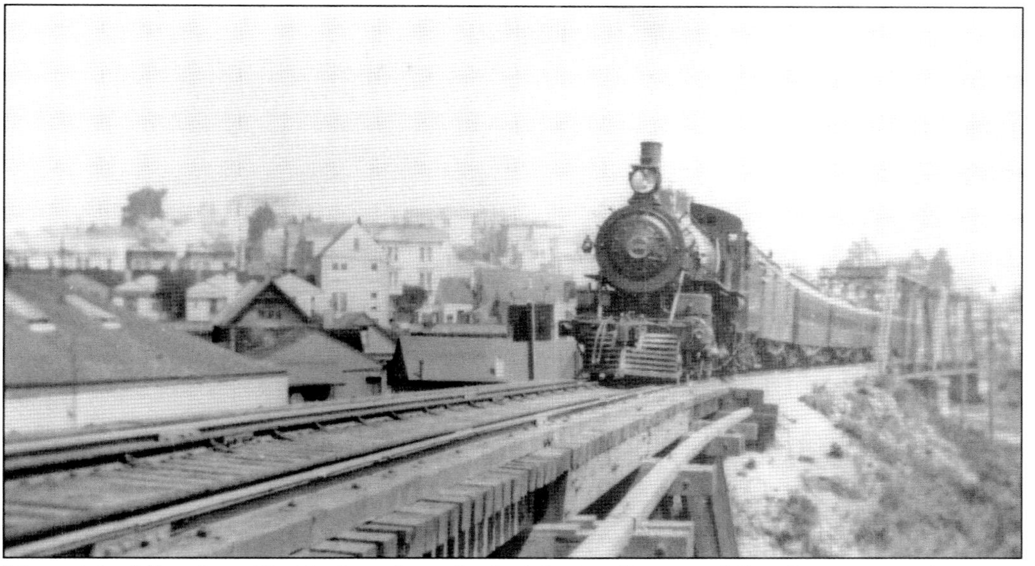

The original Southern Pacific line through the Mission District of San Francisco is shown in this Robert H. McFarland photograph, c. 1905, as SP 1456 crosses the Dolores Street Bridge. Work had begun to build a new main line along the waterfront before the 1906 earthquake, and Harriman persevered with the construction, opening the Bayshore Cutoff on December 8, 1907. (Tom Gray collection.)

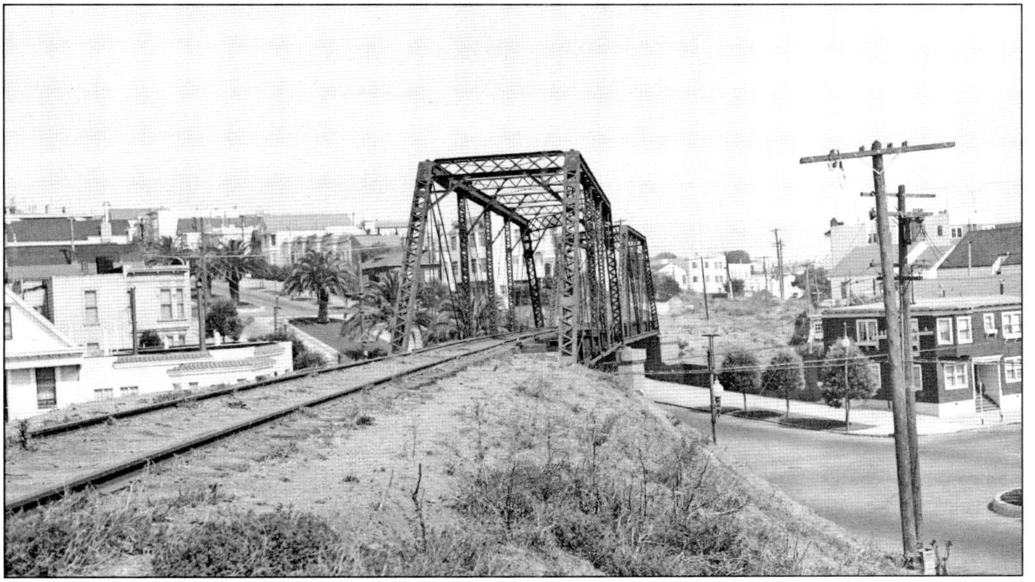

After the Bayshore Cutoff opened, the main line saw less and less use. Until 1930, one passenger train a day operated on what had become a branch line, and the last through freight train use was in 1942, when the middle section was abandoned. The Dolores Street Bridge was one of the last remnants in San Francisco. (Arthur Lloyd collection.)

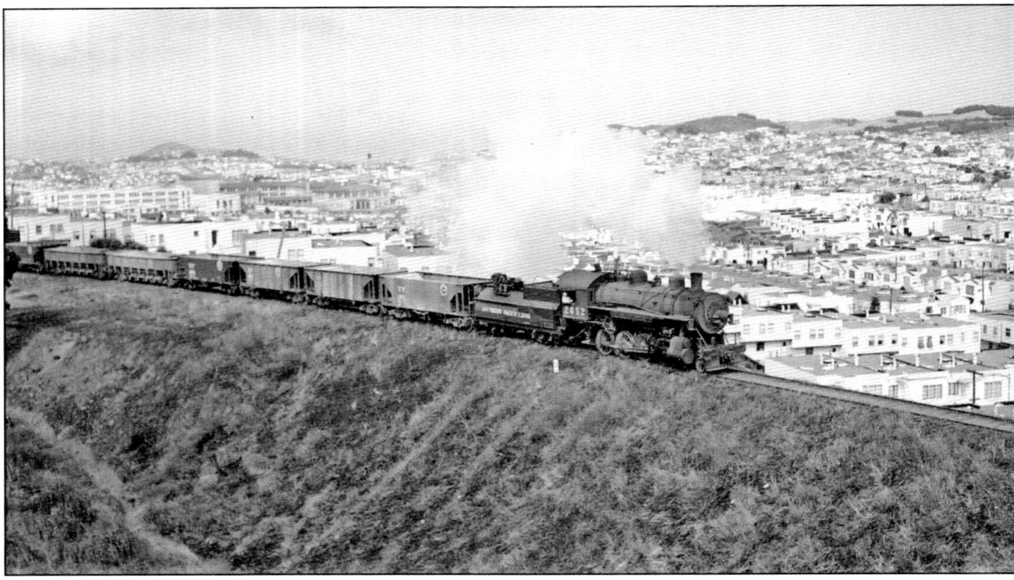

The line between San Bruno and Daly City and a section within the limits of the San Francisco yard to the Elkton/Market Street Railway shops at Geneva and San Jose Avenues were the remaining sections of the original main line. Bay Area Rapid Transit District trains operate today on the right-of-way in this picture. (Arthur Lloyd collection.)

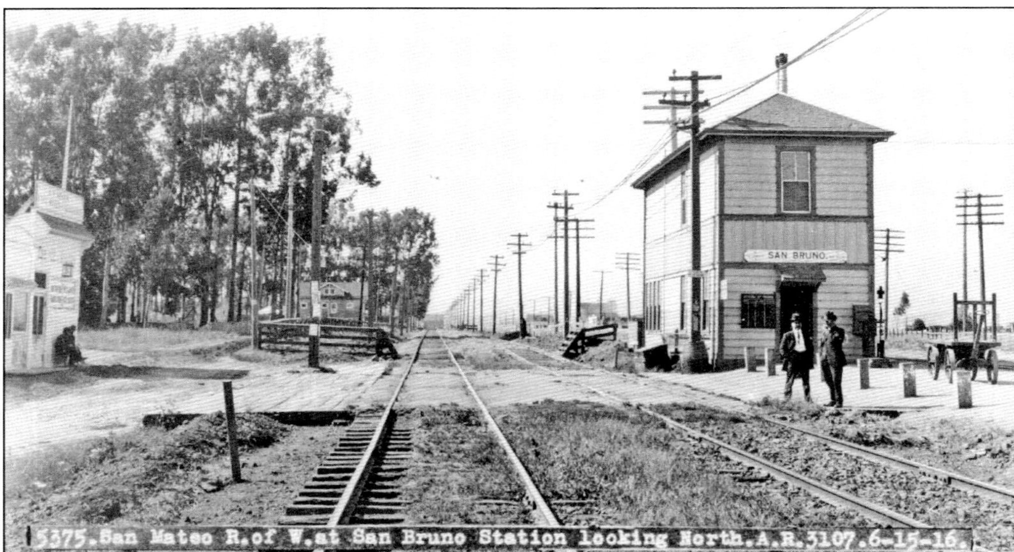


When the Bayshore Cutoff was completed in 1907, the new waterfront alignment connected with the old SP main line at San Bruno. A depot was built at the junction. In the center is the United Railroads interurban line, which continued south to San Mateo. In 1916, a two-story depot replaced the first San Bruno depot. Remodeled to one story in 1953, it survived until 1963. (Henry Bender collection.)

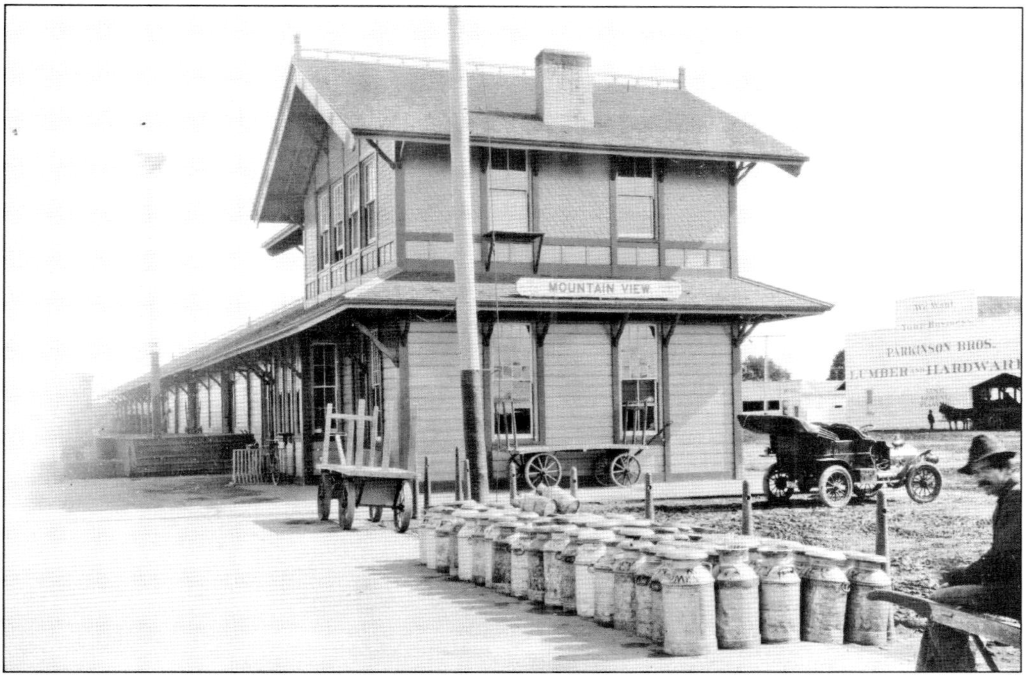


The milk cans in the foreground of this 1912 view of the Mountain View depot are a reminder how farmers depended on the train to transport products. Built in 1888, the two-story depot survived until SP closed the freight and ticket office in 1959. When the city celebrated its centennial, a replica of this depot was constructed in 2002. (Tom Gray collection.)

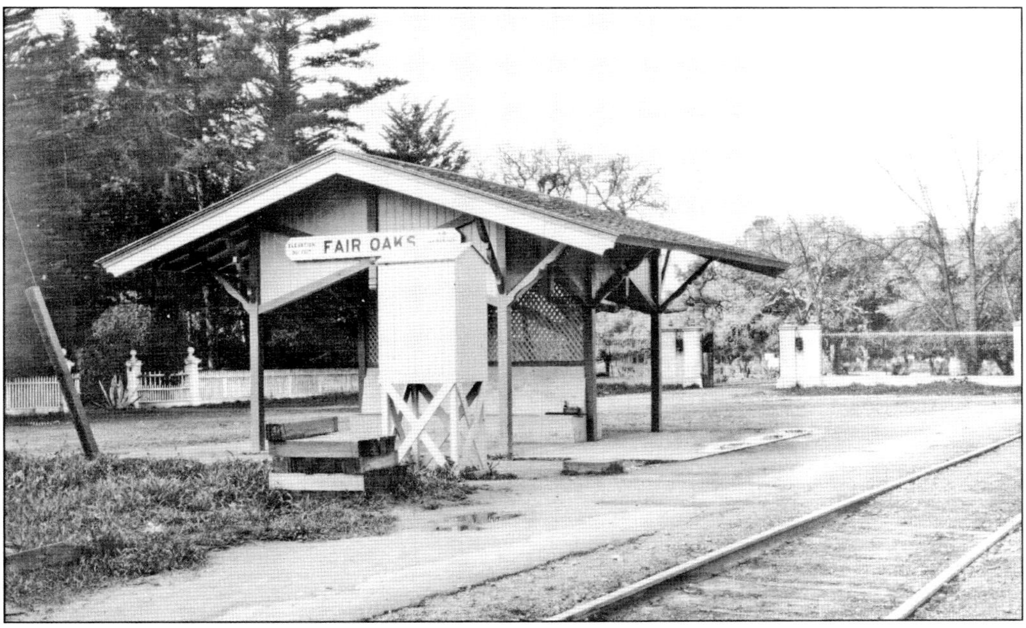


Originally called Fair Oaks, the first Atherton stop was served by a 14-by-20-foot open shelter with a lattice partition. The station was renamed for hide-and-tallow merchant Faxon Atherton in 1912, about when this photograph was taken. (Henry Bender collection.)

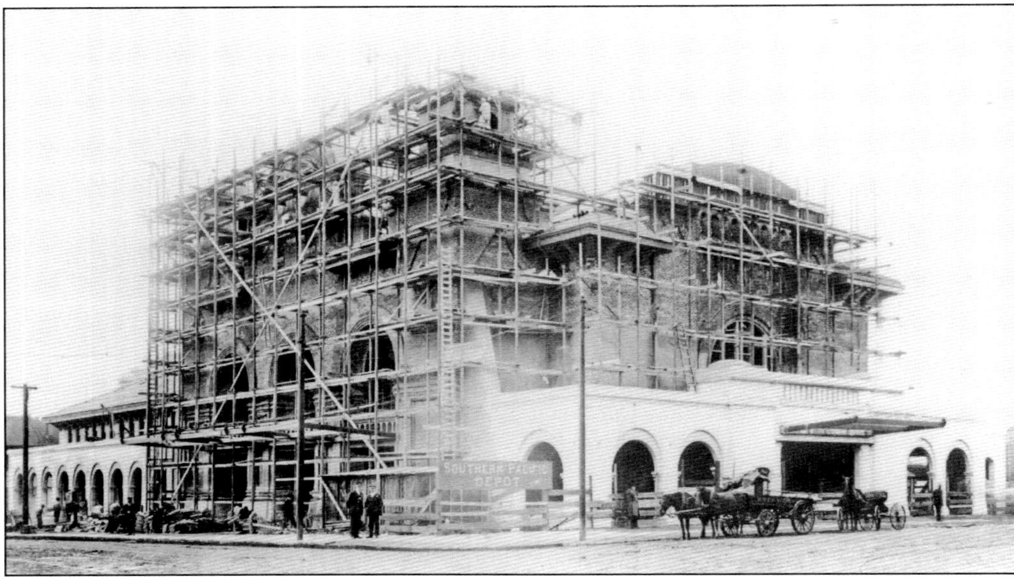


The Mission-style terminal at Third and Townsend Streets was built in 1914–1915 as a "temporary" station in time for the opening of the Panama-Pacific International Exposition. The World's Fair provided a stage to showcase The City's revival after the devastating 1906 earthquake, as well as to mark the completion of the Panama Canal. The first photograph was taken in February 1915, when the terminal was still under construction, and the second after it opened. A baggage room building, commissary, and Pullman storeroom were provided, as SP prepared to welcome the world to San Francisco. (Above, Henry Bender collection; below, courtesy Union Pacific Museum.)

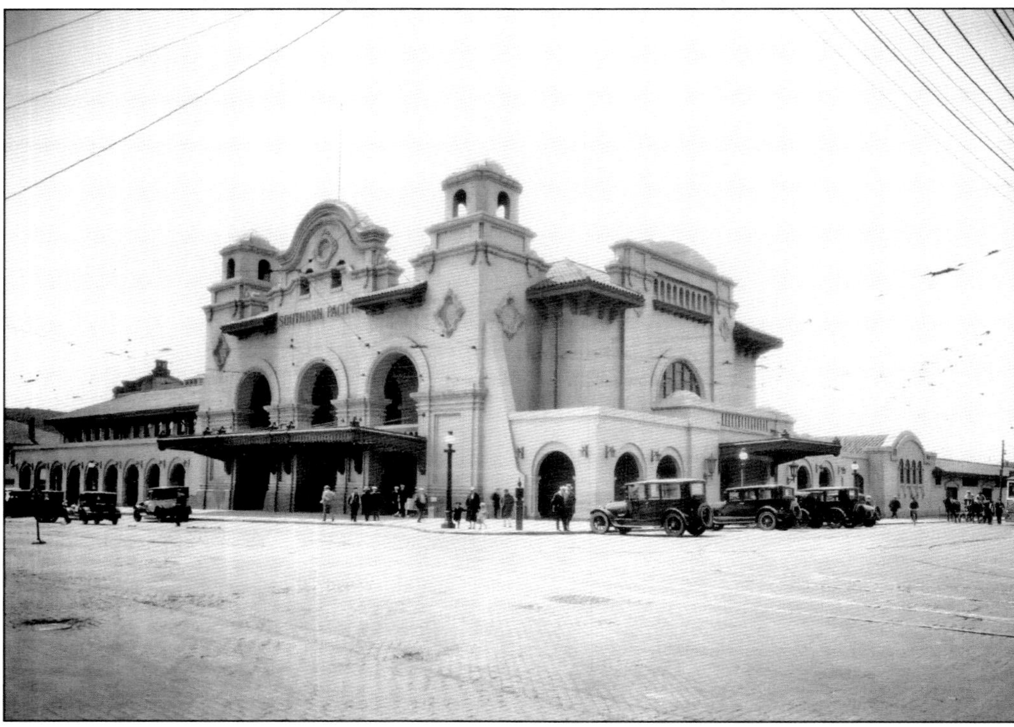

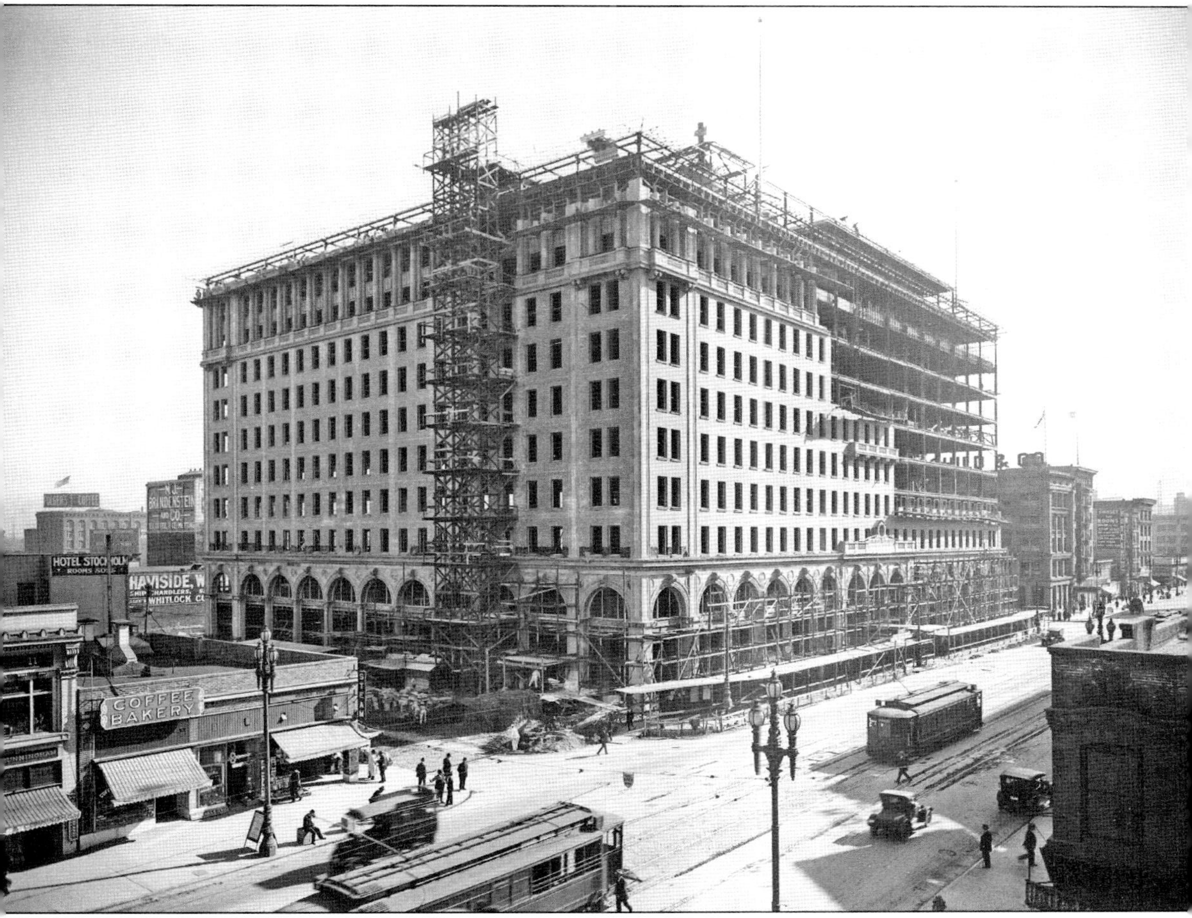


The railroad rented space for 10 years until the new SP headquarters was constructed at 65 Market Street. This April 3, 1917, photograph taken from the corner of Sacramento and Market Streets, also gives a glimpse of the city's Phoenix-like rise after the earthquake. According to the *Southern Pacific Bulletin*, nearly 2.5 million bricks, 50 miles of wiring, and 40,000 barrels of cement went into the construction of what was then the largest office building in the West. Designed by architects Bliss and Faville, the building took nearly a year to construct and required some of the tallest pile drivers in the world to sink piles 130 feet below the street level. The building featured 275 feet of frontage on Market Street and two 209-foot-long wings. Some 2,500 employees, who had been working at offices in the Flood Building, occupied the new headquarters by September 1917. (Courtesy California State Railroad Museum.)

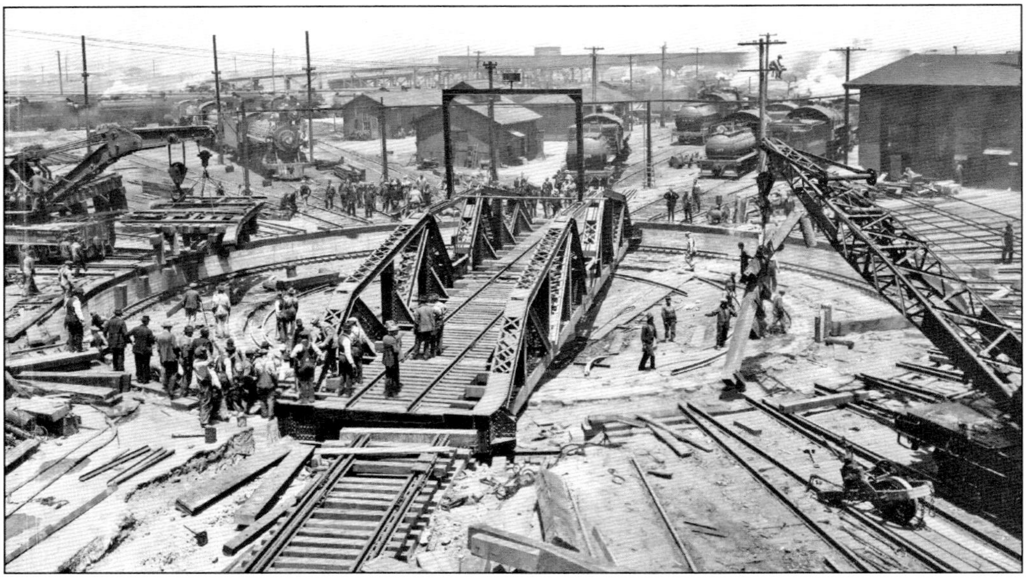

The Mission Bay roundhouse maintained the growing fleet of Southern Pacific passenger cars and locomotives, and provided good jobs for skilled blue-collar workers. These two photographs show locomotives approaching and then on the giant turntable before heading into the roundhouse for maintenance. Turntables are used to put the engines front-end first into the roundhouse and then turn them so they are headed in the right direction when they return to the main line for duty. These pictures were taken in July 1924. Around that time, SP was replacing 70-foot turntables with 100-foot turntables in several rail yards, including San Francisco's, to accommodate larger locomotives. (Both, courtesy California State Railroad Museum.)

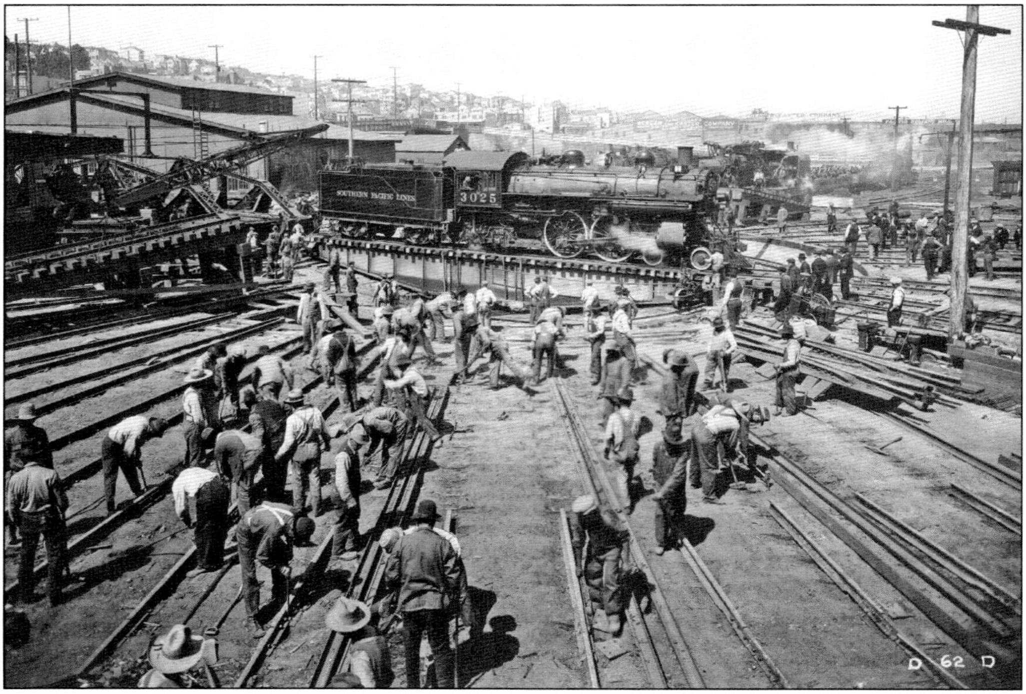

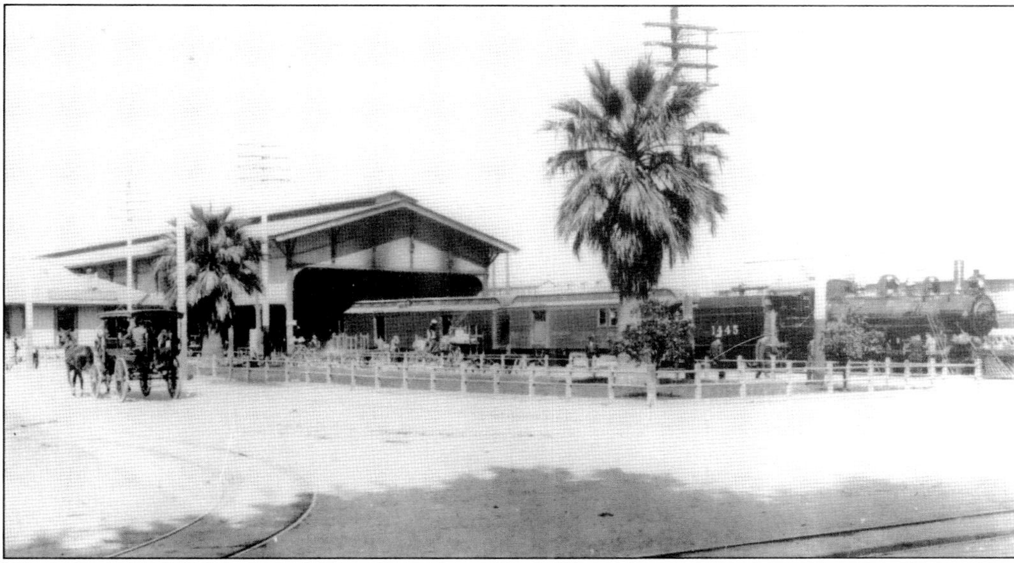

The end-of-the-line for the SF&SJ Railroad in 1864 was at San Pedro Street just north of Bassett, but freight and passenger facilities were later expanded. This photograph, taken around 1907, is of the depot at Market and Bassett Streets, built in 1883. As automobile use expanded early in the 20th century, operating trains along Fourth Street through San Jose was an increasing problem. (Tom Gray collection.)

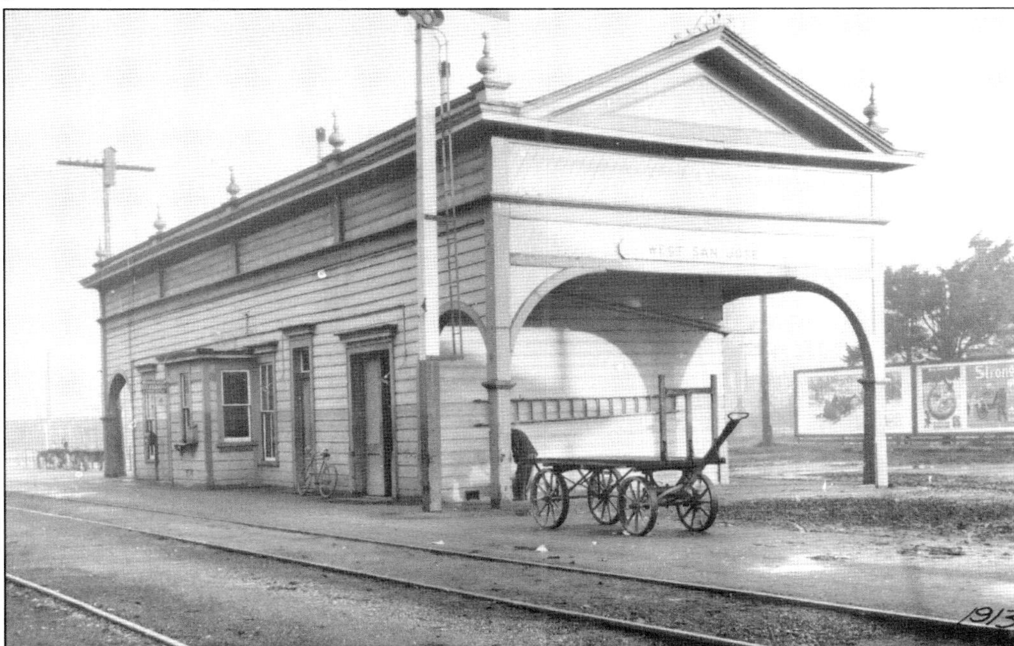


The West San Jose depot is shown here, around 1912. It was built in 1878 by the South Pacific Coast Railroad, a narrow-gauge line, which ran from Alameda via Newark to Santa Cruz. When the San Jose terminal was relocated, it moved to this building site on Cahill Street. (Tom Gray collection.)

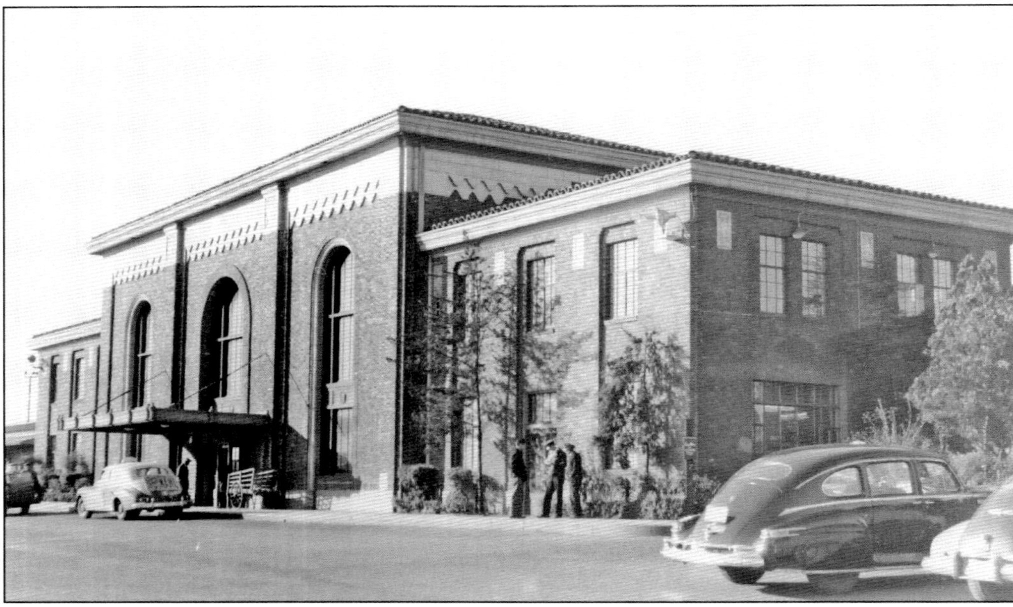

The relocation of the SP main line off of Fourth Street in San Jose required a major track relocation project, nine grade separations through the central city, and a new depot. By December 1935, everyone was ready to celebrate the completion of the $3.3-million project and the opening of the handsome new Cahill Street terminal. (Henry Bender collection.)

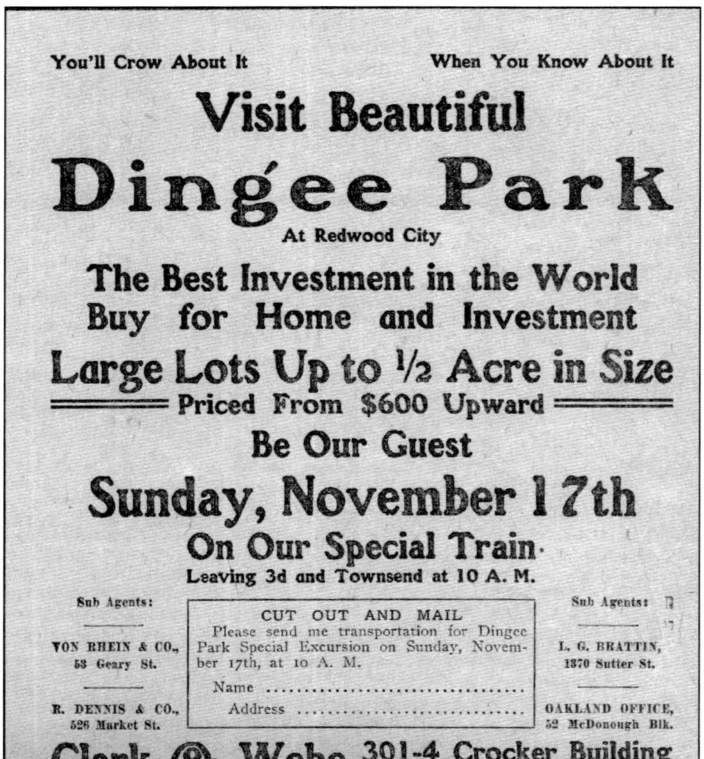


In this 1907 advertisement, prospective purchasers of land in the area that is now part of Sequoia High School were invited to take a special train to Redwood City to see the real estate in person. The same year, the *San Carlos Park Syndicate* promoted the fact that there was "excellent transportation via the Bayshore Cutoff of the Southern Pacific." (Nicholas and Betty Veronico collection.)

# *Two*

# Espee and the Peninsula Commute Service

The pace of growth on the Peninsula accelerated, and the availability of rail and passenger service from San Francisco to San Jose facilitated this transition. San Mateo County population more than doubled from 1920 to 1930. The Espee, which prided itself on being "Your Friendly Railroad," accommodated this burgeoning population by providing reliable commute service, as well as trains for special events and weekend jaunts. Midday, SP operated mail trains, and for decades, a steam locomotive pulling both passenger cars and a railway post office car was a common sight. At the same time, SP provided freight service over the same tracks, serving a changing array of businesses and industries, from farms and canneries to steel mills and electronics companies. For a time, an interurban railway from San Francisco to San Mateo and a railway from San Jose extending north to Palo Alto and west to Los Gatos and Saratoga provided connecting service for SP riders. The railroad's fortunes, however, were not immune to outside forces. Nationally, the transportation of military personnel comprised 45 percent of SP's passenger revenue in 1944, an all-time high to that date. Similarly, Peninsula Commute Service ridership jumped 43 percent from 1941 to 1942, peaking at 9.5 million in 1944. Postwar ridership dipped—but then rebounded—to 9.2 million in 1952. After that, steady erosion began, reaching a low of about 4.4 million in 1977. The completion of the Bayshore Freeway in 1962, followed by the construction of Interstate 280, made it increasingly difficult for the railroad to compete with automobiles. Finding itself trapped by spiraling costs, the SP attempted to raise fares and ultimately to jettison the service. But frustrated passengers and public officials were not willing to give up on a transportation service that had been a fact of life for more than a century. Intensive negotiations led, in 1980, to a new phase—and the new name CalTrain—for the railroad, which so long had served the public.

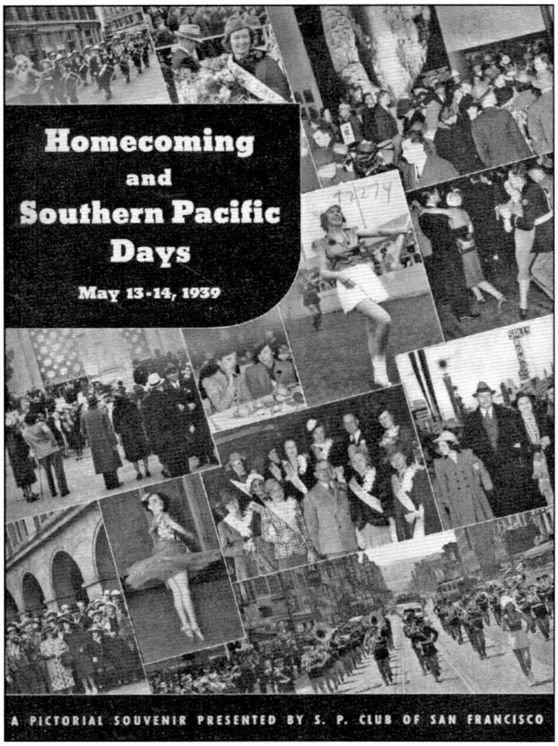


Employees and their families from the entire Southern Pacific system poured into the Third and Townsend Streets station and the Ferry Building in 1939 for Homecoming and SP Days, a two-day celebration of the railroad's 70th anniversary, which was held during the Golden Gate International Exposition. The SP Club Band performed for parades, concerts, and wherever the rail line went, riding in its own cars painted in *Daylight* colors. The band paraded up Market Street and then entertained arriving guests at the fair at Treasure Island. Of the 73,663 who attended on May 14, more than 50,000 were said to be there because of SP Day. The SP Club of San Francisco produced this booklet as a souvenir for attendees. (Left, Reg McGovern collection; below, Tom Gray collection.)

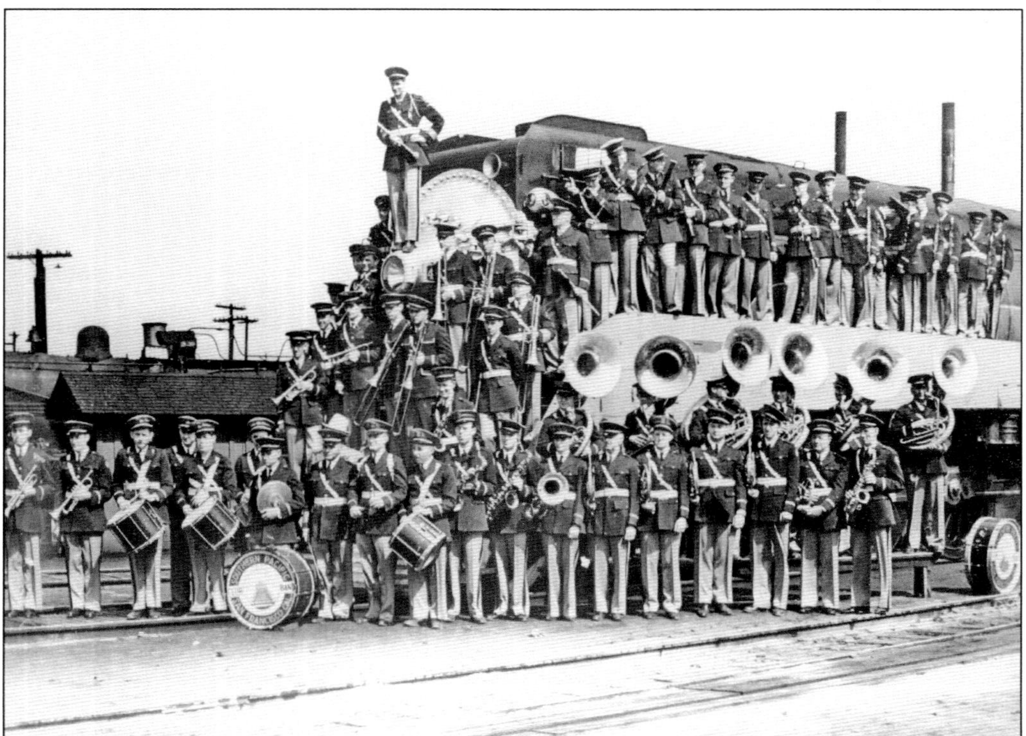

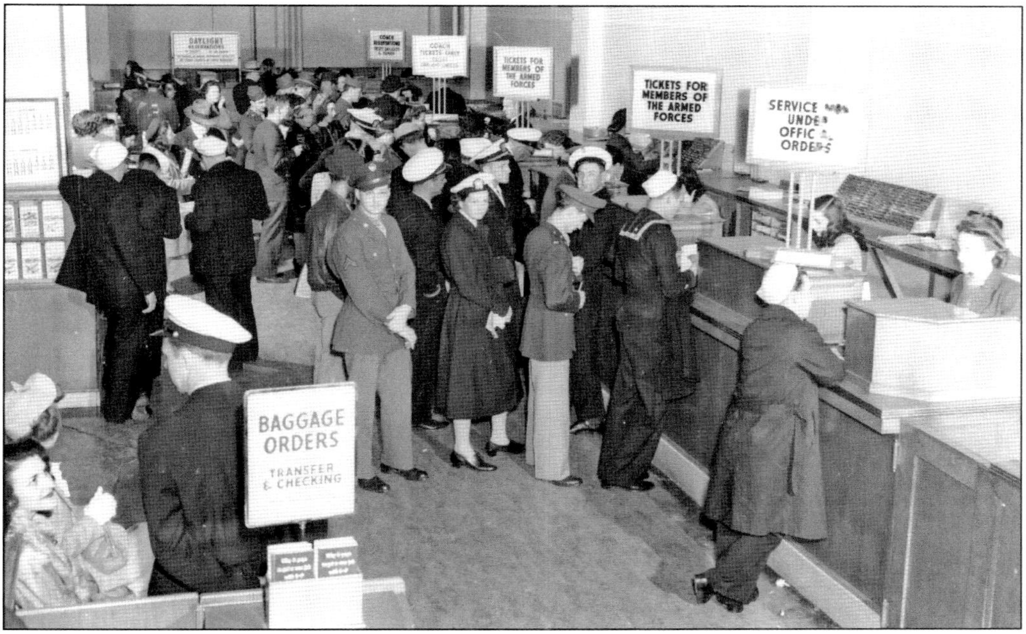


SP played a major role in moving the large numbers of military travelers during World War II, illustrated by this Will Whittaker photograph below of a troop train passing the Potrero Tower in San Francisco and the SP photograph above of servicemen and women lining up to buy tickets. A daily military "extra" ran between Monterey and San Francisco, and city ticket offices were widely available. With thousands of employees off to war, the "help wanted" sign put up at the San Francisco freight office in 1943 advertised "7,500 good-paying railroad jobs for men and women." In 1944, Vera Guthrie, who joined SP to help relieve the manpower shortage, became the first woman passenger director on the West Coast at the Third and Townsend Streets station. (Both, Henry Bender collection.)

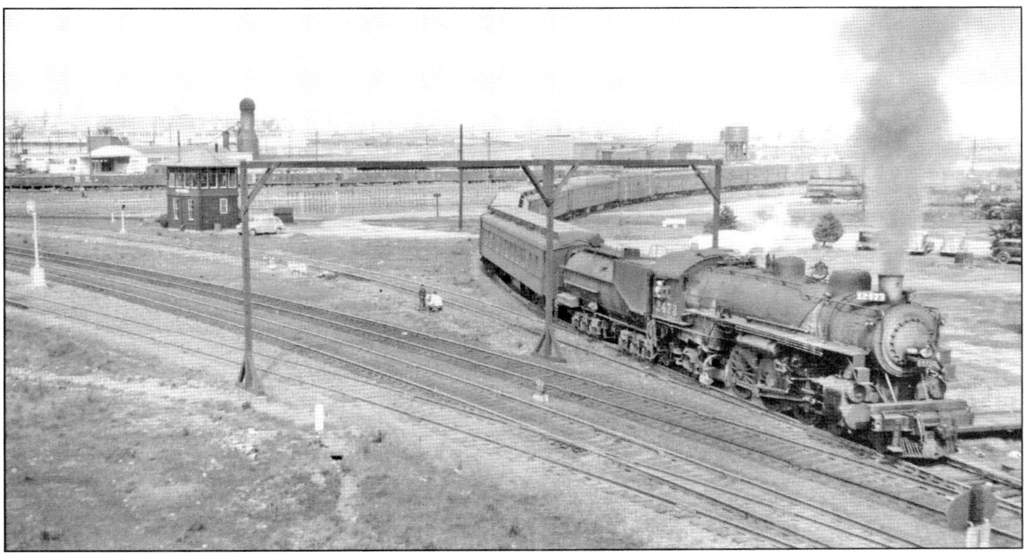

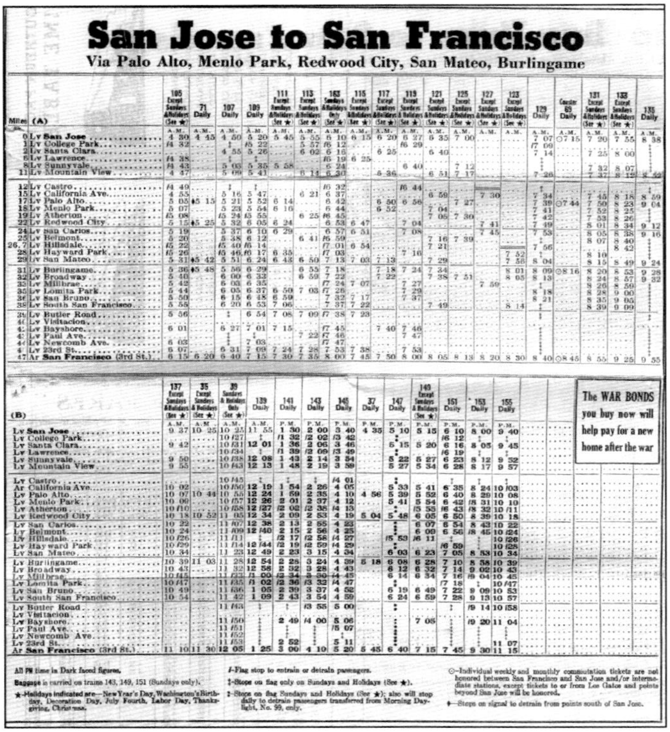
San Jose to San Francisco

Via Palo Alto, Menlo Park, Redwood City, San Mateo, Burlingame

The WAR BONDS you buy now will help pay for a new home after the war

All PM time in Dark faced figures.

Baggage is carried on trains 143, 149, 151 (Sundays only).

★-Holidays indicated are—New Year's Day, Washington's Birthday, Decoration Day, July Fourth, Labor Day, Thanksgiving, Christmas.

f-Flag stop to entrain or detrain passengers.

‡-Stops on flag only on Sundays and Holidays (See ★).

‡-Stops on flag Sundays and Holidays (See ★); also will stop daily to detrain passengers transferred from Morning Daylight, No. 99, only.

⊙-Individual weekly and monthly commutation tickets are not honored between San Francisco and San Jose and/or intermediate stations, except tickets to or from Los Gatos and points beyond San Jose will be honored.

♦—Stops on signal to detrain from points south of San Jose.

SP management and employees wholeheartedly showed their home-front support for the war effort, seeing the railroads' "Victory Trains" as vital to the nation. Employees were encouraged to buy war bonds through a payroll savings plan. Note that this 1943 commute service timetable also puts in a plug for buying bonds. (Arthur Lloyd collection.)

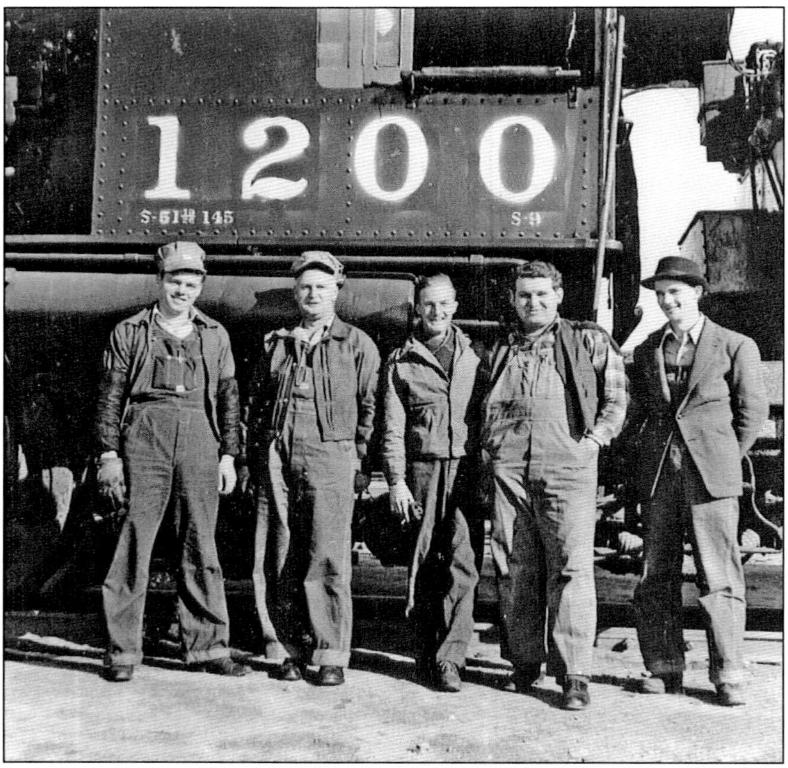


In February 1944, a Southern Pacific switching crew pauses next to the locomotive for a photograph. From left to right are fireman C.J. Rapp, engineer Herb Wenster, and three switchmen identified by last name only as Moon, Winchester, and Hicks. (Millbrae Train Museum.)

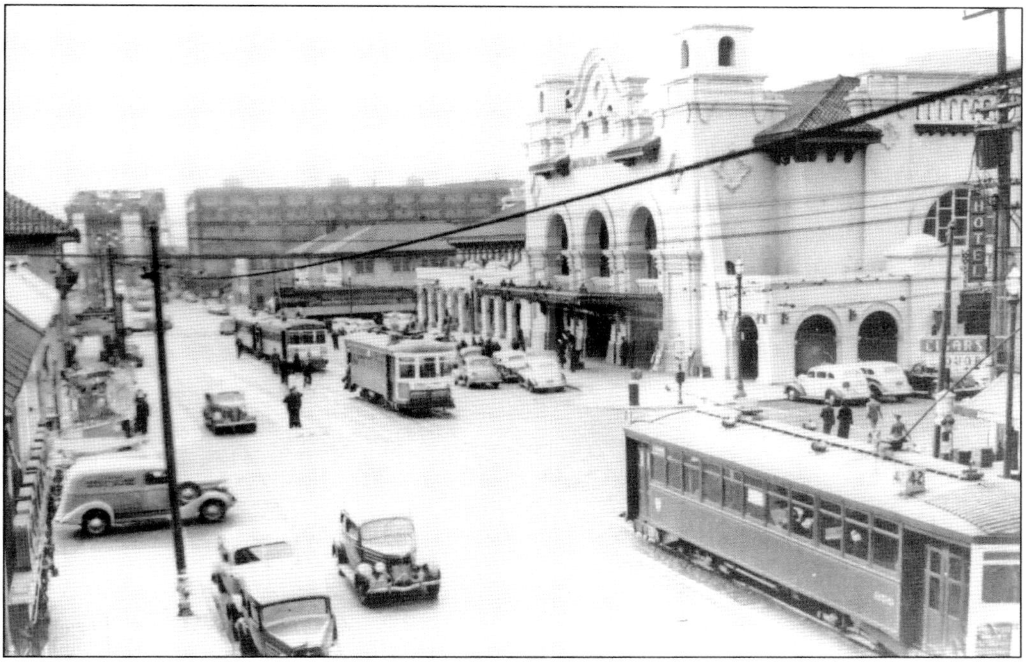


In the 1940s, the SP's San Francisco terminal was a hive of activity, with taxicabs lined up to pick up arriving passengers and streetcars providing service from the Third and Townsend Streets area to other parts of the city. Note the Third Street Bridge in the background. (Tom Gray collection.)

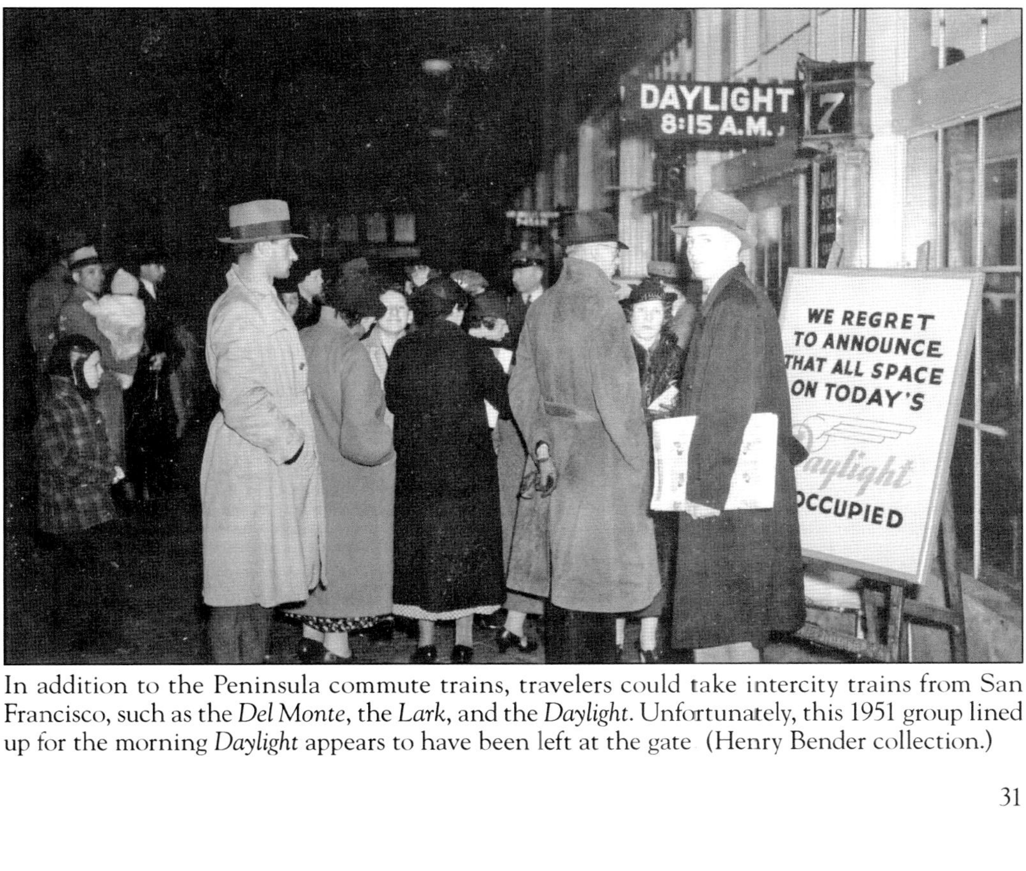


In addition to the Peninsula commute trains, travelers could take intercity trains from San Francisco, such as the *Del Monte*, the *Lark*, and the *Daylight*. Unfortunately, this 1951 group lined up for the morning *Daylight* appears to have been left at the gate (Henry Bender collection.)

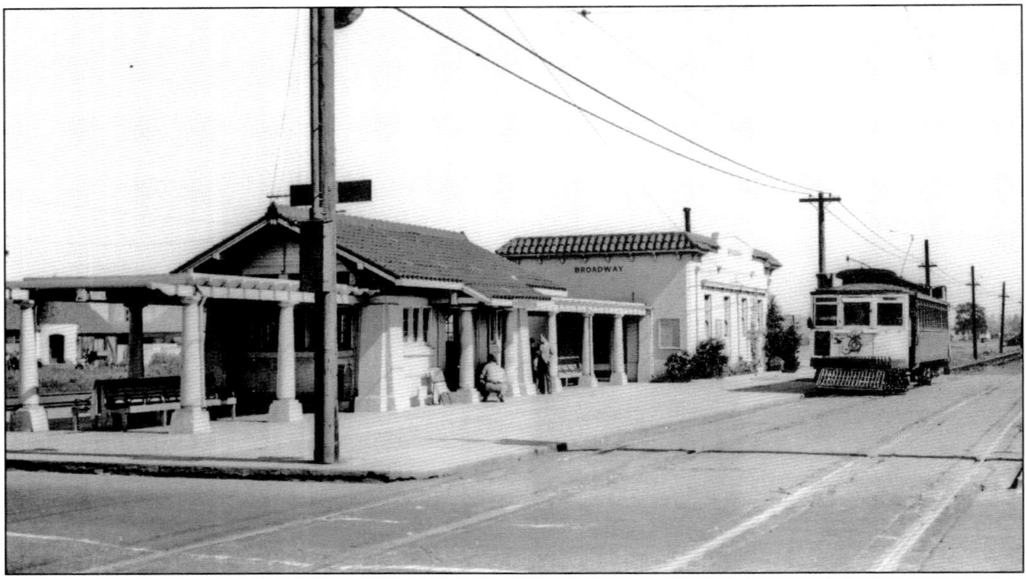

Peninsula residents had very good rail transportation options, including the Market Street Railway's 40 Line, which went from Fifth and Market Streets in San Francisco to San Mateo. The 40 Car is shown here in 1940 at the Broadway Burlingame depot, shared with Southern Pacific. The 40 Car ran on tracks west of the depot, on what is today California Drive. (Tom Gray.)

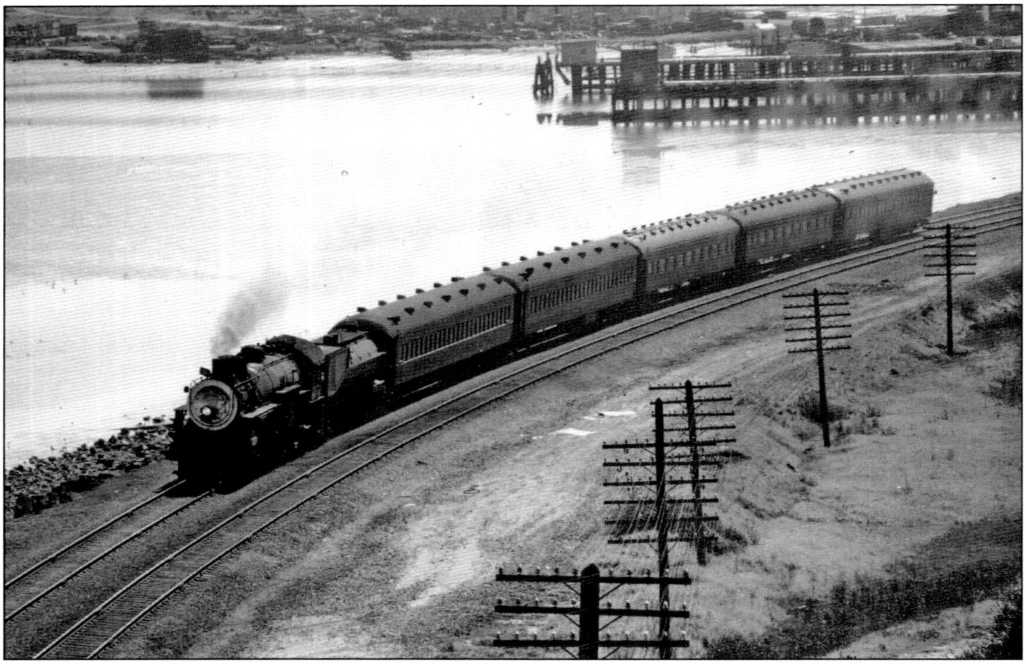

A Pacific-type engine steams along the waterfront, pulling a five-car consist north through South San Francisco, past shipyards that were kept busy during World War II. For decades until Caltrans introduced new gallery cars, rail commuters traveled in Harriman coaches built in 1911 by Pullman. These cars, which seated 68 passengers, had arched roofs and seats that would "flip" for the direction of travel. (Reg McGovern.)

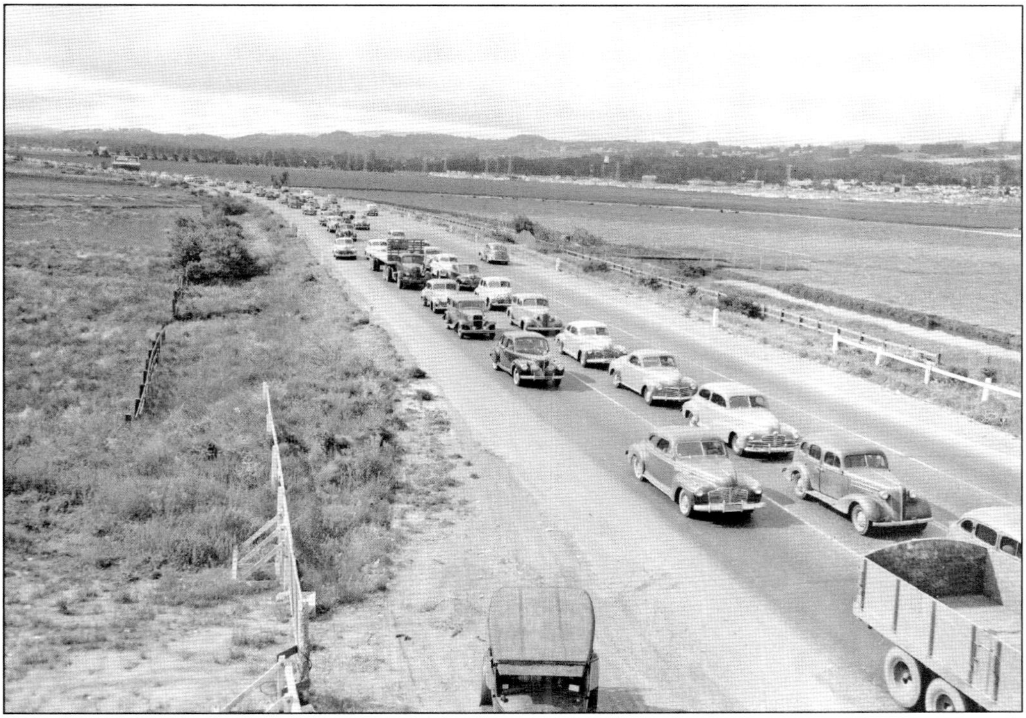

The 1947 photograph above, taken near Mills Field (the future San Francisco International Airport), shows bumper-to-bumper conditions on the highway that was the alternative to taking the train. "Bayshore Highway," as it was called, was only two lanes in each direction. Below, SP 2474 barrels through Millbrae, as work progresses on a temporary bridge over the tracks, used to transport construction materials to Mills Field, where work was underway on the new airport. A crane can be seen setting the bridge in place, and on the left are the 40 Line tracks. (Above, Reg McGovern; below, Tom Gray.)

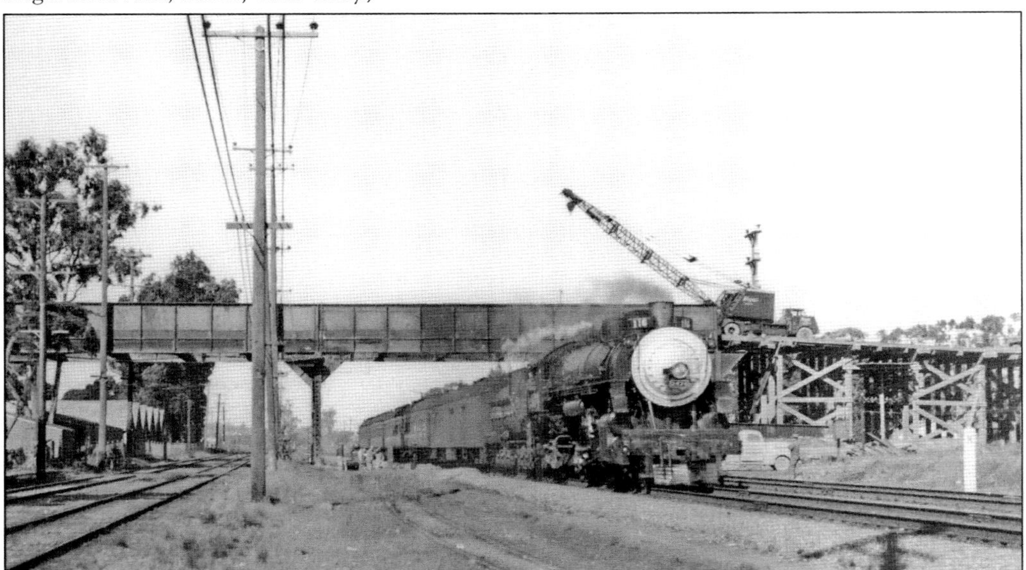

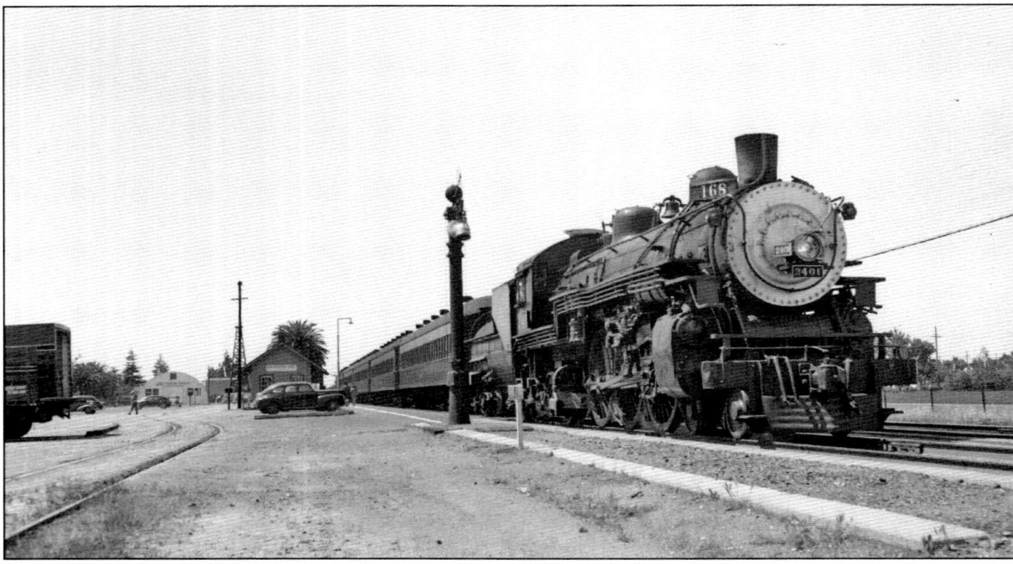

Train No. 168 stops in May 1949 at Palo Alto's California Avenue depot to pick up passengers. Note the water column for steam engines to take water and the spur track on the left side past the station to the freight shed. The Will Whittaker photograph below shows a closer view of the building itself, taken during World War II, with an SP poster reading "The Victory Trains Come First" on the exterior. Palo Alto's bike-friendly attitude seems to be deeply rooted, judging by the bike rack next to the building. (Above, Arthur Lloyd collection; below, Tom Gray collection.)

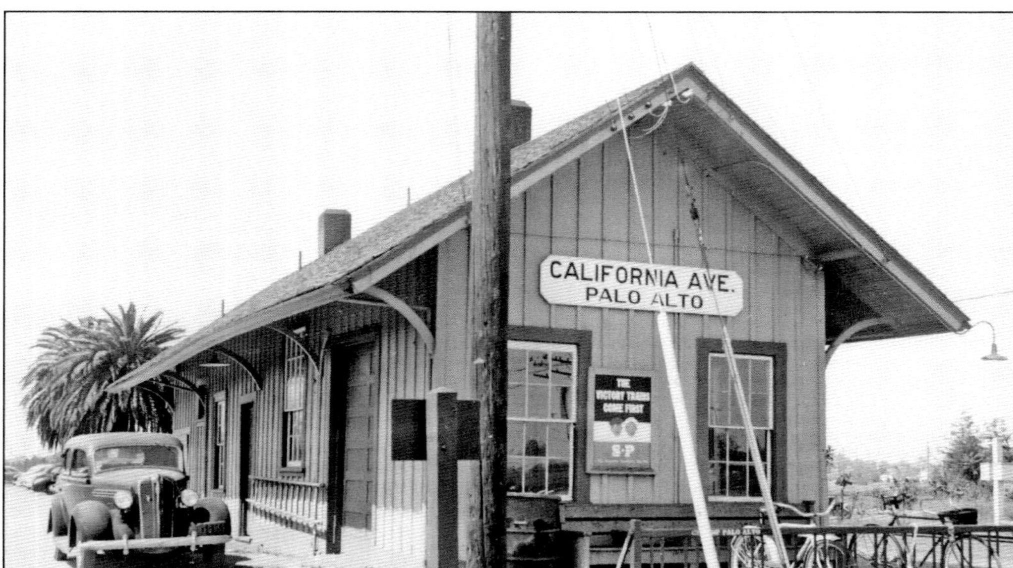

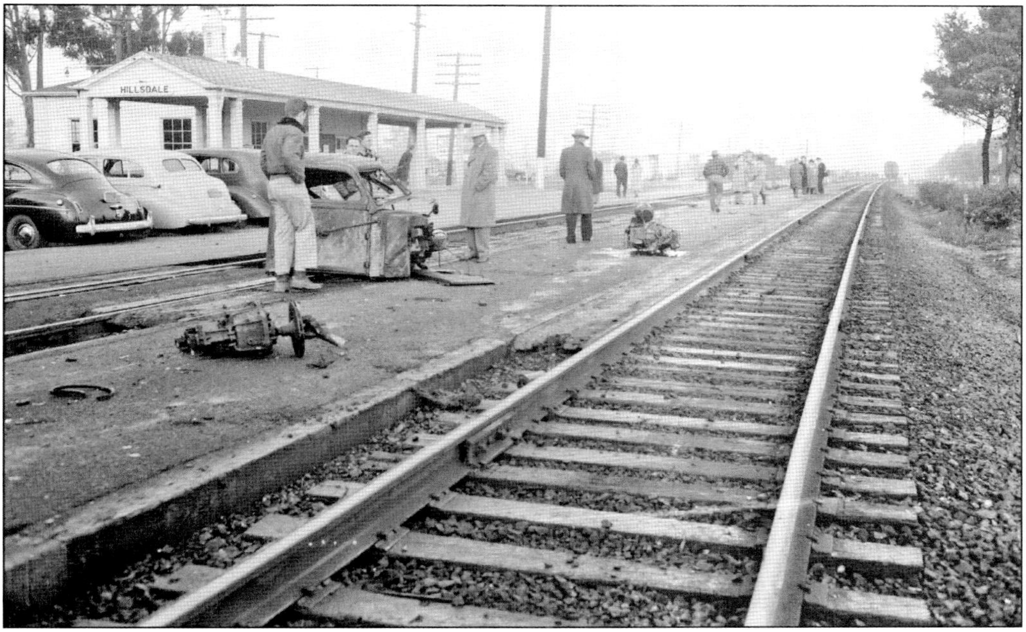


Collisions between trains and vehicles are a sad fact of life for any railroad, and over the decades, a number of safety improvements have been made to reduce opportunities for these tragedies on the rail corridor. This 1948 photograph above shows the aftermath when an unloaded dump truck stalled on the Hillsdale crossing near Bay Meadows Racecourse, strewing metal parts hundreds of yards, after a commute train collided with the truck. In later years, the Hillsdale crossing was grade-separated, eliminating the possibility for a train-vehicle crash. Because of their weight, trains often emerge unscathed from collisions, so the battering that this train took in Redwood City in 1952 from a large cement truck and trailer was a bit unusual. (Both, Reg McGovern.)

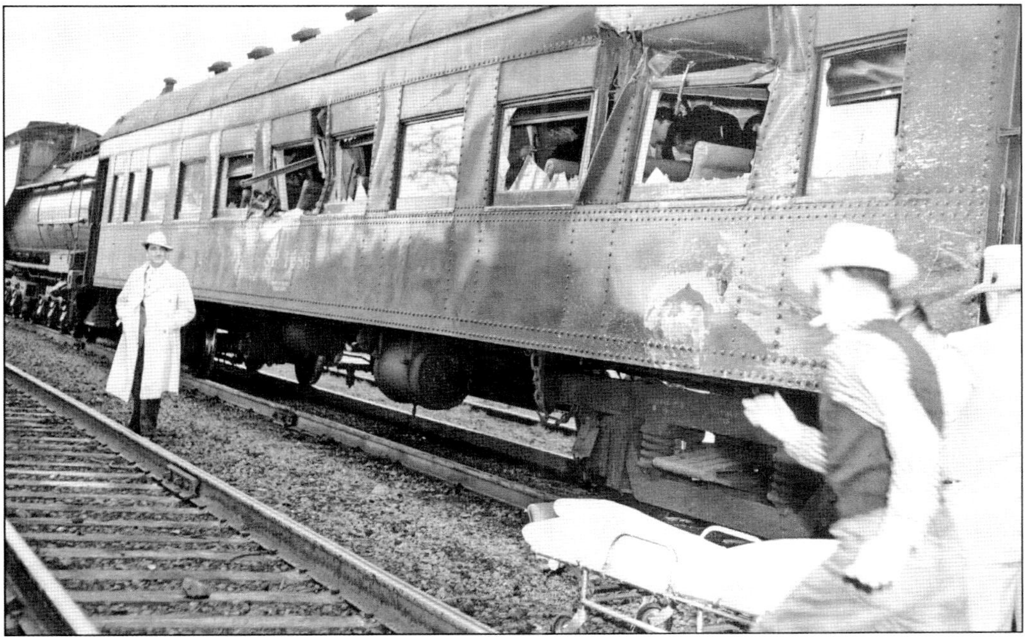

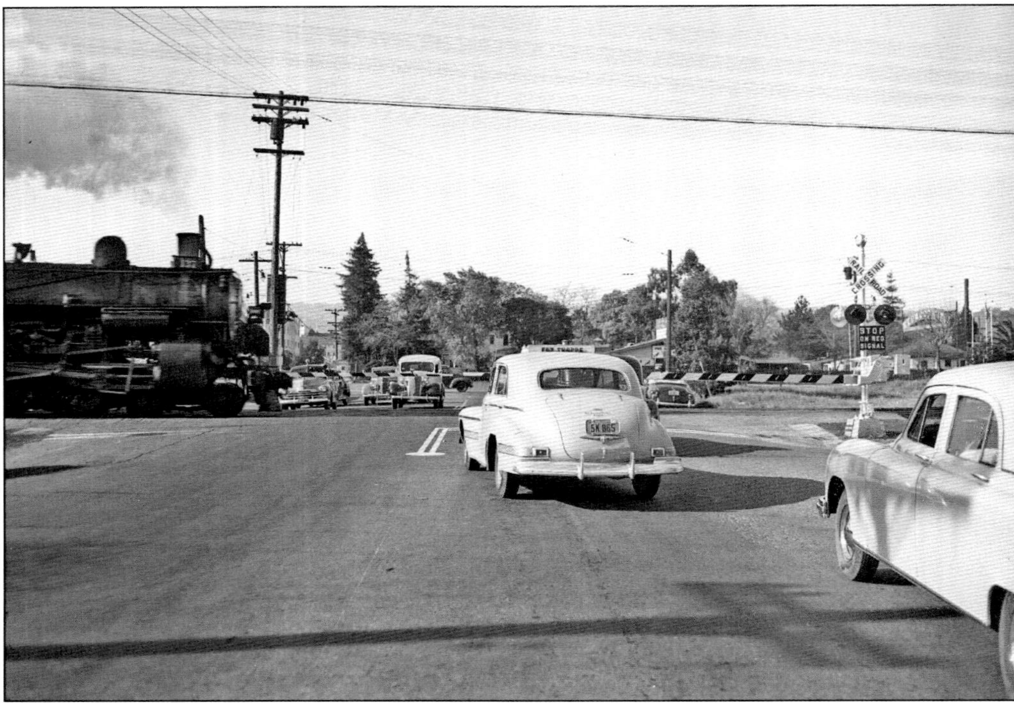


After a half-dozen people had been killed or injured at the Whipple Avenue crossing over two decades, in 1948 SP installed electrically operated gates. Prior to that, the Redwood City crossing was unguarded. Installed at a cost of $8,000, the gates operated much as they do today, with arms automatically lowering and bells sounding as a train approaches. (Reg McGovern.)

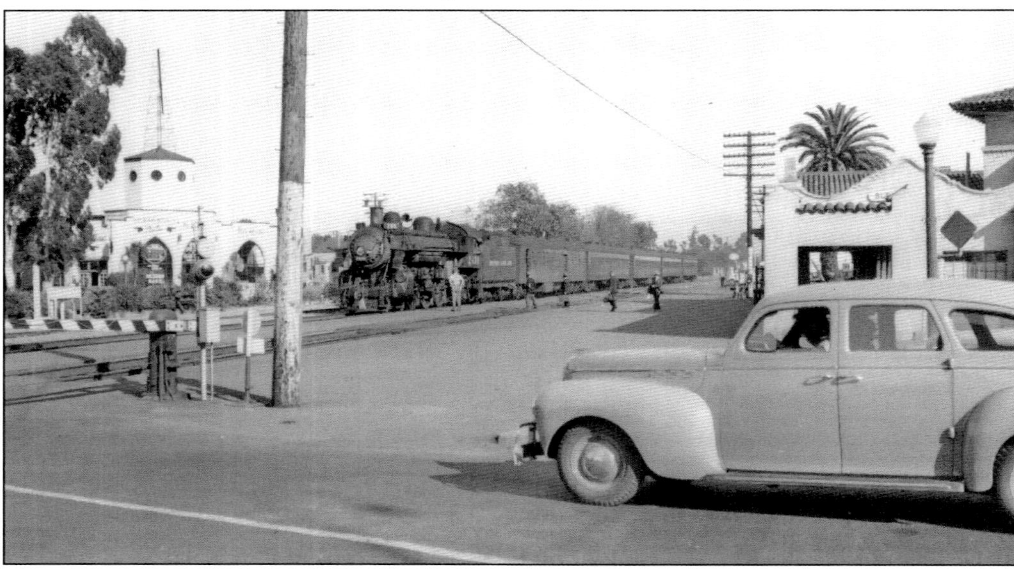

Except for the steam engine and the car stopped at the automatic gate, this 1945 scene looked remarkably similar to the Burlingame Avenue grade crossing and station area until 2008, when major pedestrian and safety improvements were made. The automobile dealership building across the street from the station is still there and the historic depot is essentially unchanged. (Tom Gray.)

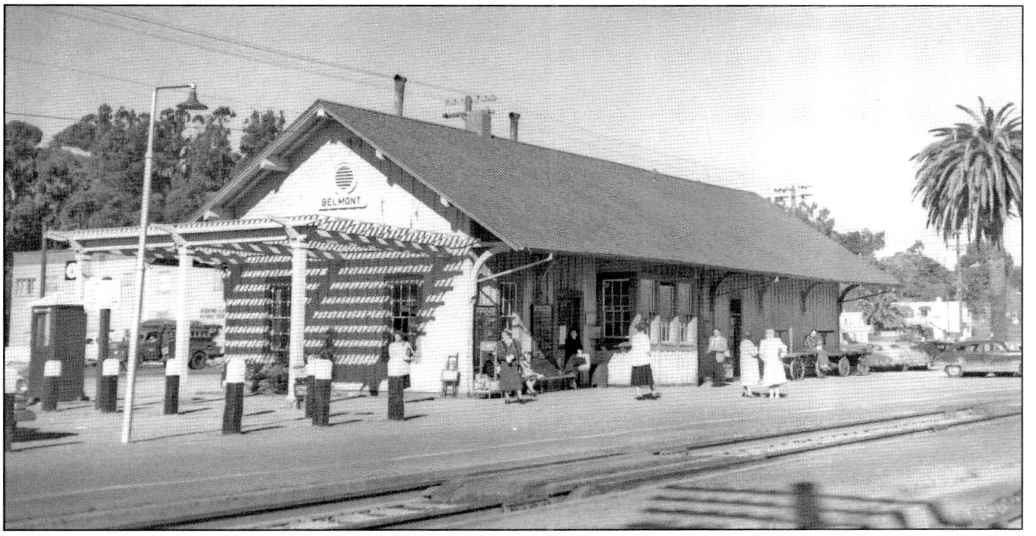


The first Belmont depot was hauled there from Menlo Park in 1867 but destroyed in a fire in 1872 and then replaced by this structure, shown in a 1940s Will Whittaker photograph. In style, it was similar to other SF&SJ board-and-batten depots, including the one at Santa Clara. The depot was closed in 1960 and later replaced by shelters. (Tom Gray collection.)

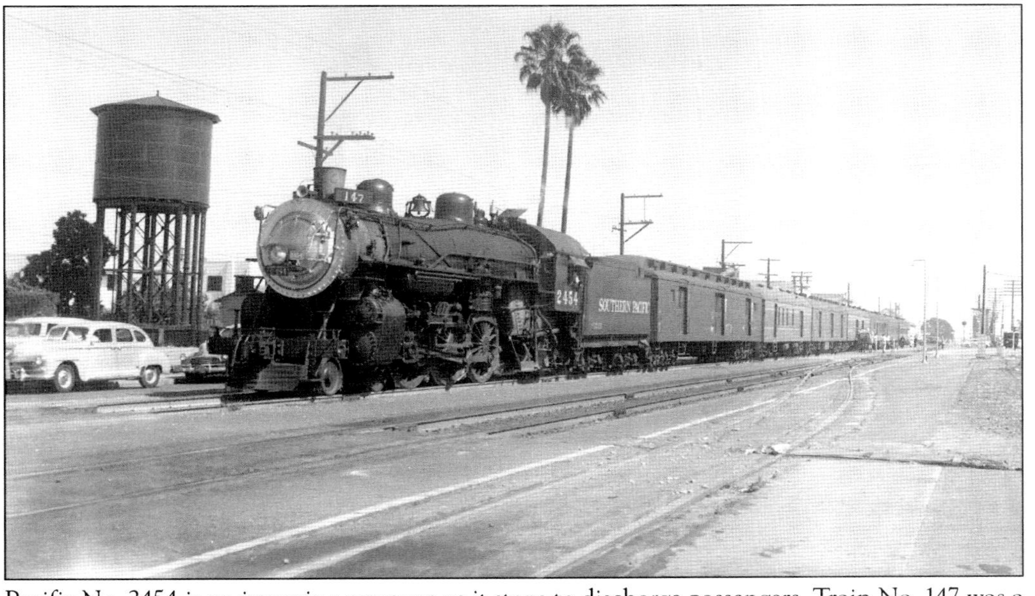


Pacific No. 2454 is an imposing presence as it stops to discharge passengers. Train No. 147 was a midday train and included both baggage-express cars and a railway post office (RPO) car along with the passenger cars. The post office trains ran at 11:00 a.m. and 3:00 p.m. Outgoing mail was hung on a mail crane at the stations and snatched into the RPO car. (Arthur Lloyd collection.)

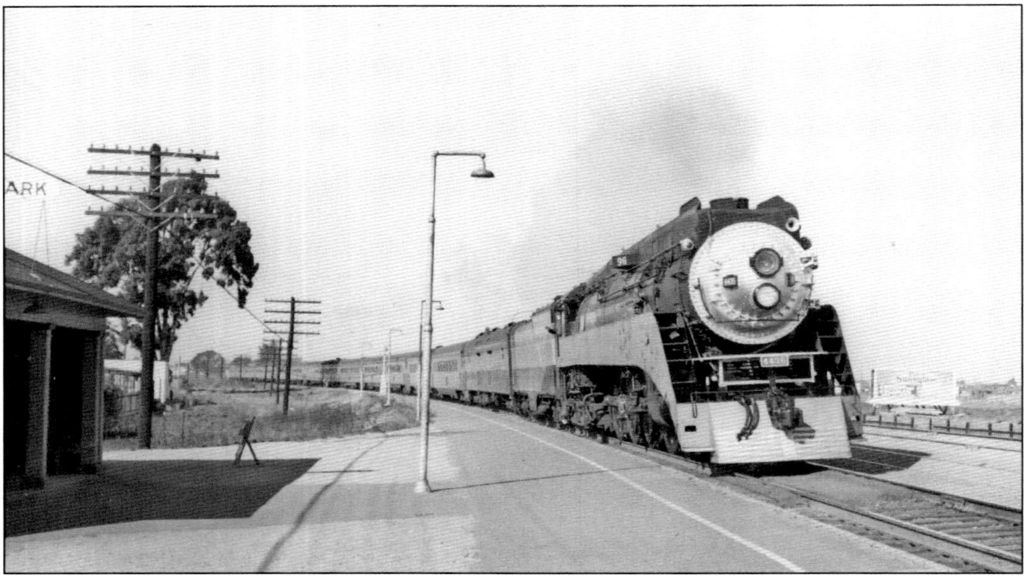

A *Daylight* engine 4435 pulling train No. 96 approaches the Hayward Park station. Originally named Leslie, the station was renamed in 1936, though the stucco shelter dated from 1925. It featured square columns and a hipped roof. A Lexan shelter replaced the deteriorating structure in 1985. (Tom Gray.)

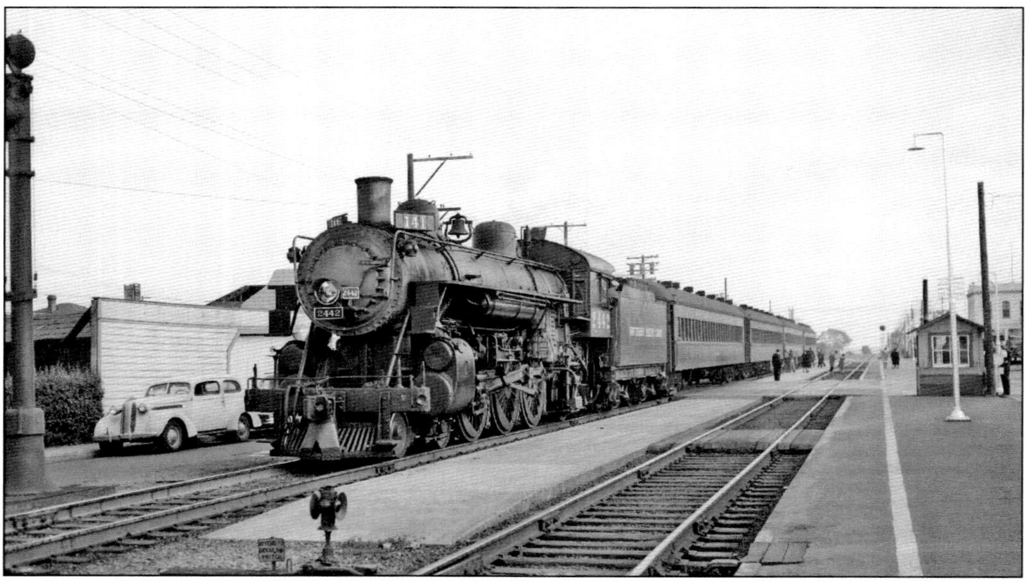

The guard's shack is visible on the right in this scene when Pacific locomotive No. 2442 delivers train No. 141 and its passengers to downtown San Mateo in October 1945. Guard shacks like this one were manned, and when the train approached, the guard would wave a flag or lantern to warn drivers a train was coming. (Arthur Lloyd collection.)

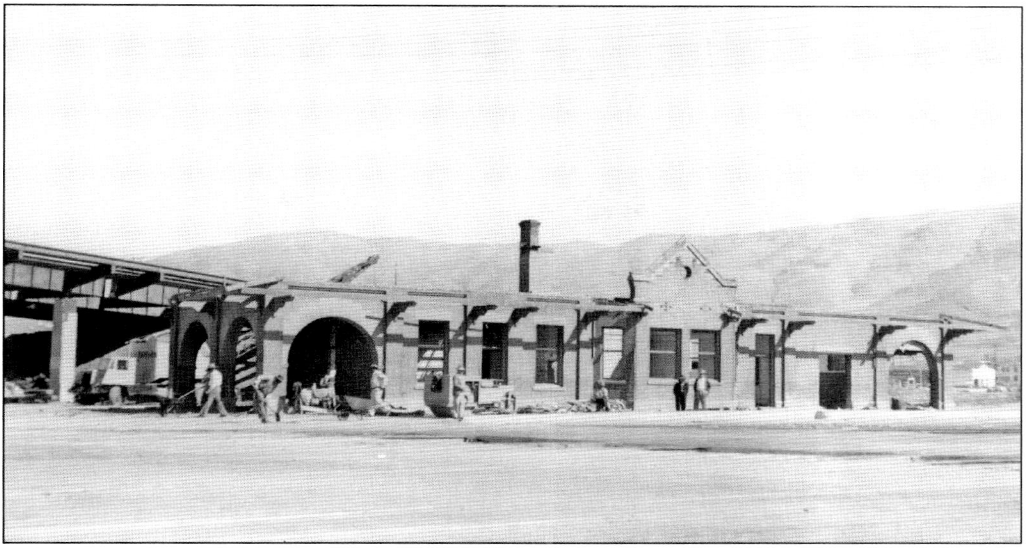

The South San Francisco depot is shown in this Alvon Thoman photograph taken in June 1948 in the process of being wrecked to make way for the approaches to the Bayshore Freeway and the widening of Grand Avenue. This depot had been replaced by a one-story redbrick structure, which was used by commuters until 1989. (Henry Bender collection.)

**TO OUR PENINSULA COMMUTERS ON TRAIN 127:**

We are sorry that our commuters on Train 127 were delayed 29 minutes in arriving at San Francisco yesterday morning (Thursday).

Because of a *very heavy fog* on the peninsula decreasing the visibility of signals and necessitating slowing down of operations in order to make them safe, a number of commuter trains were delayed slightly yesterday morning. However, in the case of Train 127, a combination of factors caused the train to be unusually late. The fog situation delayed a freight train, which, in turn, got in the way of Train 127 and delayed it 15 minutes for that reason alone. The fog also caused an operating situation delaying the starting of the train from San Jose and then slowed down its normal operations. The total delay in this case was unusually large and irritating, we know, to No. 127's passengers.

CLAUDE E. PETERSON, *Vice President*
*System Passenger Traffic*

**S•P**
**The friendly Southern Pacific**

10-21-48 (1500)

Compared to the "just-the-facts" style of today's "seat drops," Southern Pacific notices like this October 1948 card had an elegant gentility. Apologies were profuse. "We have had no important delays in our commuter fleet for some time," vice president Claude E. Peterson wrote in one such message in 1950. "We are sorry and unhappy that one had to happen this morning." (Arthur Lloyd collection.)

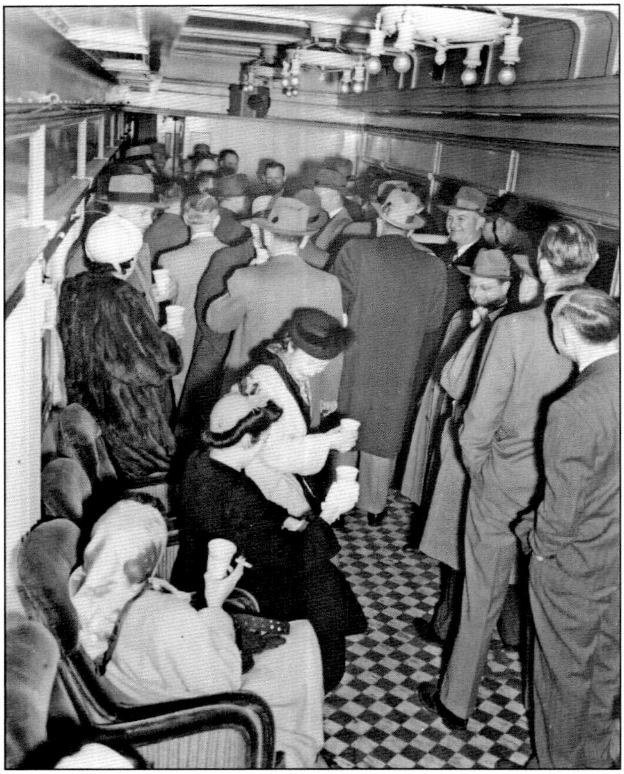

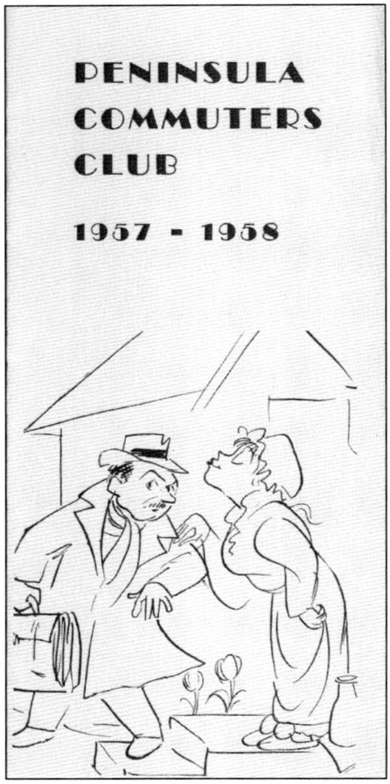


Regular riders made friends on the train and even formed the Peninsula Commuters Club for after-hours socializing and promoting civic interests. A newsletter kept them informed about subjects such as the planned Bay Area Rapid Transit District (BART). The club's board of directors examined the issue and, in 1961, went on record in opposition, concluding that BART would be too costly, and the route through Daly City too roundabout, when commuters already had good rail service. A Christmas party such as one in 1949, when a lounge car was added to the head end of train No. 144 in San Francisco, was an annual event. Members could enjoy some "Christmas cheer" on the way home. (Both, Arthur Lloyd collection.)

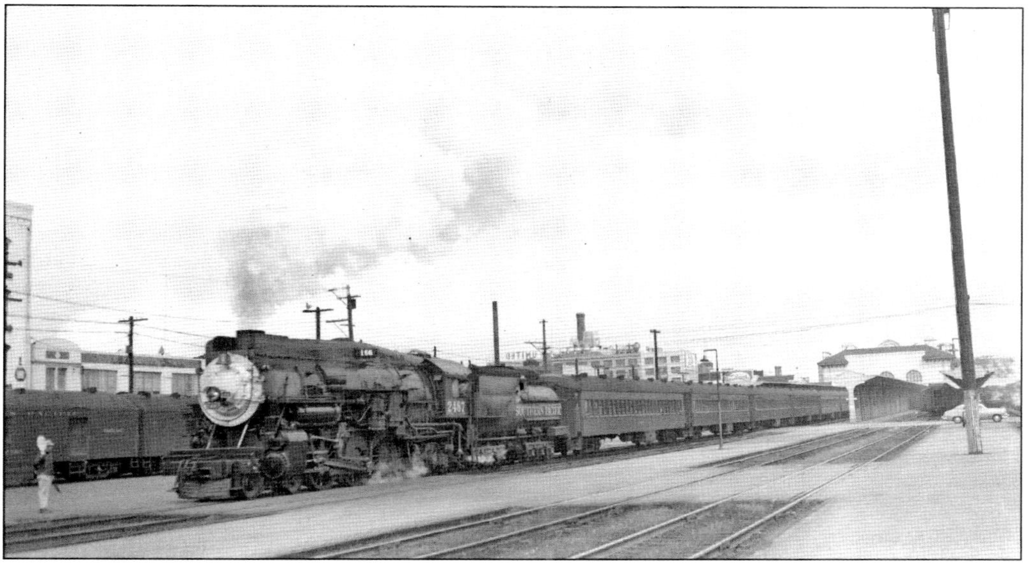


A train fireman leans out the window for a look as train No. 166 begins to roll in this 1950 photograph. The consist stretches well past the umbrella sheds at the Third and Townsend Streets terminal in San Francisco, pulled by Pacific 2487. (Arthur Lloyd collection.)

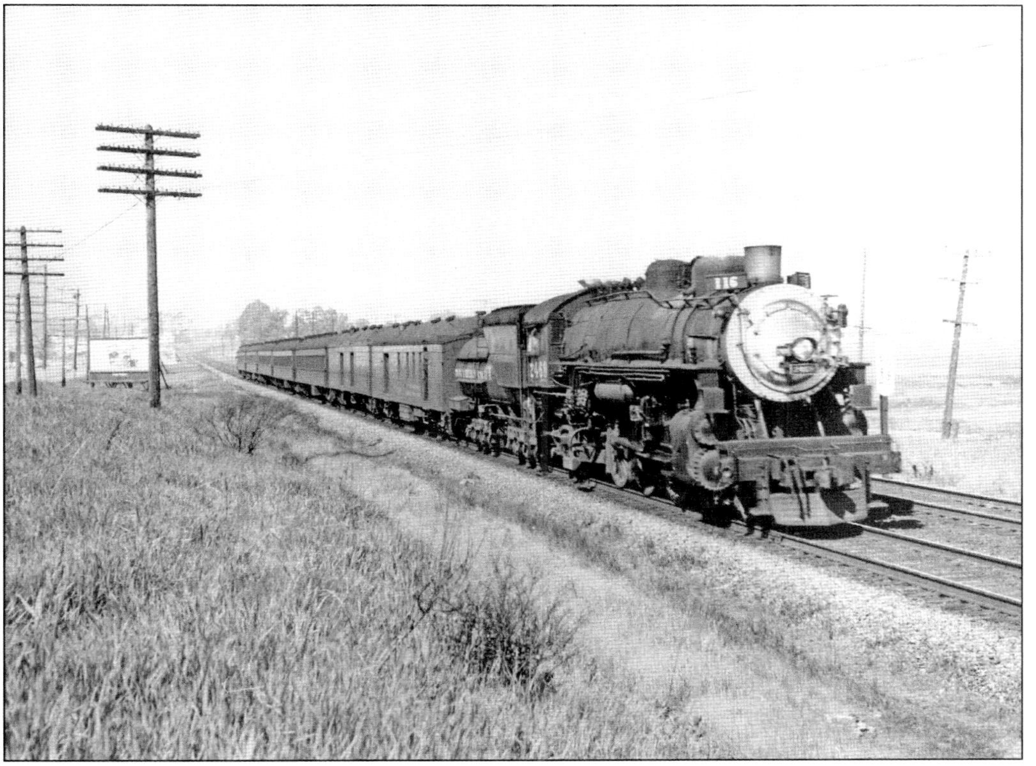


Train No. 116 highballs through San Mateo, with one mile to go to Hillsdale, pulling a consist of Harriman cars. To modern eyes, the bucolic setting through which the train is passing is a startling reminder of how much the Peninsula has changed since World War II. (Reg McGovern.)

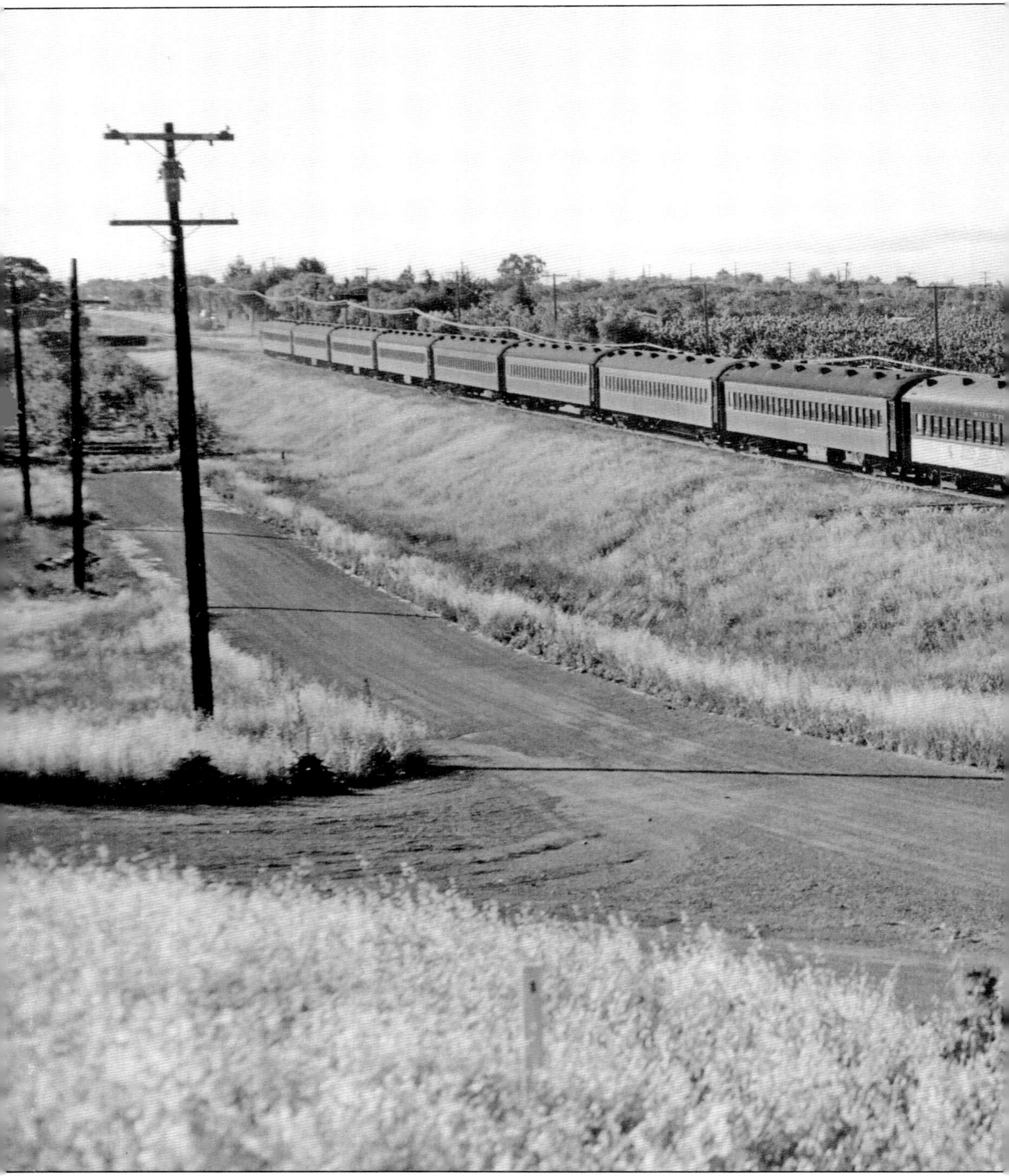

In this 1948 photograph, SP 2401 steams over the track between Los Altos and Loyola on the alignment of the old Peninsular Railroad Company. SP trains to Los Altos used that rail line between Mayfield (today's California Avenue station in Palo Alto) through Los Altos, Monta Vista, and on to Los Gatos. Trains passed through the orchards, making various stops along the

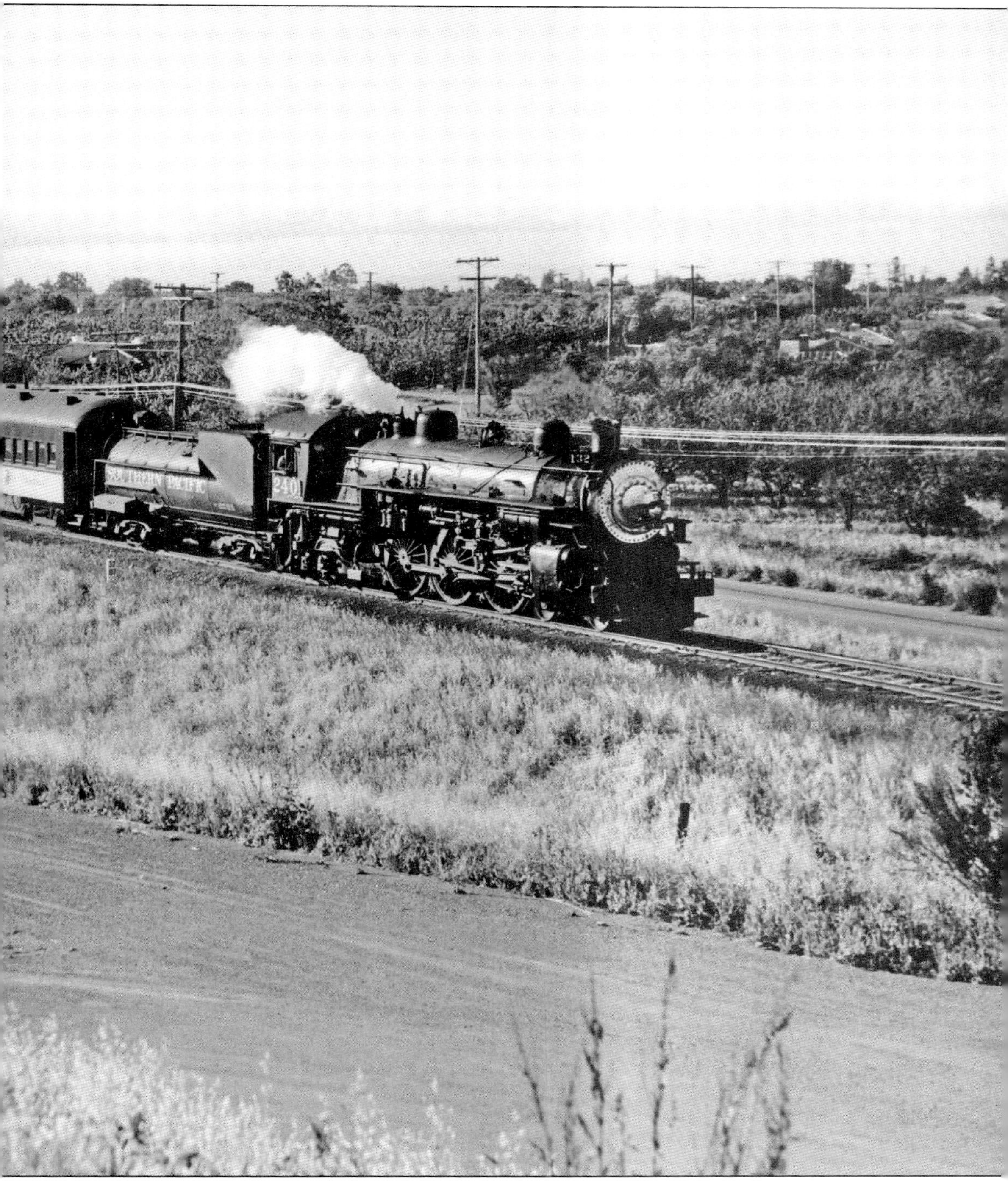


way. It is hard to reconcile this view with the fact that the Foothill Expressway, constructed in the 1960s, occupies the former railroad alignment. In the photograph, a blast of steam curls back over the nine-car consist. Just below the windows of the second car is a recruitment advertisement for the US Marines, both the Marine Corps and the Marine Reserve. (Reg McGovern.)

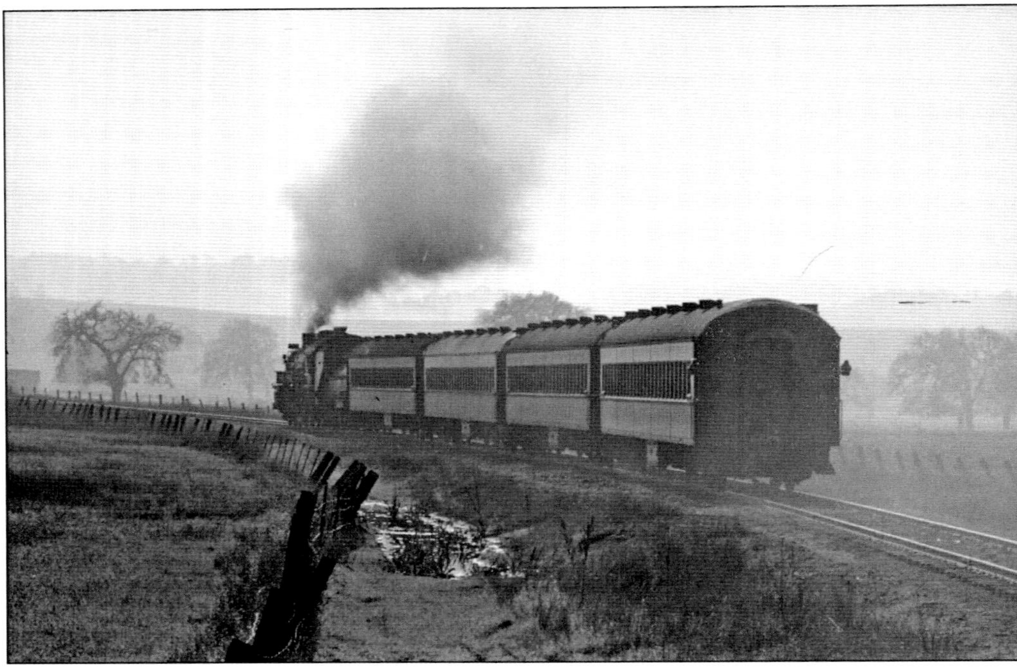

Southern Pacific's commute train No. 168 headed for the open country after leaving the main line at California Avenue in this April 1953 photograph. This 19-mile branch line took it through the backcountry and to Los Gatos. By 1953, Saturday trains had been discontinued but one weekday commute train each way was still run from Los Gatos to San Francisco. The Campbell depot was on SP's line, which snaked its way from Los Gatos to San Jose. The present Santa Clara Valley Transportation Authority Vasona Light Rail Line stops at the same location. (Above, Reg McGovern; below, Tom Gray.)

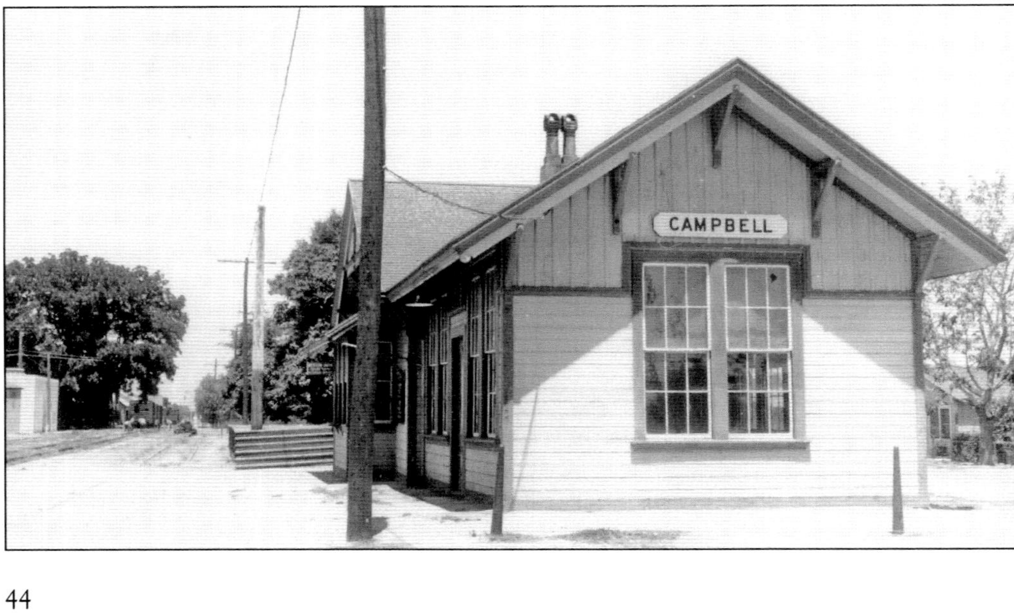

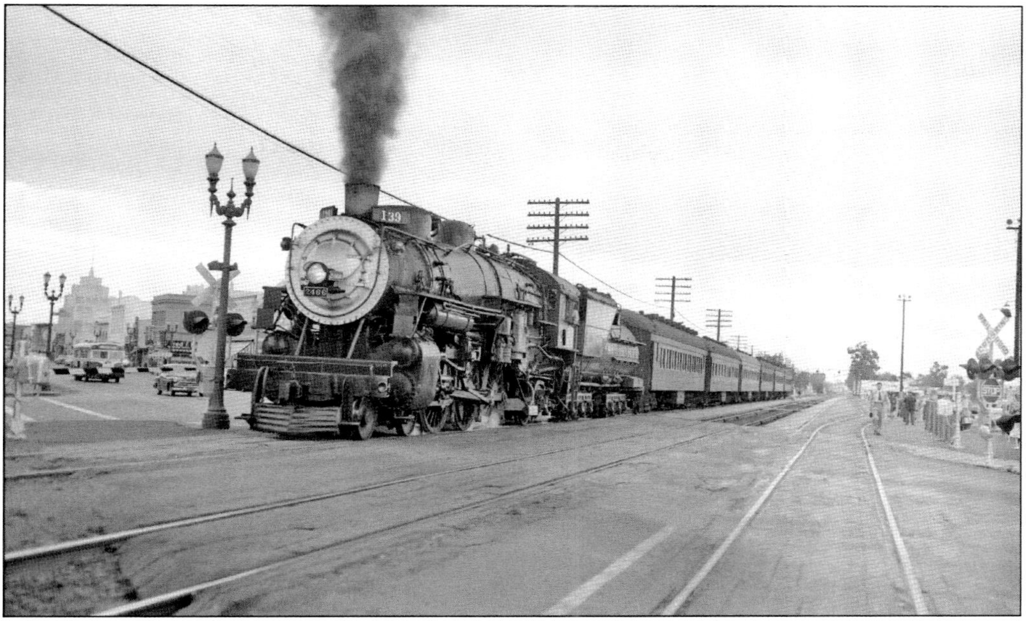


These photographs, taken weeks apart in 1954 at the Broadway grade crossing in Redwood City, illustrate the transition that was underway as diesels began to replace steam engines on the Peninsula Commute Service. SP 2466 (above), powering train No. 139, sent a blast of steam skyward, as if to ask people to take a good look. Below, a diesel enters the crossing. SP had been converting to diesel motive power on other passenger trains but the Peninsula Commute Service was the last to make the switch. By 1954, three of 22 locomotives in service were diesels, a change offering many efficiencies. Turntables were no longer needed, and diesels were more able to operate in forward or reverse direction than steam locomotives. (Both, Reg McGovern.)

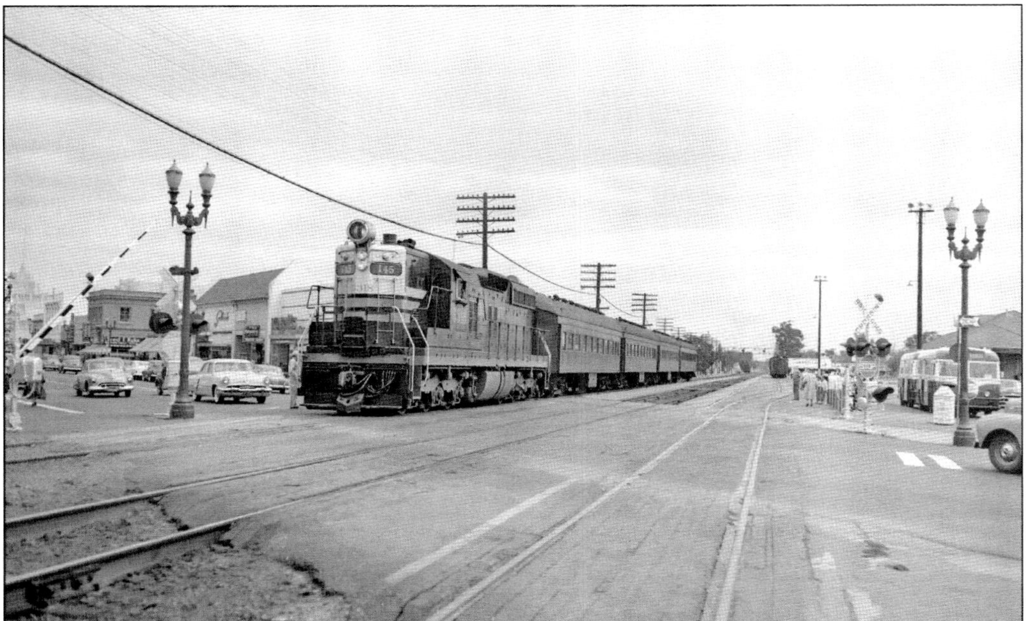

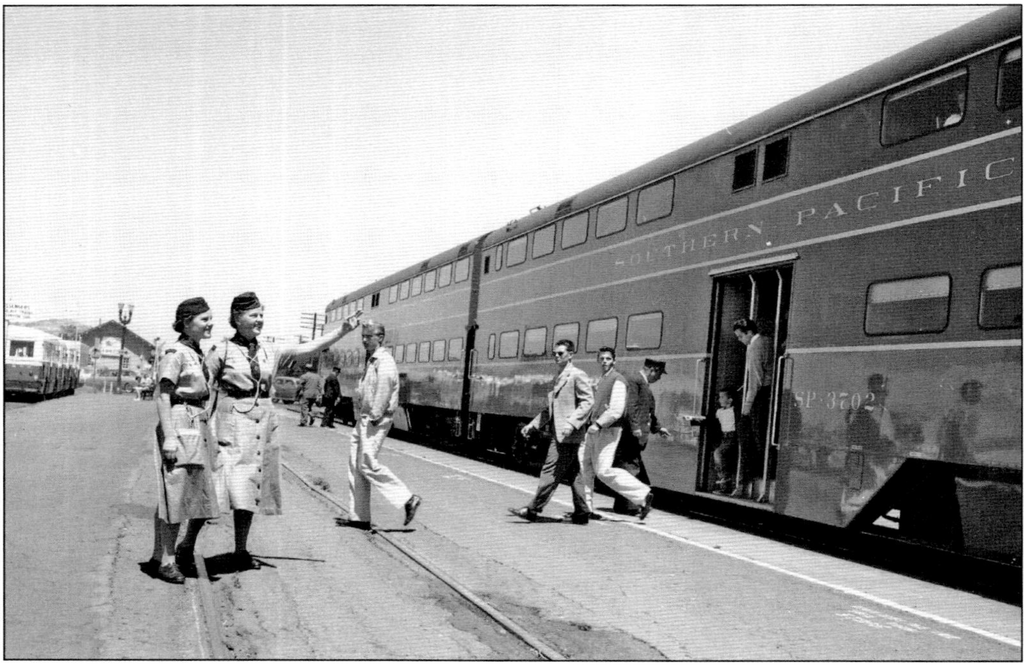


Visiting New Zealanders Helen Patten and Alison Stout checked out one of 10 new two-level SP commute coaches, the first of which went into service on the San Francisco Peninsula in June 1955. Equipped with automatic sliding doors in the center, the double-deck coaches seated 145 passengers, requiring a smaller fleet. (Reg McGovern.)

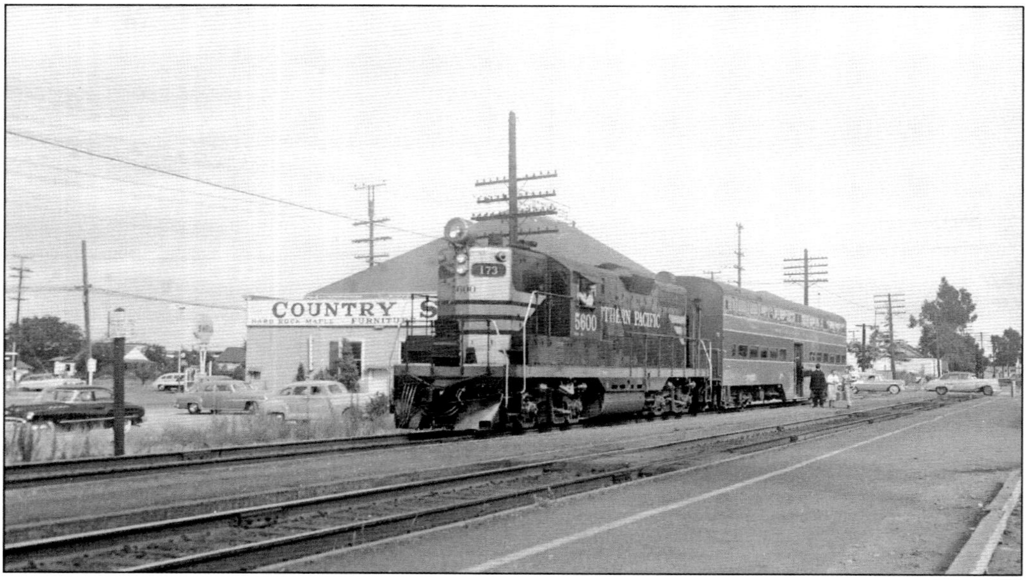


Stopped at Belmont, train No. 173 was a midday train, pulling just one of the new double-decker coaches. They were so popular that SP quickly ordered 21 more. Claude E. Peterson, vice president in charge of passenger public relations, explained that SP wanted to continue its high service standards "until such time as a Bay Area rapid transit system of some kind may go into effect." (Arthur Lloyd collection.)

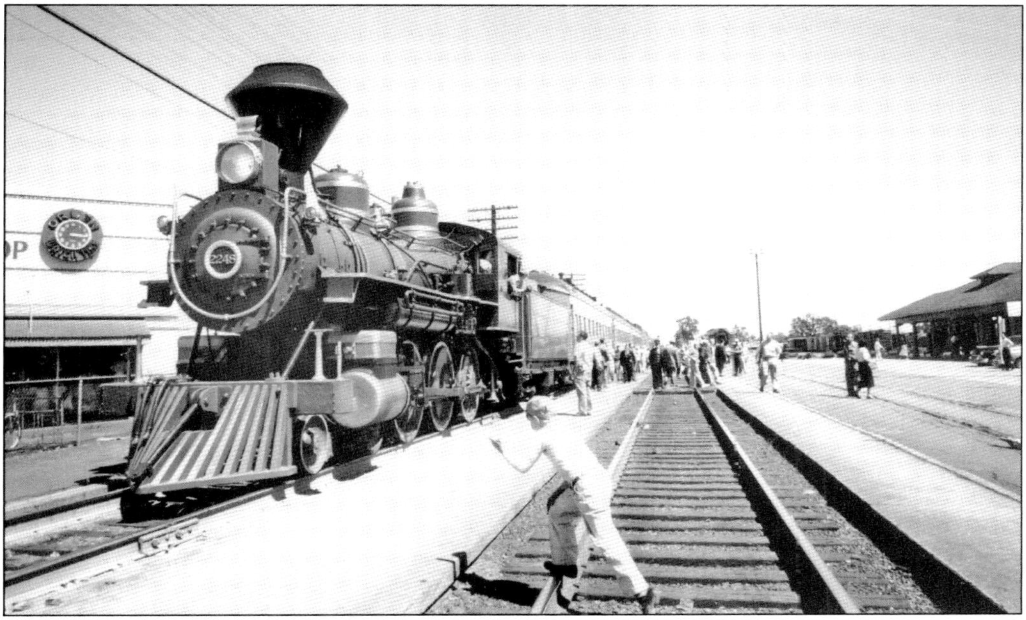

A rail fan special train in 1957 saluted the fading away of nearly a century of steam service on the Peninsula, and organizers brought locomotive 2248 out of retirement from Sacramento for a day of nostalgia and a salute to T. Louis Chess on his retirement. The San Francisco district passenger agent since 1939 was a beloved railroad man who customers affectionately called "Mr. SP." Chess is shown greeting friends as they rode to Los Gatos to the Billy Jones Wildcat Railway. Chess was elected in 1959 to the San Mateo County Board of Supervisors. Chess Boulevard in Foster City is named in his honor. Built in 1896 by the Cooke Locomotive Works, No. 2248 now runs on the "Tarantula" tourist train in Grapevine, Texas. (Both, Reg McGovern collection.)

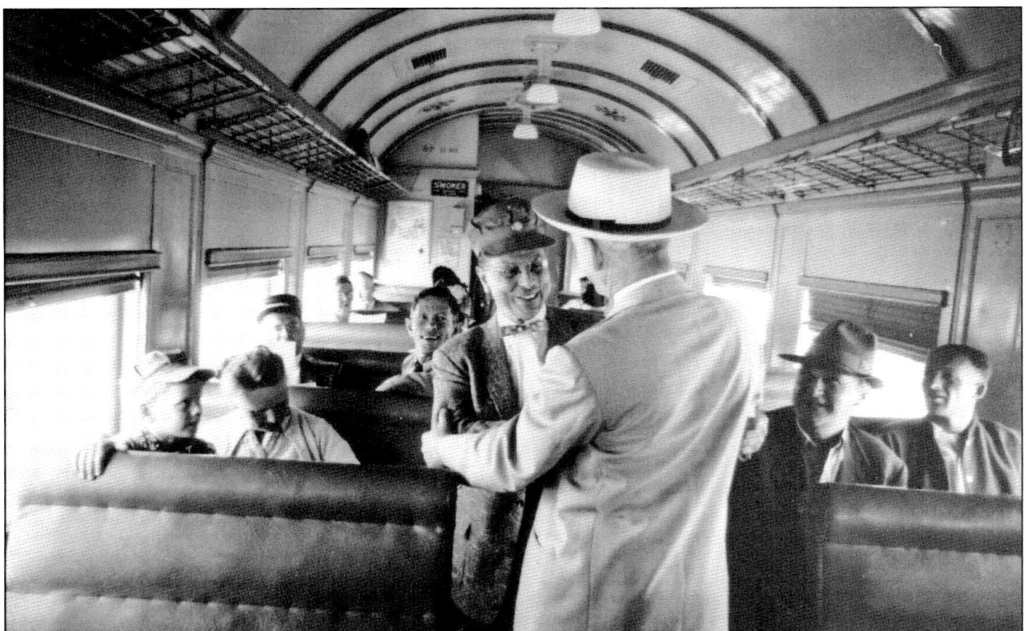

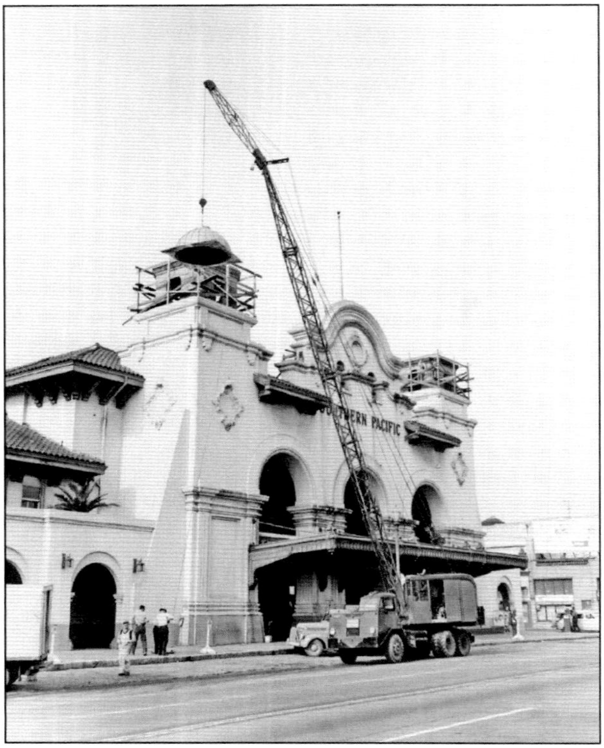

The dome of the Southern Pacific depot at Third and Townsend Streets needed to be replaced, and a crane was brought in to do the job, as is shown in this February 17, 1955, photograph. (Courtesy Union Pacific Museum.)

The San Francisco terminal 10 years later was still a hub for taxicab drivers, connecting passengers to destinations in the city. For almost as long as SP existed, the terminal's location about a mile from the city center was a major complaint and was considered a detriment to increasing patronage. Riders had to board a Muni bus, walk, or grab a cab. (Courtesy Union Pacific Museum.)

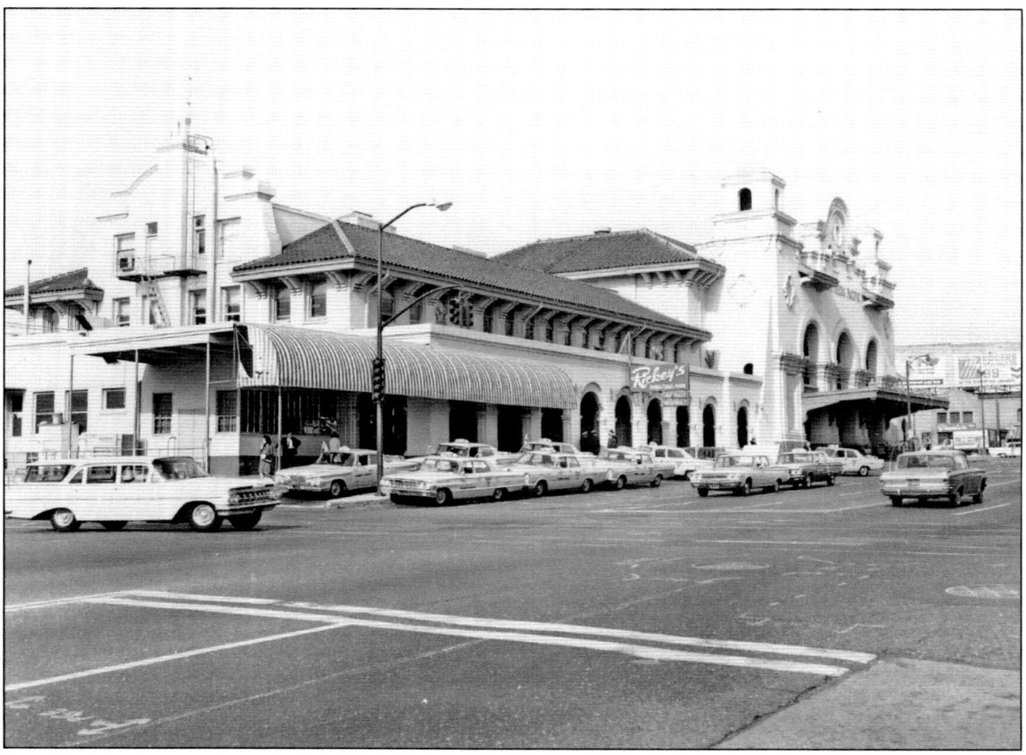

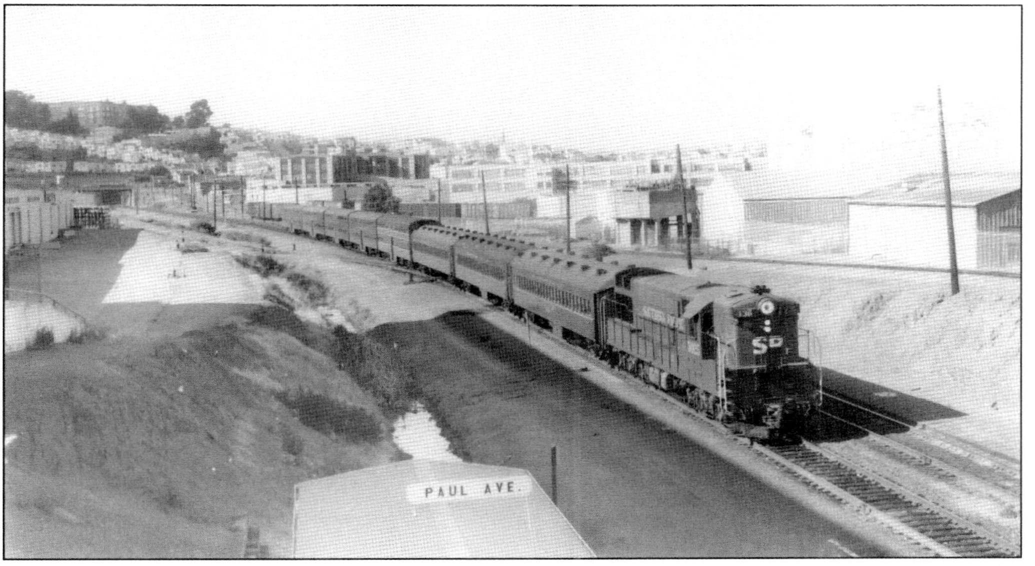


With a Fairbanks-Morse Train Master H-24-66 unit on the head end, train No. 136 passes by the Paul Avenue station in this 1970 shot. When SP replaced steam locomotives, Train Masters—rated at 2,400 horsepower—had the power and acceleration required for the Peninsula Commute Service, where stations were often only a mile or two apart. Note that this train included both double-decker cars and Harriman coaches. (Tom Gray.)

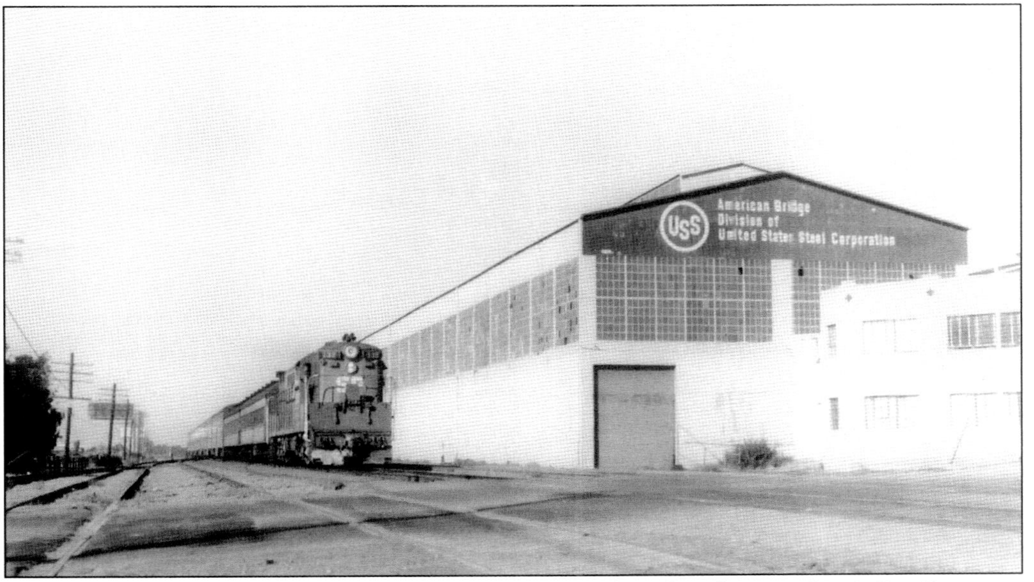


Early industries, including meat-packing, ship-building and steel works, gave South San Francisco its identity as "the Industrial City." Built in 1926, the small Butler Road shelter could hardly have been more convenient for workers taking the SP to the adjacent United States Steel mill, pictured in the early 1970s. After the mill was demolished in 1980, the Butler Road stop was eliminated. (Tom Gray.)

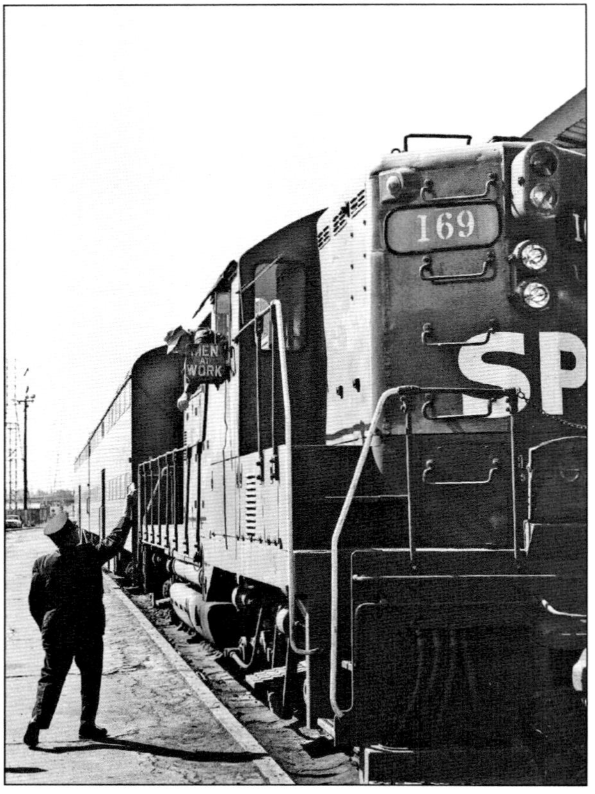


Engineers had to get clearance before departing from San Francisco or the San Jose terminal, shown here in 1972. They received train orders if there were any in effect, such as speed restrictions, and it was the conductor's job to hand them to the engineer. The two crewmembers would discuss the orders before taking off. The same happens today, but the orders are printed by computer and can be transmitted by radio should something occur after the train is under way. In the photograph below, crew dispatcher Bill Stewart is shown working in the Seventh Street Diesel Terminal Building in San Francisco. Dispatchers moved the little wooden blocks around when assigning engineers and firemen for the day. Not long after this photograph was taken, crew dispatching was computerized. (Both, Greg Welker.)

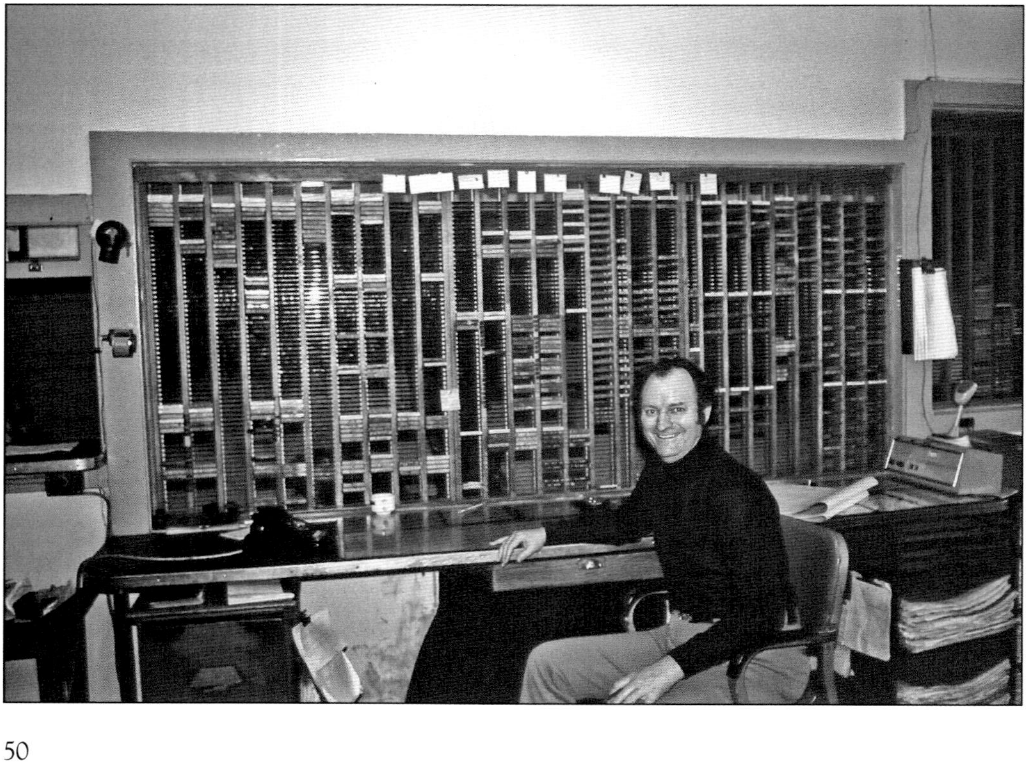

Commuters may not realize it but the view from the engineer's cab is of a highly symbolic scene in the history of the Peninsula Commute Service. In 1863, when the SF&SJ Railroad ran an inaugural trip as far as Palo Alto, the picnic celebration took place near the landmark El Palo Alto coast redwood tree on what later became the Menlo Park/Palo Alto border. (Greg Welker.)

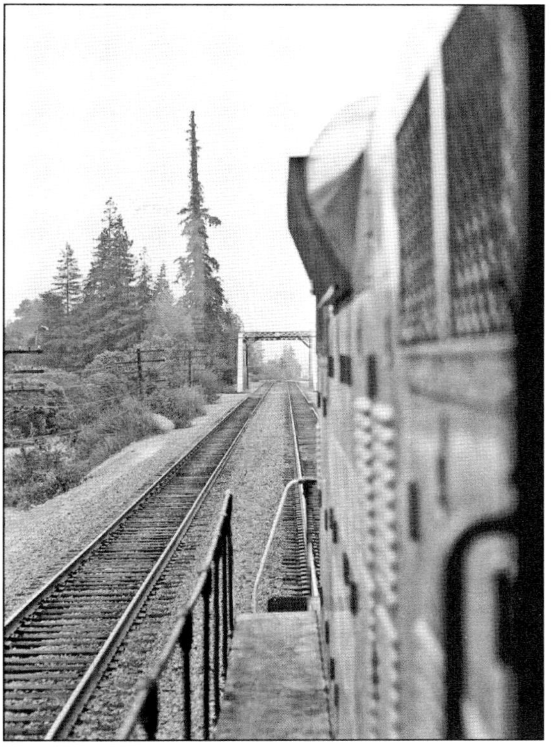

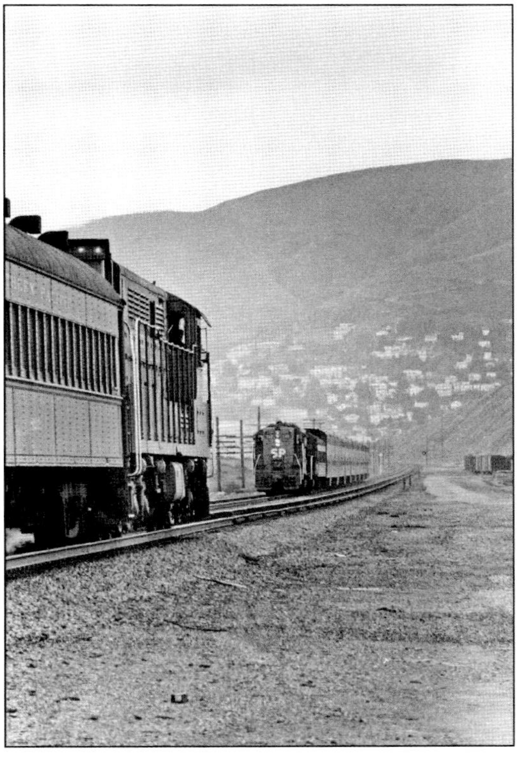


Northbound train No. 117 meets southbound train No. 112 in the Bayshore area at 7:18 a.m. in this 1973 photograph. The hillside community of Brisbane is in the distance as train No. 112 heads south past the vast Southern Pacific rail yards and roundhouse. The Bayshore yard closed in the early 1980s. (Dave Stanley.)

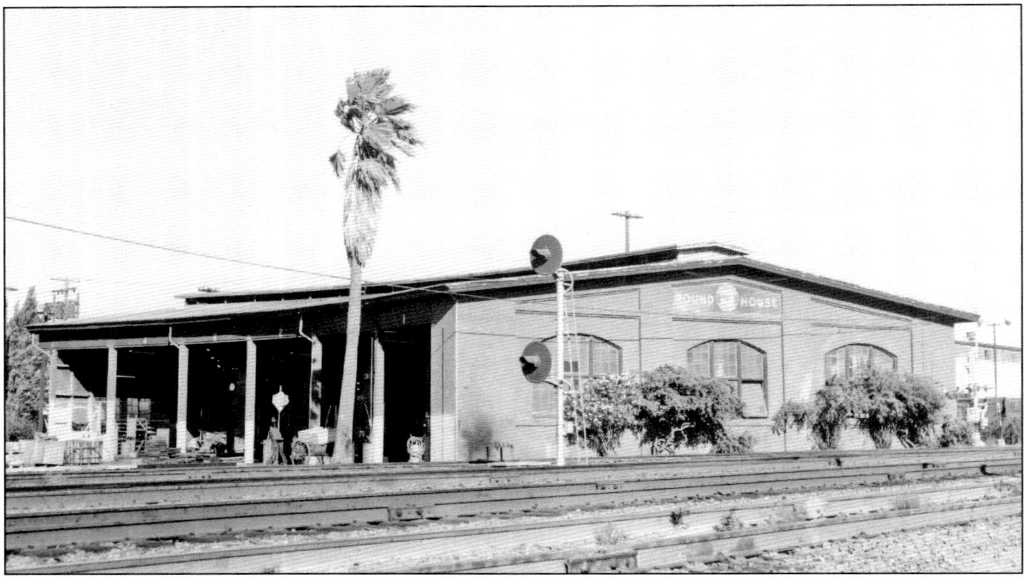


Much of the maintenance work on the commute fleet based in San Jose took place at the Lenzen Avenue Roundhouse, shown in the August 1972 photograph above. A nine-stall brick roundhouse was built toward the end of the 19th century, but it was later expanded to 15 stalls. During the steam heyday, Lenzen Avenue throbbed with activity. Hostlers who moved locomotives from one track to another moved the behemoths into a stall, where machinists, boilermakers, and laborers worked on them. With the end of steam, Lenzen Avenue was downsized to six stalls. The second photograph, taken in 1982, shows SP 3209 going into the roundhouse. A brick structure, Lenzen Avenue suffered damage in the 1989 Loma Prieta earthquake and was demolished in 1992. (Above, Henry Bender; below, Bill Kepner.)

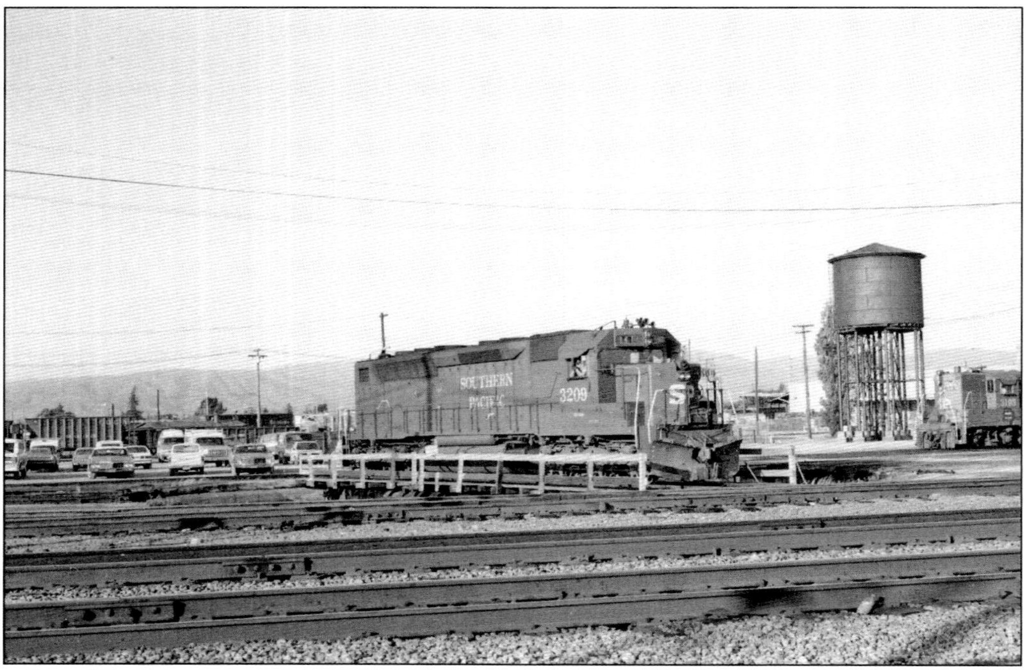

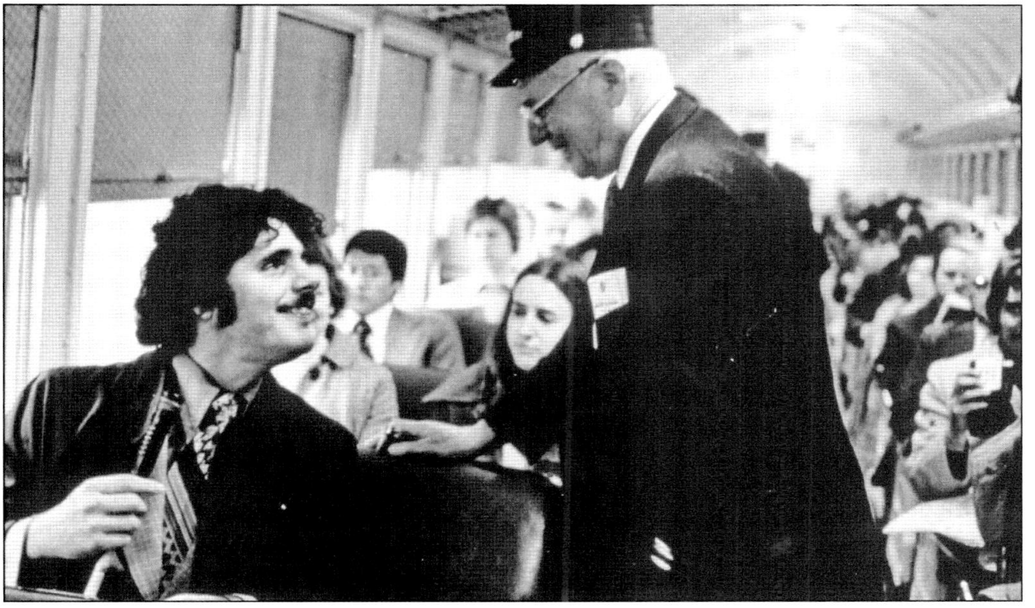

Blind since birth, Pete De Vasto (left) has long been a loyal Peninsula Commute Service commuter. In 1978, he rode from his Belmont home to work at Fireman's Fund on California Street in San Francisco. He continued to ride the train to subsequent jobs, and was still taking the train in 2011 to work at Adobe Corporation in San Jose. He often carries a scanner to track arrivals. (Reg McGovern.)

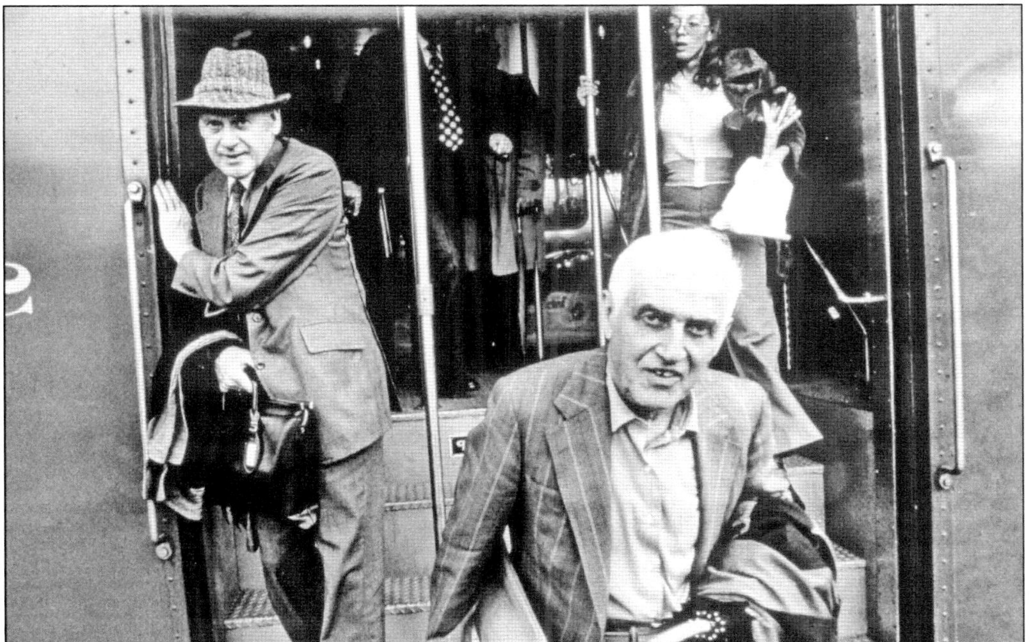

In this photograph taken in the 1970s, the doors of the double-decker cars open, and commuters disembark from the train at the Atherton station, ready to head for home after a day at work. (Reg McGovern.)

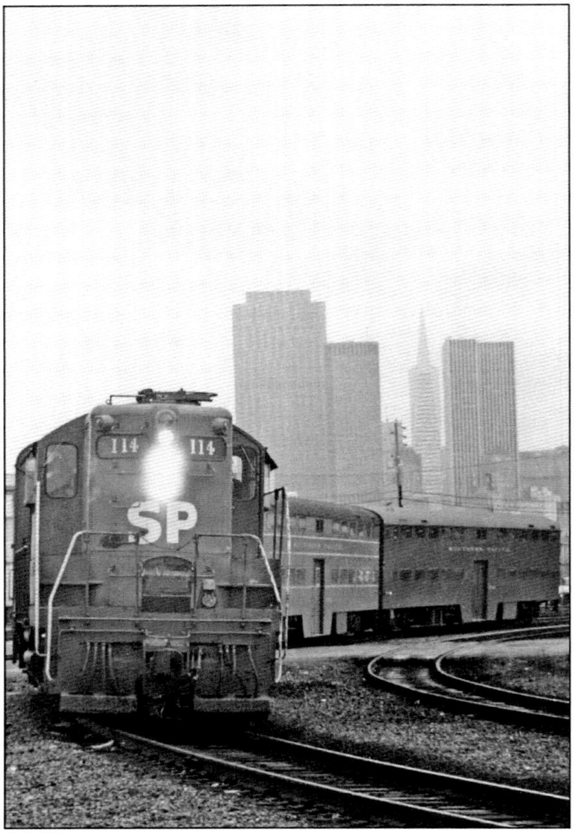


An Electro-Motive Division SD45 pulls morning commute train No. 114 in this 1972 view as it rounds the Seventh Street curve leaving San Francisco. SP at one time had a fleet of more than 350 of these engines; those used on the Peninsula Commute Service had steam generators to provide heating in the passenger cars. (Dave Stanley.)

On a Saturday morning in October 1972, two trains pass each other near the College Park interlocking tower. Built in 1927, the tower was used to control the switching of trains from the main line to the San Jose terminal, the Newhall Street yard, and other points. It closed in 1993 and vandals burned it down in 1996. (Dave Stanley.)

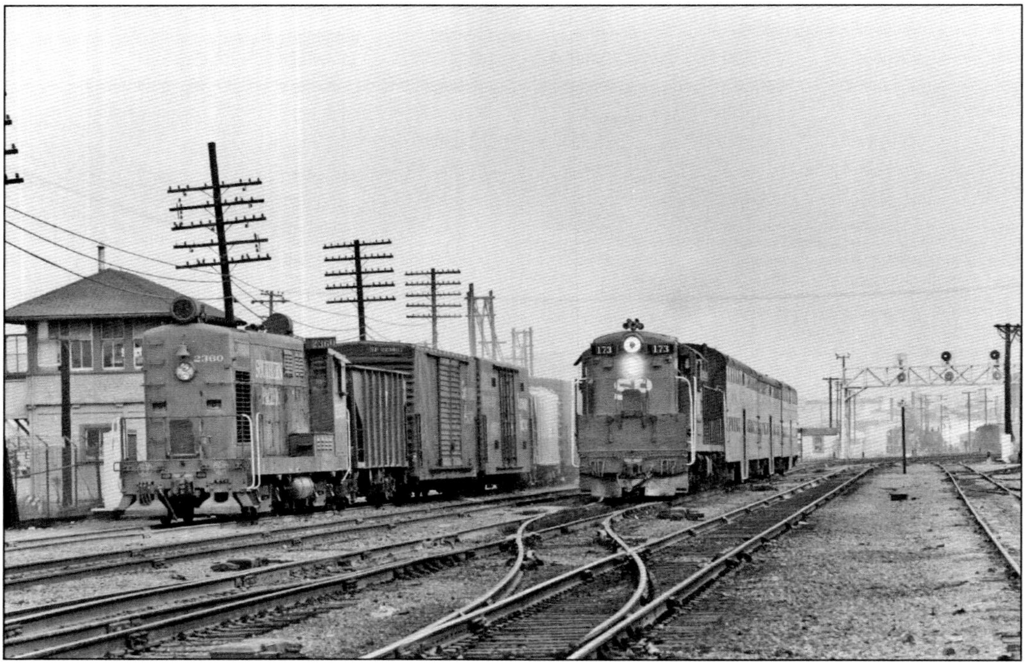

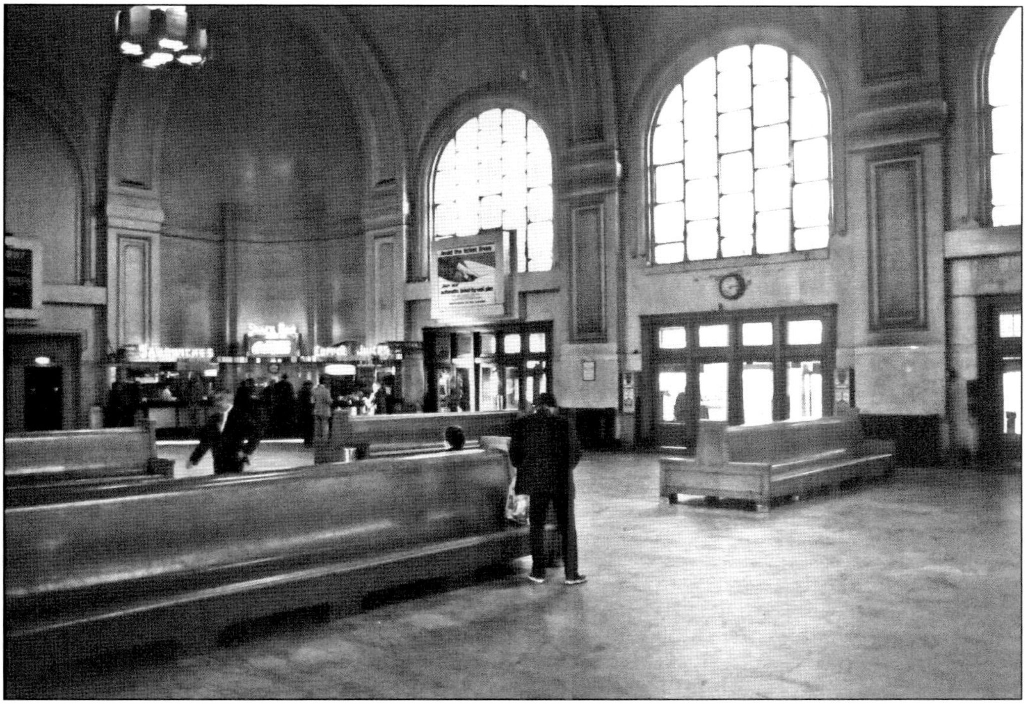

In San Francisco, travelers passed through this 64-by-110-foot waiting room, which featured a dramatic arched ceiling and amber Moss glass in the windows. Customers could buy tickets, purchase flowers, grab a snack, or pick up a newspaper for the ride home. Rickey's Coach Room, a popular restaurant with a red-and-white striped awning, offered cocktails and meals. (Greg Welker.)

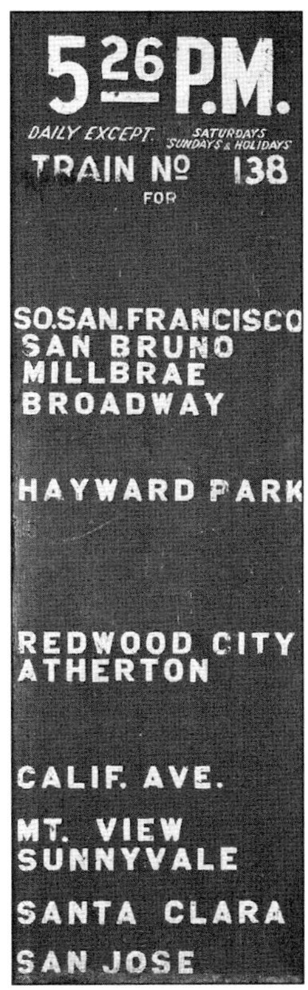


Passengers checked these signs for the correct track for the homeward trip. Southern Pacific ran peak-hour commute trains leaving San Francisco at three-minute headways, the first running nonstop to the farthest station and the next running nonstop to intermediate stations. Operating nonstop to South San Francisco, train No. 138 really made tracks, so to speak, in a skip-stop pattern that foreshadowed Caltrain's "Limiteds" in 2005. (Greg Welker.)

## PENINSULA ZONE FARES

(Effective August 6, 1977)

| BETWEEN | | San Francisco 3rd St. | | | | | |
|---|---|---|---|---|---|---|---|
| **SAN FRANCISCO** 23rd St. Paul Ave. Bayshore | O.W. | $.95 | ZONE 1 | | | | |
| | R.T. | 1.90 | | | | | |
| **(RED) ZONE 1** Butler Rd. So. San Fran. San Bruno Millbrae | O.W. | 1.45 | $.95 | ZONE 2 | | | |
| | R.T. | 2.90 | 1.90 | | | | |
| **(GREEN) ZONE 2** Broadway Burlingame San Mateo Hayw'd Park | O.W. | 1.70 | 1.30 | $.95 | ZONE 3 | | |
| | R.T. | 3.40 | 2.60 | 1.90 | | | |
| **(ORANGE) ZONE 3** Hillsdale Belmont San Carlos Redwood City | O.W. | 2.10 | 1.70 | 1.30 | $.95 | ZONE 4 | |
| | R.T. | 4.20 | 3.40 | 2.60 | 1.90 | | |
| **(BLUE) ZONE 4** Atherton Menlo Park Palo Alto Calif. Ave. | O.W. | 2.55 | 2.10 | 1.70 | 1.30 | $.95 | ZONE 5 |
| | R.T. | 5.10 | 4.20 | 3.40 | 2.60 | 1.90 | |
| **(YELLOW) ZONE 5** Castro Mount. View Sunnyvale | O.W. | 3.00 | 2.55 | 2.10 | 1.70 | 1.30 | $.95 |
| | R.T. | 6.00 | 5.10 | 4.20 | 3.40 | 2.60 | 1.90 |
| **(BROWN) ZONE 6** Santa Clara College Park San Jose | O.W. | 3.20 | 3.00 | 2.55 | 2.10 | 1.70 | 1.30 |
| | R.T. | 6.40 | 6.00 | 5.10 | 4.20 | 3.40 | 2.60 |

**ZONE 6**

Between Any Two Stations Santa Clara To San Jose

One Way .... $ .95
Round Trip .. 1.90

O.W. denotes **ONE WAY** • R.T. denotes **ROUND TRIP**

In addition to purchasing tickets at staffed stations, SP customers could buy them on the train from conductors. They carried a mini fare chart like this one from 1977 so they could easily compute a one-way or round-trip ticket sale on board the train. Conductors were issued a punch with a unique design, which they used in hole-punching tickets. When conductors sold tickets or fare-inspected for tickets or passes, they would place a "hat check" under a metal clip above the passenger's seat to indicate that the customer had paid. Passengers were charged by the number of zones traveled, and at this particular time, SP had six fare zones. The Butler Road station was still open in South San Francisco and the Twenty-second Street station was listed as Twenty-third Street, before it was "moved" because of the Interstate 280 construction project. (Patty Doolette collection.)

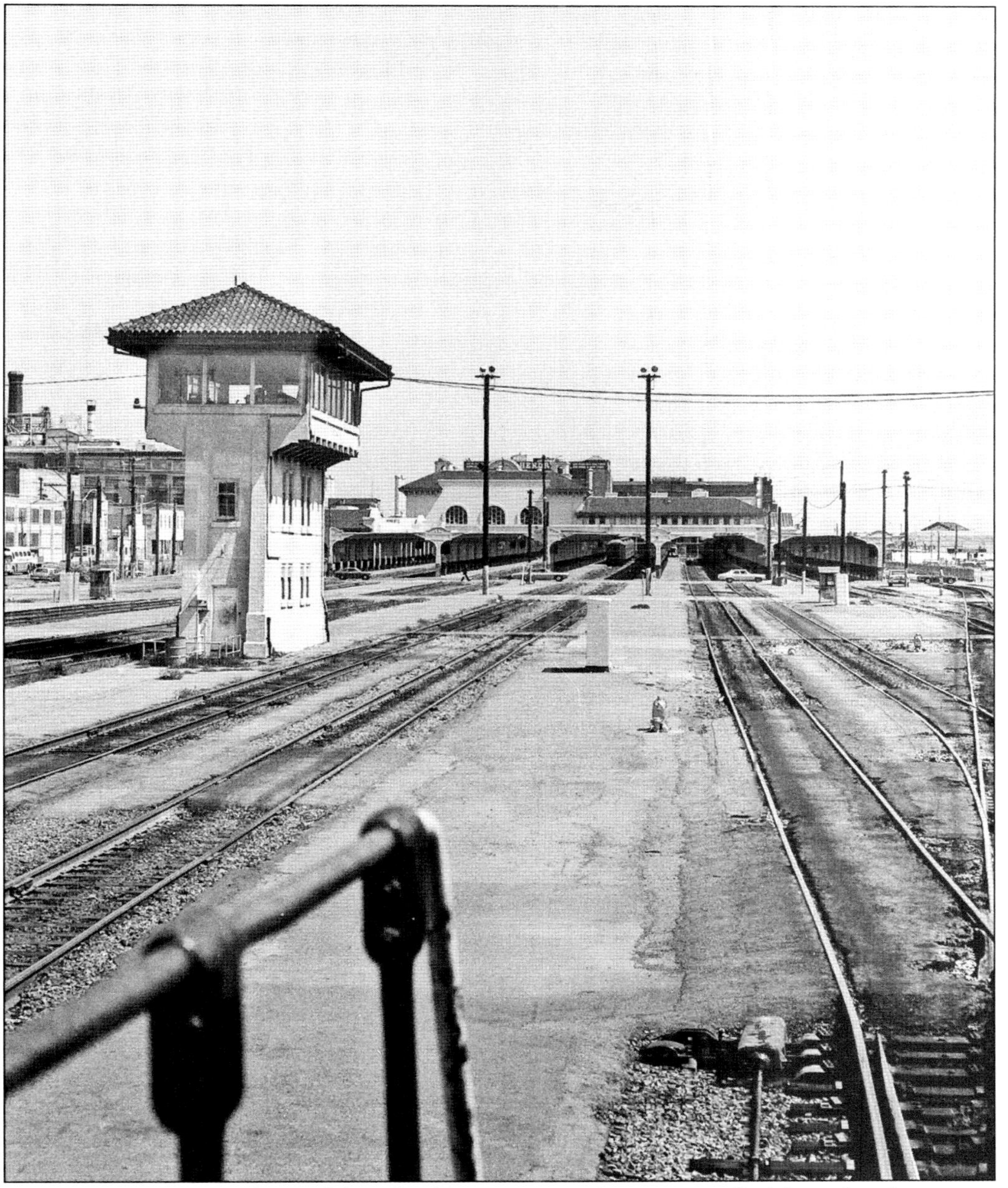

Train movements in and out of the Third Street terminal were controlled from this three-story interlocking tower near the Fourth Street end of the station. The towerman's office had cantilevered sides, and from his perch high above the tracks, the towerman was kept busy controlling a variety of train movements. Commute trains were arriving or departing. Switch engines would couple onto the rear of an arriving train after the passengers departed, and then reposition it, depending on where it was going. Engines might be taken to the Bayshore yard or to the Seventh Street Diesel Terminal for servicing. When the Fourth and Townsend terminal opened in 1975, a new smaller tower was built near Fifth Street on the north side of the rail yard. For many years, the former depot track area shown in the photograph was occupied by a recreational vehicle parking lot. (Greg Welker.)

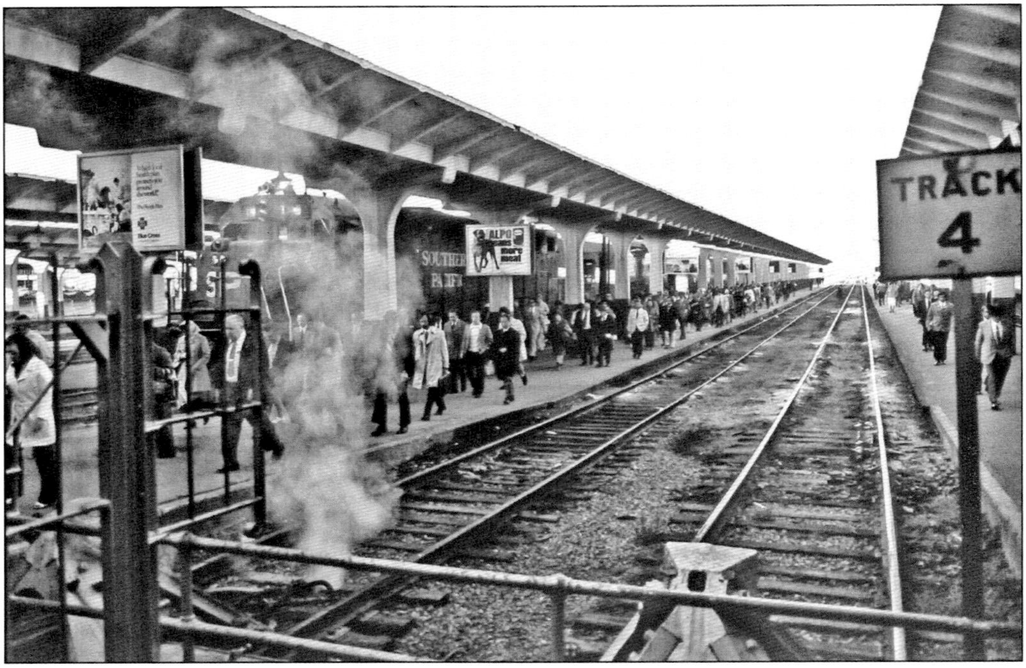


A train has pulled into Third Street and passengers pour onto the platform in this 1972 photograph. All the platforms had reinforced concrete, "butterfly"–type sheds, which extended to Fourth Street to shelter passengers from the elements. (Greg Welker.)

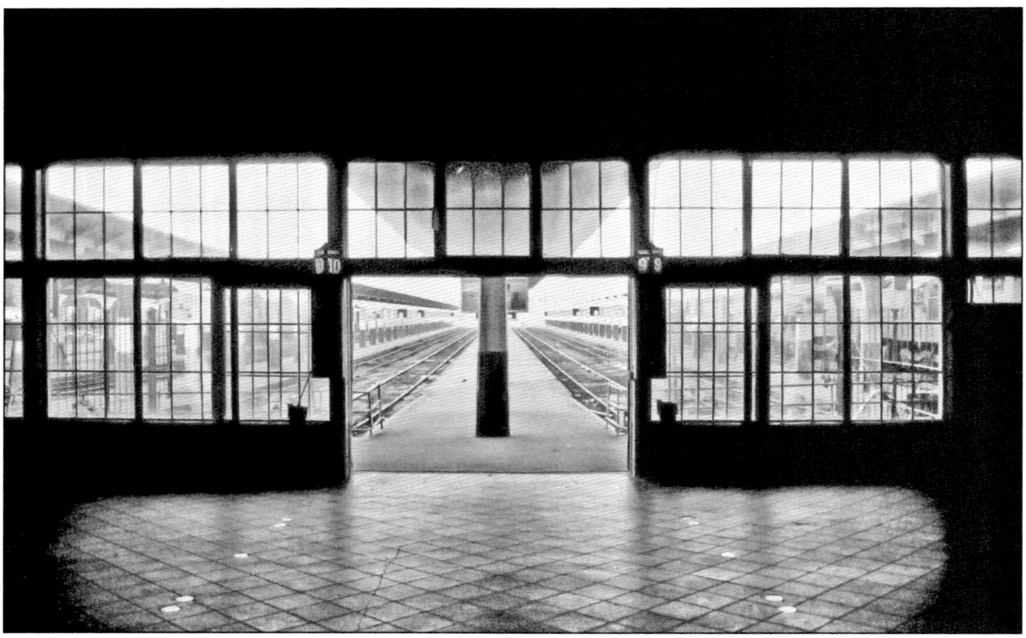

This dramatic view from the concourse has a mournful quality, befitting the end of an era. For 60 years, passengers flowed through the doors to catch a train, but the perennial rail rival—the automobile—was about to end it. Demolition of the terminal would eliminate the need to construct an overpass and ramp to connect Interstate 280 to the San Francisco waterfront. (Greg Welker.)

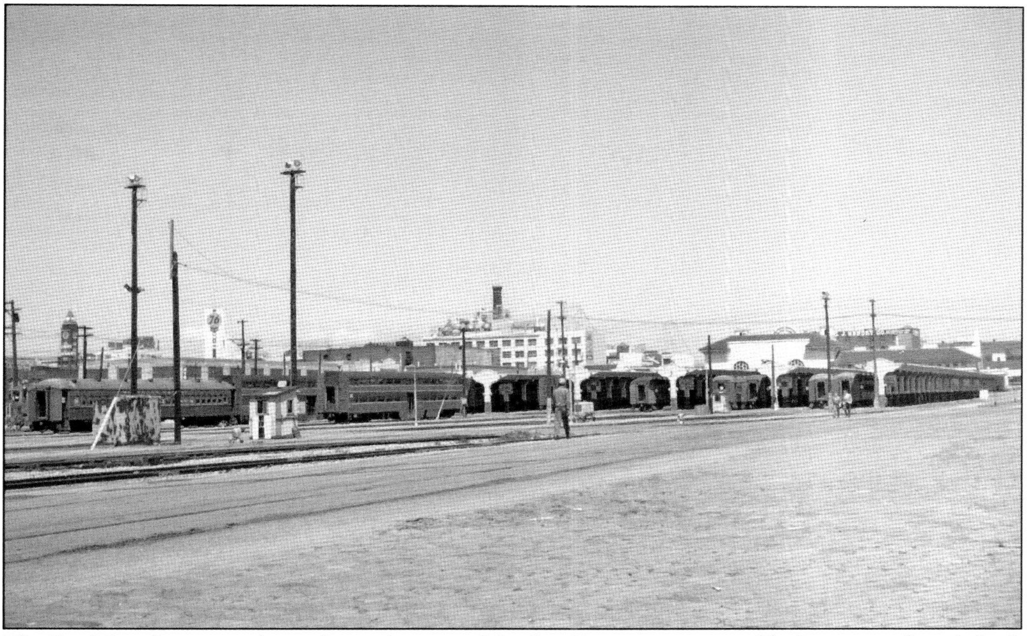

The Fred Stindt picture above shows the rear of the San Francisco terminal before it was demolished. The replacement structure, a utilitarian design, opened in June 1975. A $200,000 one-story precast concrete building with a waffle-type slab roof, the terminal provided ticket sales space, restrooms, a snack bar, and a newsstand. For the June 23, 1975, opening, SP also introduced a new locomotive, decked out in a bicentennial theme. No. 3197 was the first of three GP40P-2s that were brought in to power the Peninsula commute trains and it made an inaugural run down the Peninsula that day, captured in another Stindt photograph. (Both, Arthur Lloyd collection.)

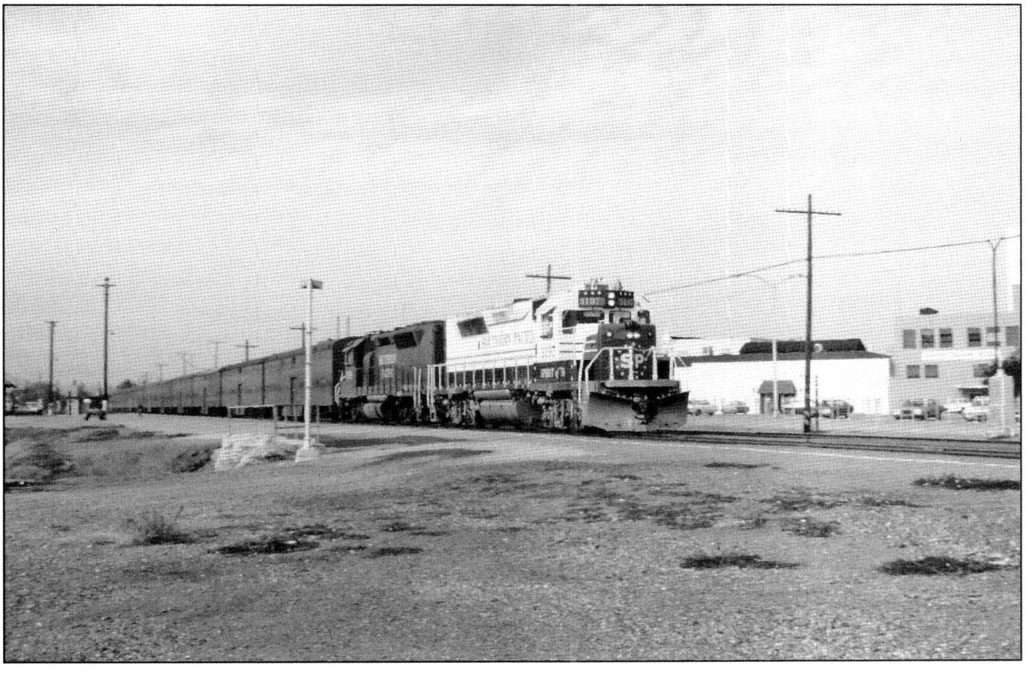

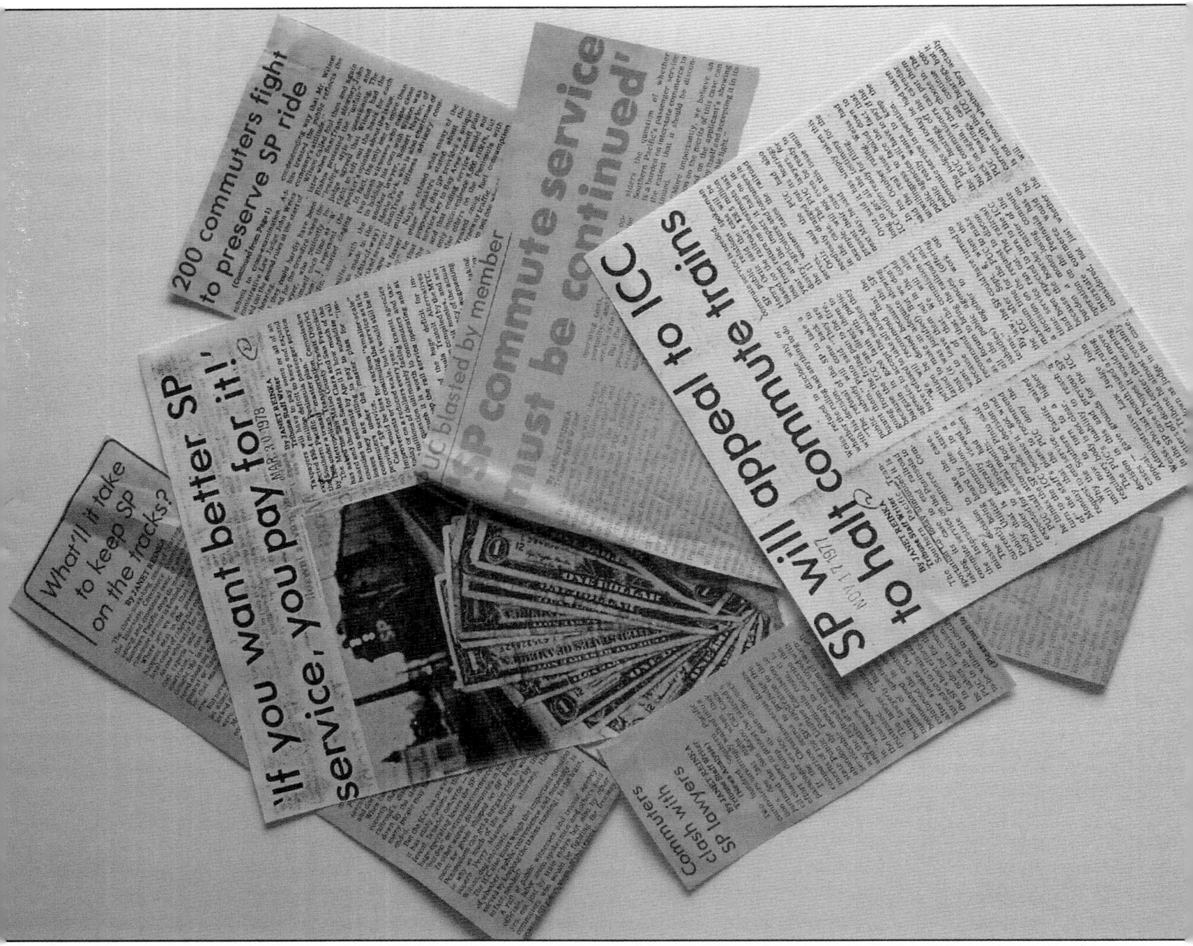


Jittery commuters watched the news closely in 1977 when, following years of deficits, Southern Pacific filed first with the California Public Utilities Commission (PUC) and then the Interstate Commerce Commission (ICC) for permission to discontinue passenger service. Commuters and public officials contended that shutting down rail service would have a catastrophic impact on traffic, the environment, and the economy. A PUC administrative law judge had said that the railroad could not be expected to pick up the deficits indefinitely. An initial decision by an ICC administrative law judge in 1979 granted the discontinuance unless a public subsidy was forthcoming. The hearings brought into sharp focus the question whether the train was in fact needed and how much the public would be willing to pay to keep it going. Ultimately, the state legislature authorized Caltrans to negotiate a purchase of service agreement with SP and the Peninsula Commute Service was saved. (Janet McGovern collection.)

# *Three*

# Caltrans and a New Name

The era of management of the Peninsula rail service by the California Department of Transportation (Caltrans) placed a public agency in the role of administering service that the Southern Pacific still operated. Yet, Caltrans was far from a caretaker, and left a remarkable record of accomplishment in just 12 years. Though supposedly "highway people," Caltrans's Peninsula Commute Service attracted staff members from throughout the country excited about the potential for a rail service many believed had been stymied by lack of investment. Caltrans set about revamping schedules unchanged for years, expanding weekday service from 44 to 46 trains. Schedules were reoriented to serve the increasing "reverse commute" market of commuters traveling south instead of the traditional pattern into San Francisco. New ticket types were created, along with transfer privileges from the train to connecting transit, and the first ticket vending machines were purchased. One of Caltrans's greatest achievements was an aggressive program to restore and upgrade stations, from adding parking to cleaning up platforms. Recognizing the rail system's historic assets, the work to list depots in the National Register of Historic Places intensified, along with seismic and other restoration to deteriorating properties. Artwork was installed at several stations, as well as monument signs at entrances. Dodgy old rail cars dating from the 1920s and the locomotive fleet were replaced. Gallery-type cars, capable of being operated from the cab end instead of being pulled by locomotives that had to be repositioned at terminal stations, enabled a far more efficient way of running the railroad. Caltrans initiated a program of free shuttles to connect commuters to their jobs, which expanded in subsequent decades. And befitting these dramatic changes, the familiar "Espee" nickname faded into history when "CalTrain" was renamed to reflect its new lease on life. However, with Gov. George Deukmejian's belief that Peninsula rail service should be a regional rather than a state responsibility, Caltrans worked with the three counties for the handoff in 1992, although the 50 percent state subsidy of the operating deficit continued until 1993.

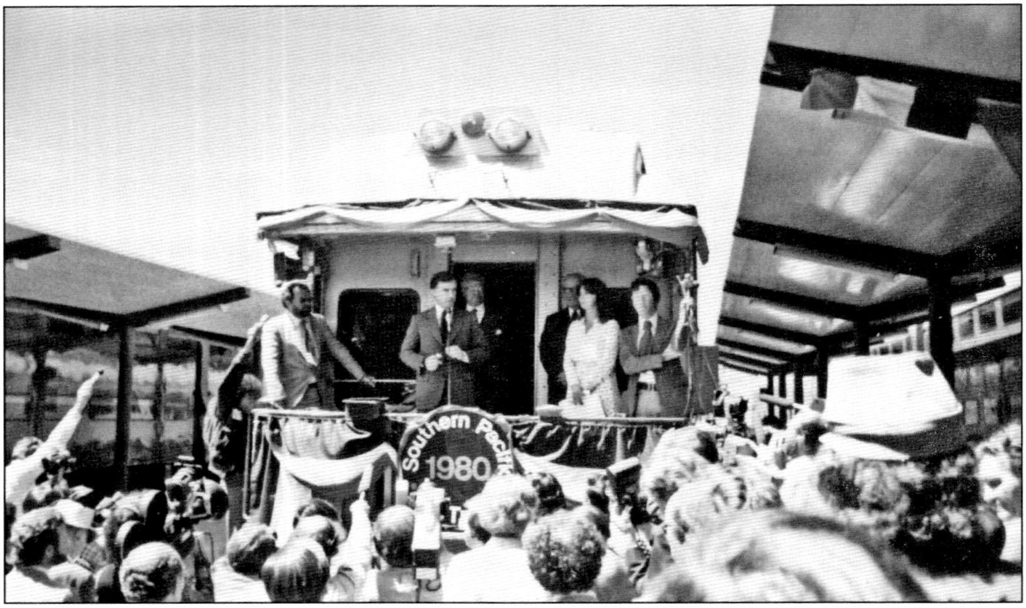


Gov. Edmund G. Brown Jr. signed legislation in 1977 that started a two-year process leading to the transfer of management of the Peninsula Commute Service to Caltrans. Brown said the 1980 agreement would allow trains to run at least another 10 years. He is pictured with other dignitaries aboard a July 7, 1980, train, where SP chairman Benjamin Biaggini presented gold spikes and "keys" to the railroad. (Dana Dillard.)

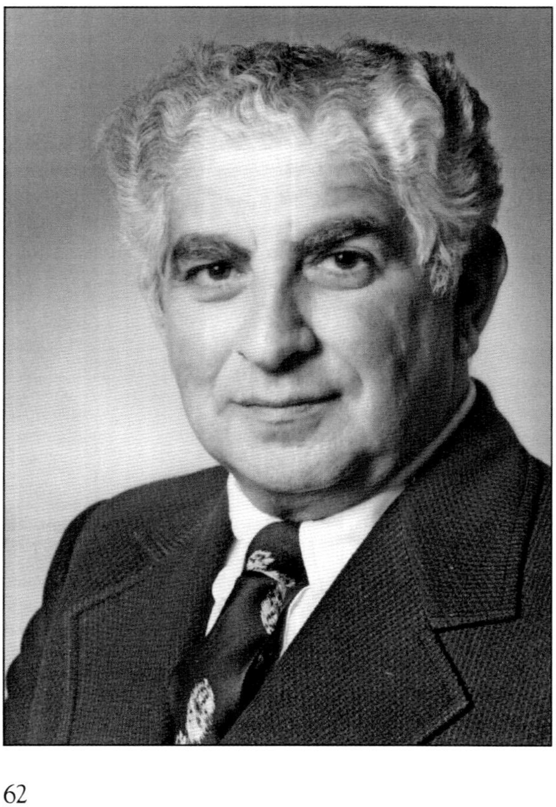

John T. Mauro was a pivotal figure in a 1978 fare stabilization program that halted a two-decade ridership decline. To overcome SP's objections to a public subsidy, SamTrans' general manager came up with a plan to buy rail tickets and sell them back to riders at a 30-percent discount. Santa Clara County joined in and ridership rebounded. Mauro died in 1981 at 58 years of age. (SamTrans.)

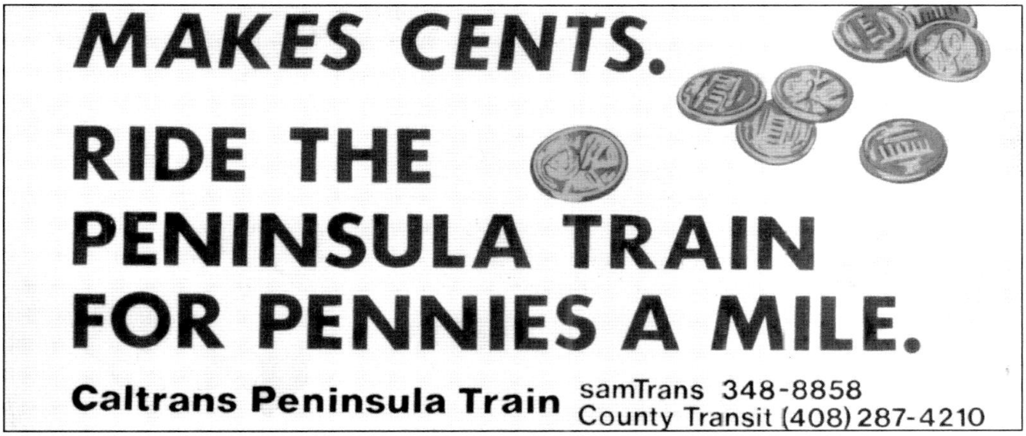


Caltrans and the transit agencies in San Francisco, San Mateo, and Santa Clara Counties worked in tandem to build ridership, with promotional messages such as this cost-focused advertisement. In 1982, Caltrans also embarked on an expanded program to sell tickets at participating companies, such as Hewlett Packard, SRI International, and GTE Lenkurt. (SamTrans.)

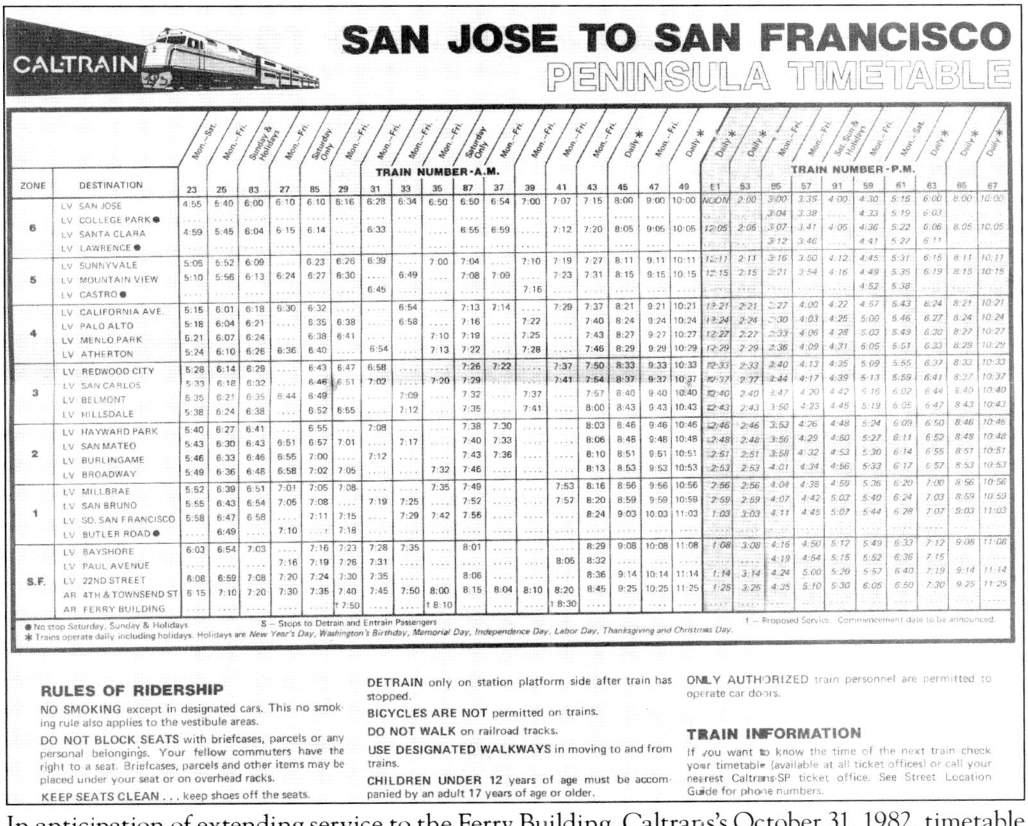

CALTRAIN

SAN JOSE TO SAN FRANCISCO
PENINSULA TIMETABLE

TRAIN NUMBER - A.M.

| ZONE | DESTINATION | 23 Mon.-Sat. | 25 Mon.-Fri. | 83 Sunday & Holidays | 27 Mon.-Fri. | 85 Saturday Only | 29 Mon.-Fri. | 31 Mon.-Fri. | 33 Mon.-Fri. | 35 Mon.-Fri. | 87 Saturday Only | 37 Mon.-Fri. |
|---|---|---|---|---|---|---|---|---|---|---|---|---|
| 6 | LV SAN JOSE | 4:55 | 5:40 | 6:00 | 6:10 | 6:10 | 6:16 | 6:28 | 6:34 | 6:50 | 6:50 | 6:54 |
| | LV COLLEGE PARK ● | .... | .... | .... | .... | .... | .... | .... | .... | .... | .... | .... |
| | LV SANTA CLARA | 4:59 | 5:45 | 6:04 | 6:15 | 6:14 | .... | 6:33 | .... | .... | 6:55 | 6:59 |
| | LV LAWRENCE ● | .... | .... | .... | .... | .... | .... | .... | .... | .... | .... | .... |
| 5 | LV SUNNYVALE | 5:05 | 5:52 | 6:09 | .... | 6:23 | 6:26 | 6:39 | .... | 7:00 | 7:04 | .... |
| | LV MOUNTAIN VIEW | 5:10 | 5:56 | 6:13 | 6:24 | 6:27 | 6:30 | .... | 6:49 | .... | 7:08 | 7:09 |
| | LV CASTRO ● | .... | .... | .... | .... | .... | .... | 6:45 | .... | .... | .... | .... |
| 4 | LV CALIFORNIA AVE. | 5:15 | 6:01 | 6:18 | 6:30 | 6:32 | .... | .... | 6:54 | .... | 7:13 | 7:14 |
| | LV PALO ALTO | 5:18 | 6:04 | 6:21 | .... | 6:35 | 6:38 | .... | 6:58 | .... | 7:16 | .... |
| | LV MENLO PARK | 5:21 | 6:07 | 6:24 | .... | 6:38 | 6:41 | .... | .... | 7:10 | 7:19 | .... |
| | LV ATHERTON | 5:24 | 6:10 | 6:26 | 6:36 | 6:40 | .... | 6:54 | .... | 7:13 | 7:22 | .... |
| 3 | LV REDWOOD CITY | 5:28 | 6:14 | 6:29 | .... | 6:43 | 6:47 | 6:58 | .... | .... | 7:26 | 7:22 |
| | LV SAN CARLOS | 5:33 | 6:18 | 6:32 | .... | 6:46 | 6:51 | 7:02 | .... | 7:20 | 7:29 | .... |
| | LV BELMONT | 5:35 | 6:21 | 6:35 | 6:44 | 6:49 | .... | .... | 7:09 | .... | 7:32 | .... |
| | LV HILLSDALE | 5:38 | 6:24 | 6:38 | .... | 6:52 | 6:55 | .... | 7:12 | .... | 7:35 | .... |
| 2 | LV HAYWARD PARK | 5:40 | 6:27 | 6:41 | .... | 6:55 | .... | 7:08 | .... | .... | 7:38 | 7:30 |
| | LV SAN MATEO | 5:43 | 6:30 | 6:43 | 6:51 | 6:57 | 7:01 | .... | 7:17 | .... | 7:40 | 7:33 |
| | LV BURLINGAME | 5:46 | 6:33 | 6:46 | 6:55 | 7:00 | .... | 7:12 | .... | .... | 7:43 | 7:36 |
| | LV BROADWAY | 5:49 | 6:36 | 6:48 | 6:58 | 7:02 | 7:05 | .... | .... | 7:32 | 7:46 | .... |
| 1 | LV MILLBRAE | 5:52 | 6:39 | 6:51 | 7:01 | 7:05 | 7:08 | .... | .... | 7:35 | 7:49 | .... |
| | LV SAN BRUNO | 5:55 | 6:43 | 6:54 | 7:05 | 7:08 | .... | 7:19 | 7:25 | .... | 7:52 | .... |
| | LV SO. SAN FRANCISCO | 5:58 | 6:47 | 6:58 | .... | 7:11 | 7:15 | .... | 7:29 | 7:42 | 7:56 | .... |
| | LV BUTLER ROAD ● | .... | 6:49 | .... | 7:10 | .... | 7:18 | .... | .... | .... | .... | .... |
| S.F. | LV BAYSHORE | 6:03 | 6:54 | 7:03 | .... | 7:16 | 7:23 | 7:28 | 7:35 | .... | 8:01 | .... |
| | LV PAUL AVENUE | .... | .... | .... | 7:16 | 7:19 | 7:26 | 7:31 | .... | .... | .... | .... |
| | LV 22ND STREET | 6:08 | 6:59 | 7:08 | 7:20 | 7:24 | 7:30 | 7:35 | .... | .... | 8:06 | .... |
| | AR 4TH & TOWNSEND ST | 6:15 | 7:10 | 7:20 | 7:30 | 7:35 | 7:40 | 7:45 | 7:50 | 8:00 | 8:15 | 8:04 |
| | AR FERRY BUILDING | .... | .... | .... | .... | .... | † 7:50 | .... | .... | † 8:10 | .... | .... |

TRAIN NUMBER - A.M. (continued) / TRAIN NUMBER - P.M.

| ZONE | DESTINATION | 39 Mon.-Fri. | 41 Mon.-Fri. | 43 Mon.-Fri. | 45 Daily * | 47 Mon.-Fri. | 49 Daily * | 51 Daily * | 53 Daily * | 55 Mon.-Fri. | 57 Mon.-Fri. | 91 Sat. Sun & Holidays | 59 Mon.-Fri. | 61 Mon.-Sat. | 63 Daily * | 65 Daily * | 67 Daily * |
|---|---|---|---|---|---|---|---|---|---|---|---|---|---|---|---|---|---|
| 6 | LV SAN JOSE | 7:00 | 7:07 | 7:15 | 8:00 | 9:00 | 10:00 | NOON | 2:00 | 3:00 | 3:35 | 4:00 | 4:30 | 5:15 | 6:00 | 8:00 | 10:00 |
| | LV COLLEGE PARK ● | .... | .... | .... | .... | .... | .... | .... | .... | 3:04 | 3:38 | .... | 4:33 | 5:19 | 6:03 | | |
| | LV SANTA CLARA | .... | 7:12 | 7:20 | 8:05 | 9:05 | 10:05 | 12:05 | 2:05 | 3:07 | 3:41 | 4:05 | 4:36 | 5:22 | 6:06 | 8:05 | 10:05 |
| | LV LAWRENCE ● | .... | .... | .... | .... | .... | .... | .... | .... | 3:12 | 3:46 | .... | 4:41 | 5:27 | 6:11 | .... | .... |
| 5 | LV SUNNYVALE | 7:10 | 7:19 | 7:27 | 8:11 | 9:11 | 10:11 | 12:11 | 2:11 | 3:16 | 3:50 | 4:12 | 4:45 | 5:31 | 6:15 | 8:11 | 10:11 |
| | LV MOUNTAIN VIEW | .... | 7:23 | 7:31 | 8:15 | 9:15 | 10:15 | 12:15 | 2:15 | 3:21 | 3:54 | 4:16 | 4:49 | 5:35 | 6:19 | 8:15 | 10:15 |
| | LV CASTRO ● | 7:16 | .... | .... | .... | .... | .... | .... | .... | .... | .... | .... | 4:52 | 5:38 | .... | .... | .... |
| 4 | LV CALIFORNIA AVE. | .... | 7:29 | 7:37 | 8:21 | 9:21 | 10:21 | 12:21 | 2:21 | 3:27 | 4:00 | 4:22 | 4:57 | 5:43 | 6:24 | 8:21 | 10:21 |
| | LV PALO ALTO | 7:22 | .... | 7:40 | 8:24 | 9:24 | 10:24 | 12:24 | 2:24 | 3:30 | 4:03 | 4:25 | 5:00 | 5:46 | 6:27 | 8:24 | 10:24 |
| | LV MENLO PARK | 7:25 | .... | 7:43 | 8:27 | 9:27 | 10:27 | 12:27 | 2:27 | 3:33 | 4:06 | 4:28 | 5:03 | 5:49 | 6:30 | 8:27 | 10:27 |
| | LV ATHERTON | 7:28 | .... | 7:46 | 8:29 | 9:29 | 10:29 | 12:29 | 2:29 | 3:36 | 4:09 | 4:31 | 5:05 | 5:51 | 6:33 | 8:29 | 10:29 |
| 3 | LV REDWOOD CITY | .... | 7:37 | 7:50 | 8:33 | 9:33 | 10:33 | 12:33 | 2:33 | 3:40 | 4:13 | 4:35 | 5:09 | 5:55 | 6:37 | 8:33 | 10:33 |
| | LV SAN CARLOS | .... | 7:41 | 7:54 | 8:37 | 9:37 | 10:37 | 12:37 | 2:37 | 3:44 | 4:17 | 4:39 | 5:13 | 5:59 | 6:41 | 8:37 | 10:37 |
| | LV BELMONT | 7:37 | .... | 7:57 | 8:40 | 9:40 | 10:40 | 12:40 | 2:40 | 3:47 | 4:20 | 4:42 | 5:16 | 6:02 | 6:44 | 8:40 | 10:40 |
| | LV HILLSDALE | 7:41 | .... | 8:00 | 8:43 | 9:43 | 10:43 | 12:43 | 2:43 | 3:50 | 4:23 | 4:45 | 5:19 | 6:05 | 6:47 | 8:43 | 10:43 |
| 2 | LV HAYWARD PARK | .... | .... | 8:03 | 8:46 | 9:46 | 10:46 | 12:46 | 2:46 | 3:53 | 4:26 | 4:48 | 5:24 | 6:09 | 6:50 | 8:46 | 10:46 |
| | LV SAN MATEO | .... | .... | 8:06 | 8:48 | 9:48 | 10:48 | 12:48 | 2:48 | 3:56 | 4:29 | 4:50 | 5:27 | 6:11 | 6:52 | 8:48 | 10:48 |
| | LV BURLINGAME | .... | .... | 8:10 | 8:51 | 9:51 | 10:51 | 2:51 | 2:51 | 3:58 | 4:32 | 4:53 | 5:30 | 6:14 | 6:55 | 8:51 | 10:51 |
| | LV BROADWAY | .... | .... | 8:13 | 8:53 | 9:53 | 10:53 | 2:53 | 2:53 | 4:01 | 4:34 | 4:56 | 5:33 | 6:17 | 6:57 | 8:53 | 10:53 |
| 1 | LV MILLBRAE | .... | 7:53 | 8:16 | 8:56 | 9:56 | 10:56 | 2:56 | 2:56 | 4:04 | 4:38 | 4:59 | 5:36 | 6:20 | 7:00 | 8:56 | 10:56 |
| | LV SAN BRUNO | .... | 7:57 | 8:20 | 8:59 | 9:59 | 10:59 | 2:59 | 2:59 | 4:07 | 4:42 | 5:03 | 5:40 | 6:24 | 7:03 | 8:59 | 10:59 |
| | LV SO. SAN FRANCISCO | .... | .... | 8:24 | 9:03 | 10:03 | 11:03 | 1:03 | 3:03 | 4:11 | 4:45 | 5:07 | 5:44 | 6:28 | 7:07 | 9:03 | 11:03 |
| | LV BUTLER ROAD ● | .... | .... | .... | .... | .... | .... | .... | .... | .... | .... | .... | .... | .... | .... | .... | .... |
| S.F. | LV BAYSHORE | .... | .... | 8:29 | 9:08 | 10:08 | 11:08 | 1:08 | 3:08 | 4:16 | 4:50 | 5:12 | 5:49 | 6:33 | 7:12 | 9:08 | 11:08 |
| | LV PAUL AVENUE | .... | 8:05 | 8:32 | .... | .... | .... | .... | .... | 4:19 | 4:54 | 5:15 | 5:52 | 6:36 | 7:15 | .... | .... |
| | LV 22ND STREET | .... | .... | 8:36 | 9:14 | 10:14 | 11:14 | 1:14 | 3:14 | 4:24 | 5:00 | 5:20 | 5:57 | 6:40 | 7:19 | 9:14 | 11:14 |
| | AR 4TH & TOWNSEND ST | 8:10 | 8:20 | 8:45 | 9:25 | 10:25 | 11:25 | 1:25 | 3:25 | 4:35 | 5:10 | 5:30 | 6:05 | 6:50 | 7:30 | 9:25 | 11:25 |
| | AR FERRY BUILDING | .... | † 8:30 | .... | .... | .... | .... | .... | .... | .... | .... | .... | .... | .... | .... | .... | .... |

● No stop Saturday, Sunday & Holidays.  S – Stops to Detrain and Entrain Passengers  † — Proposed Service. Commencement date to be announced.
✱ Trains operate daily including holidays. Holidays are *New Year's Day, Washington's Birthday, Memorial Day, Independence Day, Labor Day, Thanksgiving and Christmas Day.*

**RULES OF RIDERSHIP**

**NO SMOKING** except in designated cars. This no smoking rule also applies to the vestibule areas.

**DO NOT BLOCK SEATS** with briefcases, parcels or any personal belongings. Your fellow commuters have the right to a seat. Briefcases, parcels and other items may be placed under your seat or on overhead racks.

**KEEP SEATS CLEAN** . . . keep shoes off the seats.

**DETRAIN** only on station platform side after train has stopped.

**BICYCLES ARE NOT** permitted on trains.

**DO NOT WALK** on railroad tracks.

**USE DESIGNATED WALKWAYS** in moving to and from trains.

**CHILDREN UNDER 12** years of age must be accompanied by an adult 17 years of age or older.

**ONLY AUTHORIZED** train personnel are permitted to operate car doors.

**TRAIN INFORMATION**

If you want to know the time of the next train check your timetable (available at all ticket offices) or call your nearest Caltrans-SP ticket office. See Street Location Guide for phone numbers.

In anticipation of extending service to the Ferry Building, Caltrans's October 31, 1982, timetable showed tentative arrival times for three rush-hour trains via the San Francisco Belt Railway line. These were to be stops on paper only because city residents objected to trains operating on city streets. This schedule marks the opening of Sunnyvale's Lawrence station. (Arthur Lloyd collection.)

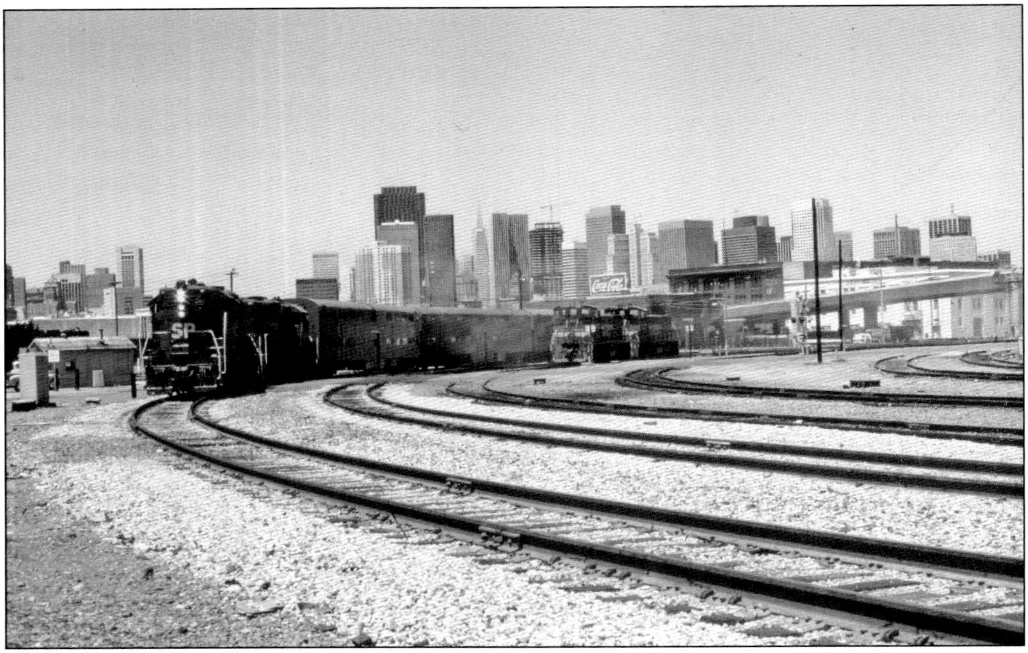


Leaving San Francisco and its skyline behind, a 2:00 p.m. Sunday train pulling double-decker gallery cars headed south in 1982. At the time of the transfer to Caltrans, SP was operating 44 weekday trains—22 in each direction. Off-peak weekday service was less frequent and in some cases, it was more than two hours between trains. Only 12 trains ran on Saturdays; nine ran on Sundays. (Bill Kepner.)

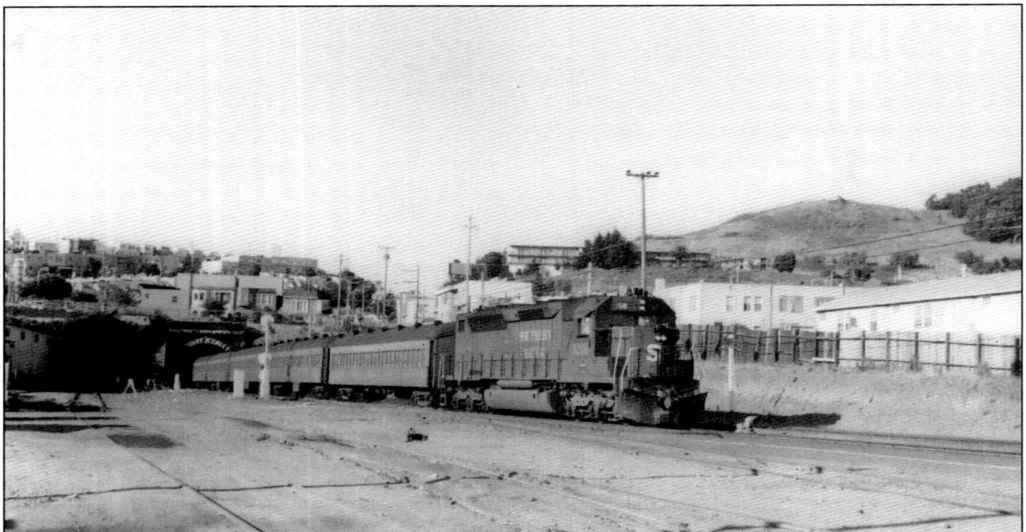

SP 3209, an Electro-Motive Division locomotive, passes through Tunnel 4 approaching the huge Bayshore Yard, around 1980. In 1982, Caltrans and the Southern Pacific Transportation Company began the first phase of a $4-million track rehabilitation program, which included surfacing and leveling of tracks between San Francisco and San Jose. Reconstruction of the track in Tunnel 4 in 1983 was a major component of the program. (Tom Gray.)

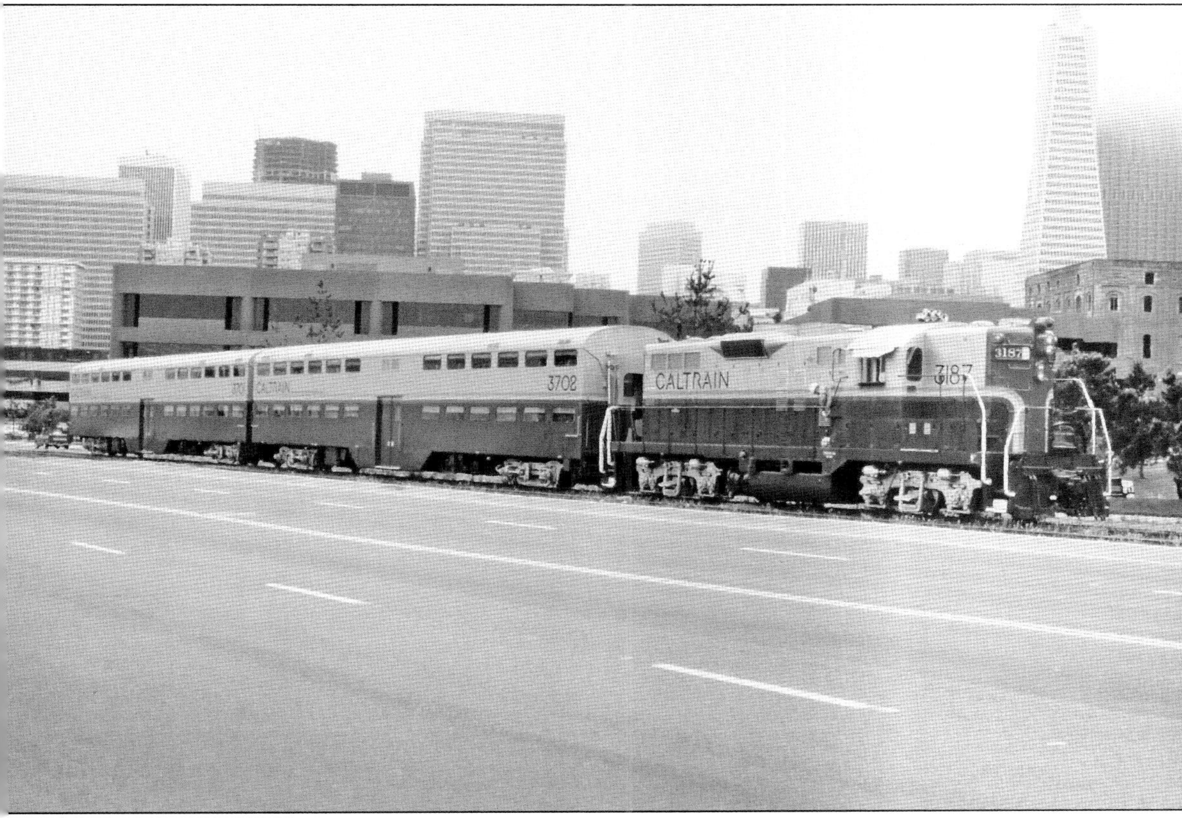


When Caltrans began subsidizing the rail service, SP's rolling stock was purchased at a nominal cost. Marketing staff thought a fresh identity was in order to replace the SP's gray color. In 1982, a new blue-and-silver color scheme, alternatively dubbed the "postal service" scheme or the "mailbox train," was tried on SP diesel 3187 and the double deck cars 3701, 3702, and 3703, along with the name "CalTrain." The result, shown here in this photograph taken by well-known rail historian Fred Stindt against a San Francisco backdrop, did not last long. In 1985, Caltrans received the first of 63 new gallery-type passenger cars from Sumitomo Corporation and Nippon Sharyo Limited, which gradually replaced the SP fleet. (Arthur Lloyd collection.)

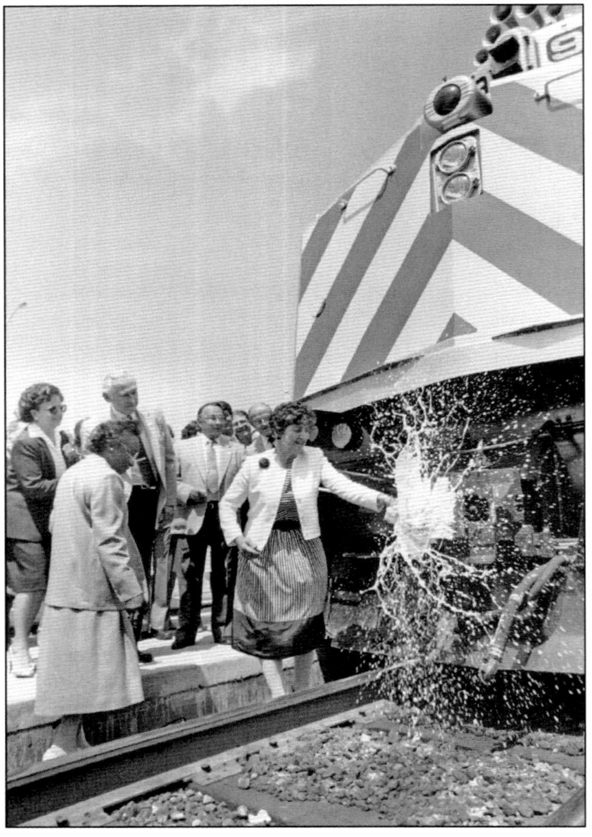

During a June 12, 1985, inaugural trip, Gloria Deukmejian, wife of Gov. George Deukmejian, christened one of the first of 18 new General Motors (EMD) "CalTrain" locomotives to go into service. Miriam Gholikely, SamTrans board chairwoman, looked on. The first of the locomotives were named in honor of each of the cities through which the train operated, and one was named after the state of California. (SamTrans.)

The northbound inaugural train, operating in the "push" mode with a cab-equipped car on the head end, smashed through a banner in San Mateo. Before Caltrans brought about the switch to push-pull mode, trains had to have a locomotive pulling the train regardless of its direction. In push-pull mode, the engineer can operate the train from either the locomotive or the cab car. (SamTrans.)

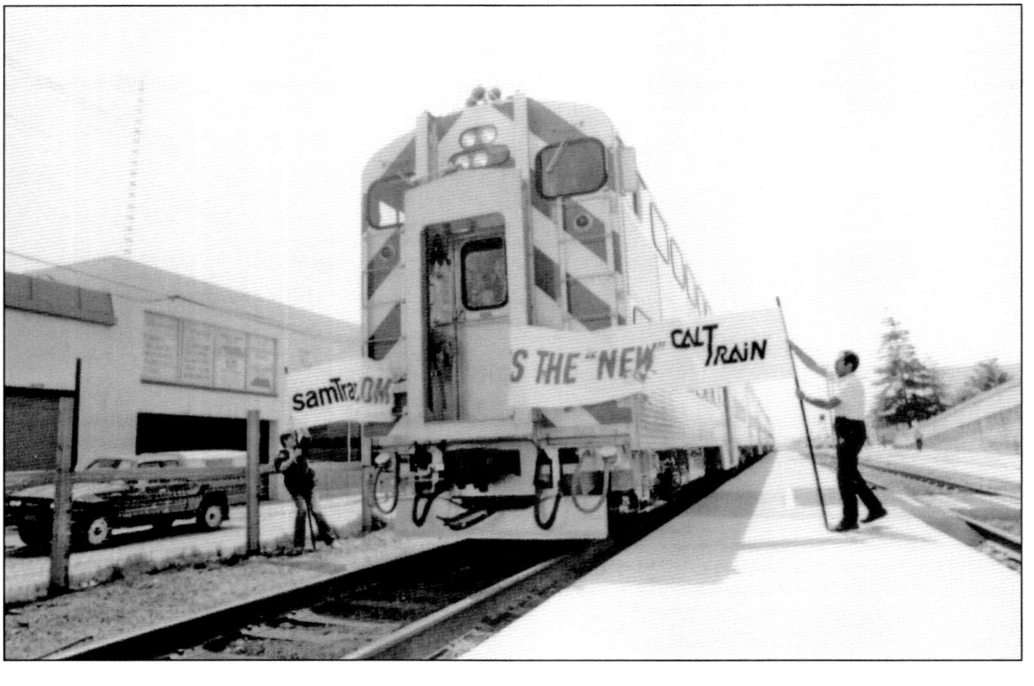

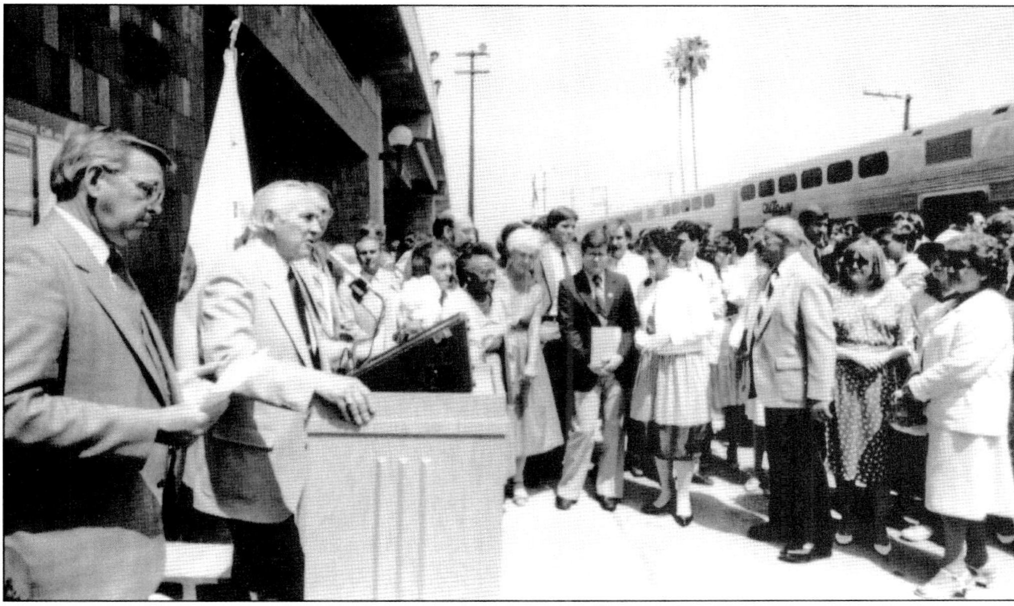

Caltrans's Burch C. Bachtold, shown here speaking at the inaugural ceremony, became District 4 director in 1983 and was chairman of the Project Management Committee for the CalTrain Peninsula Rail Service. Bachtold had earlier pledged to do everything possible to improve the effectiveness of CalTrain and increase ridership, and the new fleet helped fulfill that promise. SamTrans general manager Gerald T. Haugh is to Bachtold's right. (SamTrans.)

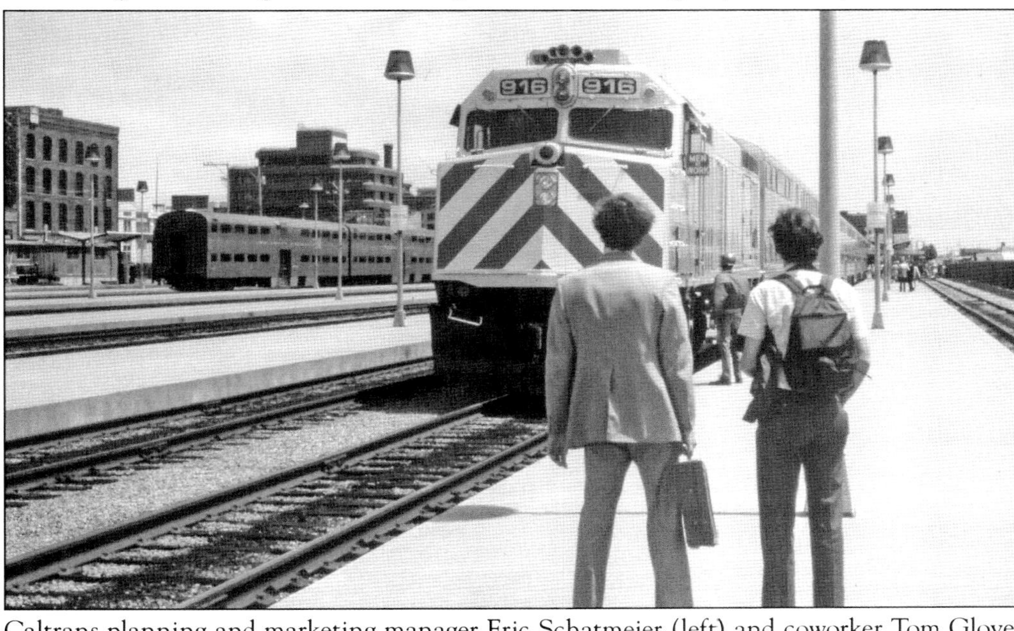


Caltrans planning and marketing manager Eric Schatmeier (left) and coworker Tom Glover admire the new locomotive, branding the CalTrain identity. The new passenger cars had orange and brown vinyl interiors, but the cab cars were ordered without carpeting because they were to be the smoking cars. When management decided to disallow smoking on them, the ban turned out to be a non-event, although about 15 percent of riders were smokers. (Steve Miller.)

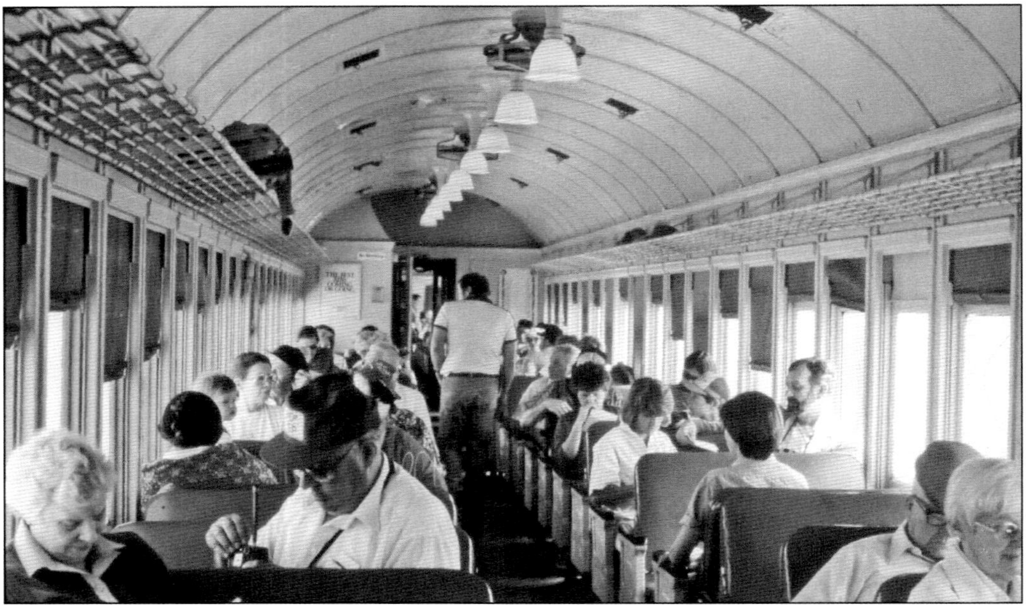

Though they were nearly 60 years old, the 96-passenger suburban cars had a certain nostalgia attached. So the weekend after the inaugural for the new cars, rail fans boarded two round-trip "Farewell to the Harrimans" excursions between San Francisco and San Jose, one with an SDP45 engine, one with two GP9s, one with two SD9s, and the final trip with the new F40 engine. (Steve Miller.)

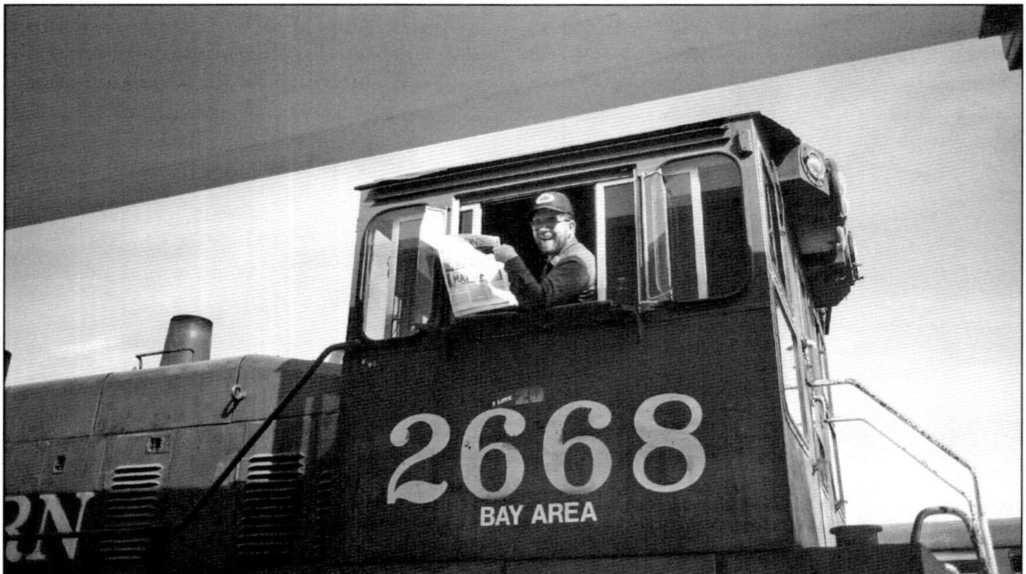


Locomotive engineer Bob Castiglione takes a break at San Francisco between runs to read a *Barrons* newspaper, possibly one left on the train by a passenger. A panoply of assignments opened for an engineer in those days in addition to running commute trains, including taking a local freight train to Millbrae, Redwood City, or the Permanente Cement plant in Cupertino. (Greg Welker.)

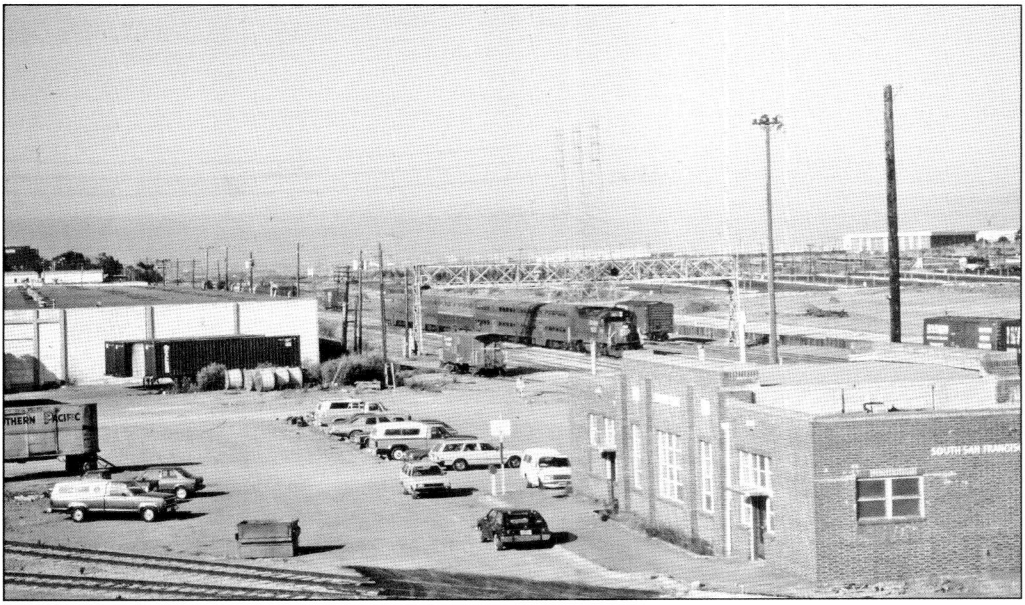

When Caltrans served South San Francisco, the city's manufacturing base east of the Bayshore Freeway had eroded from its heyday. It is remarkable how much the skyline has changed in just two decades since this picture was taken in August 1984, as high-rise construction, biotechnology companies, and office parks replaced early manufacturers. (Bill Kepner.)

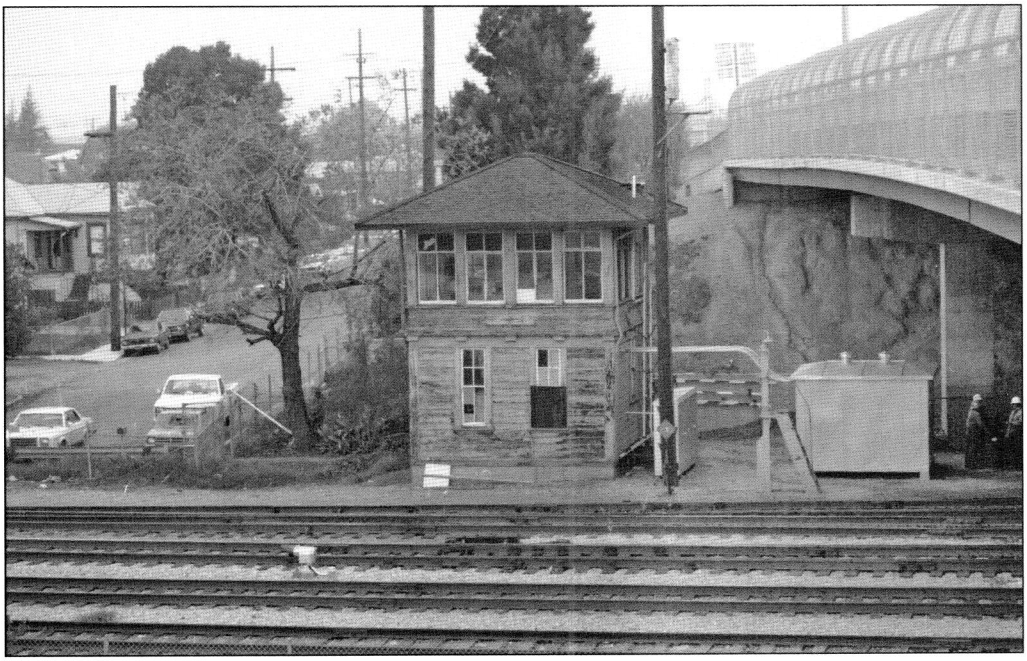

Located under the Woodside Road overpass and built in 1909, the Redwood Junction Interlocking Tower was at the junction to the Dumbarton Bridge line and was manned until 1986, five years after this photograph was taken. An arsonist set the tower afire in 1987, and the fire-gutted shell was later destroyed. (Bill Kepner.)

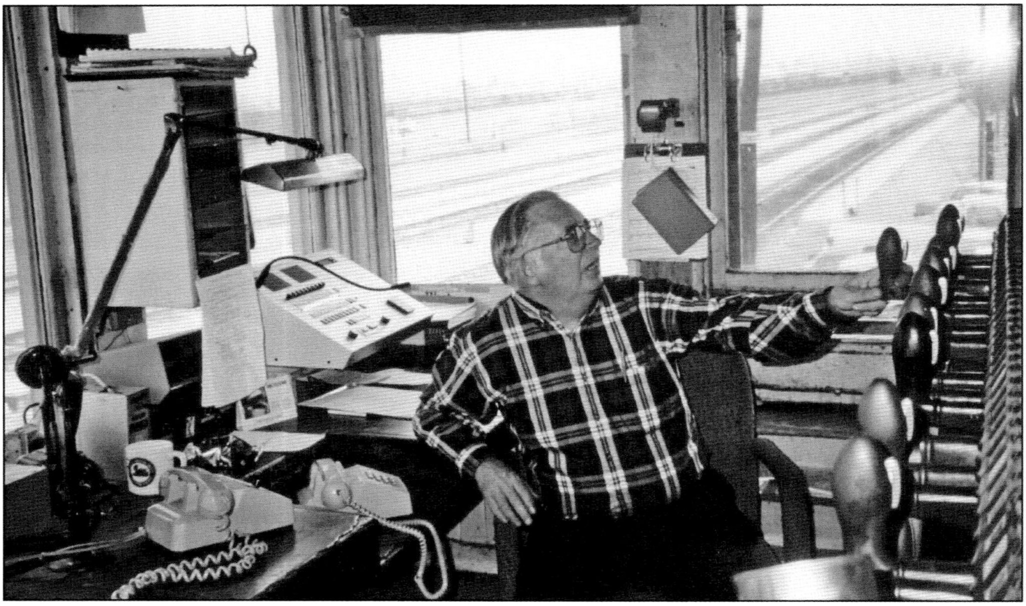

Don Douglas is shown operating the levers at the Santa Clara tower, which was used to activate switches to control train movements. Douglas had gone to work for Southern Pacific in 1955 and worked many jobs over the years, including at the Redwood City station, until his retirement in 1996. He has written numerous articles about rail history and his experiences as a railroader. (Caltrain.)

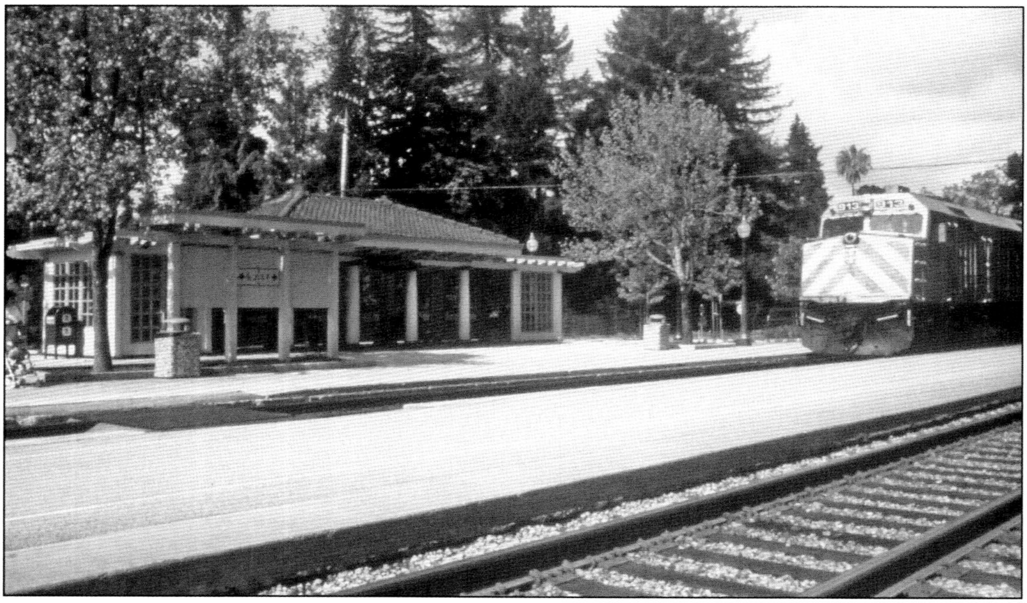

The Atherton station was restored in 1991 and was the second-to-last of the projects Caltrans undertook to restore stations, among them Burlingame, Menlo Park, Millbrae, and San Carlos. After a $200,000, eight-month project, sagging pavement and deteriorating woodwork at Atherton were corrected. The town also made its own improvements including adding old lampposts and 10-foot-high gateposts. (Caltrain.)

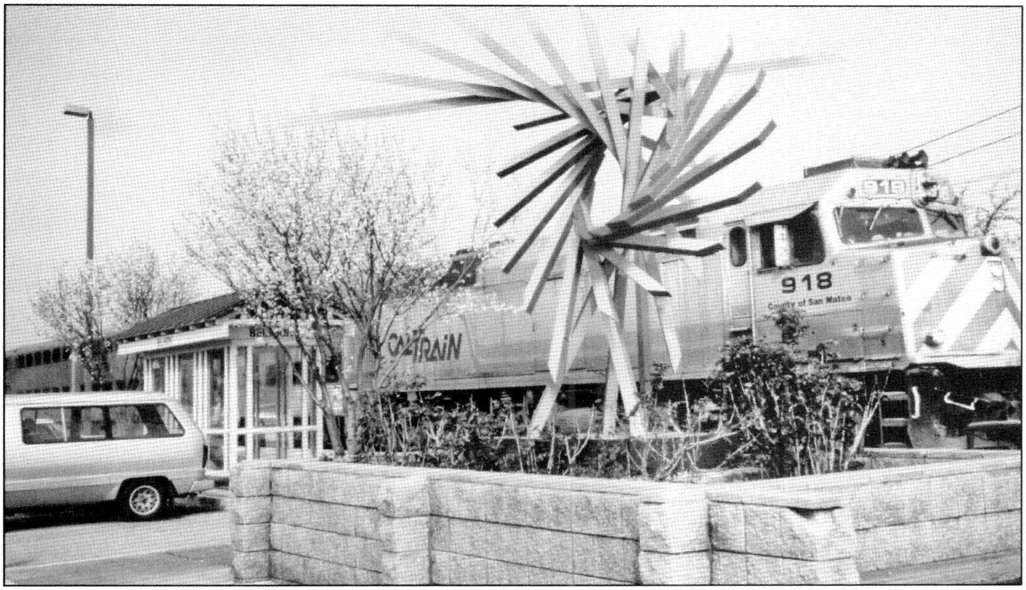


Cosponsored by Caltrans and the Office of the State Architect, the California Arts Council's ArtTrain program brought artwork to eight Caltrain stations. Among the installations was *Salsa del Sol*, a colorful sunburst at the Belmont station. The 11-foot-high sculpture was created by artist Roslyn Mazzilli. Two painted black steel chairs at the Santa Clara station were the work of Anna Valentina Murch. At San Carlos, artist Alan Shepp installed a Colorado red sandstone sculpture, while at Burlingame a gazebo with a paved pathway was designed by Gary Dwyer for integration into the landscaping. The final art project that was accomplished was *Mystical Bear*, a 12-foot-high bronze grizzly bear created by John Battenberg. It was installed at the Millbrae station in 1992. (Both, Caltrain.)

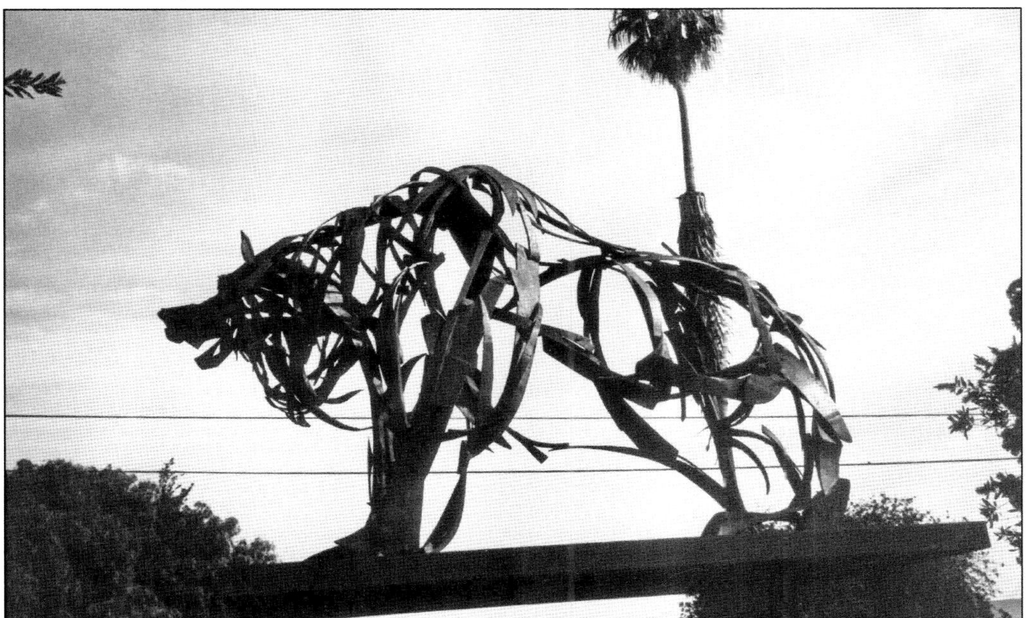

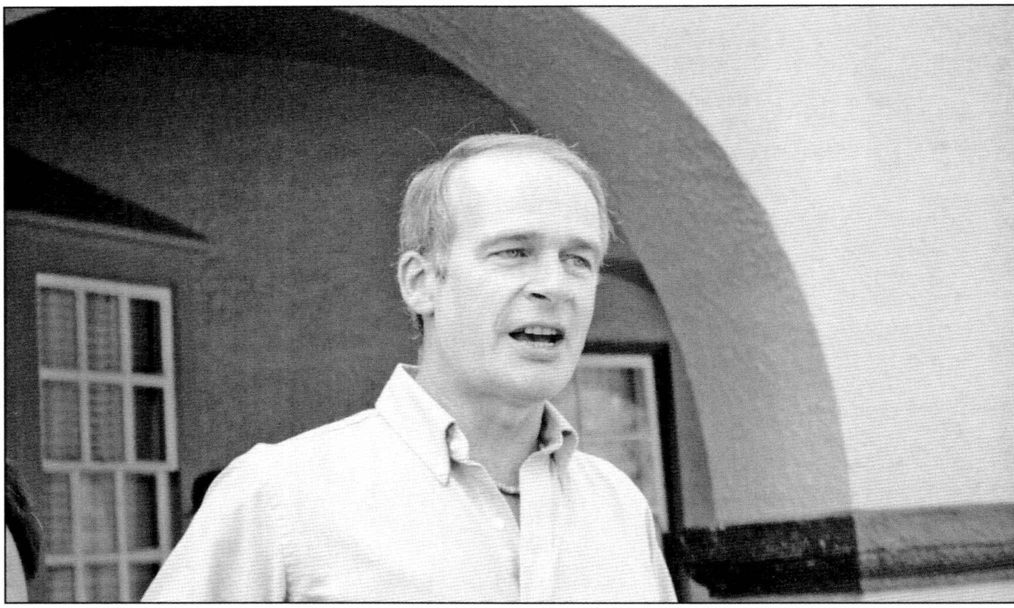

John W. Snyder, Caltrans's chief architectural historian, pictured here in a 1992 tour, is credited with ensuring the historic accuracy of the restoration work that took place during the Caltrans management of the system. Seven Caltrain depots are listed in the National Register of Historic Places: Millbrae, Burlingame, San Carlos, Menlo Park, Palo Alto, Santa Clara, and San Jose Diridon. (Caltrain.)

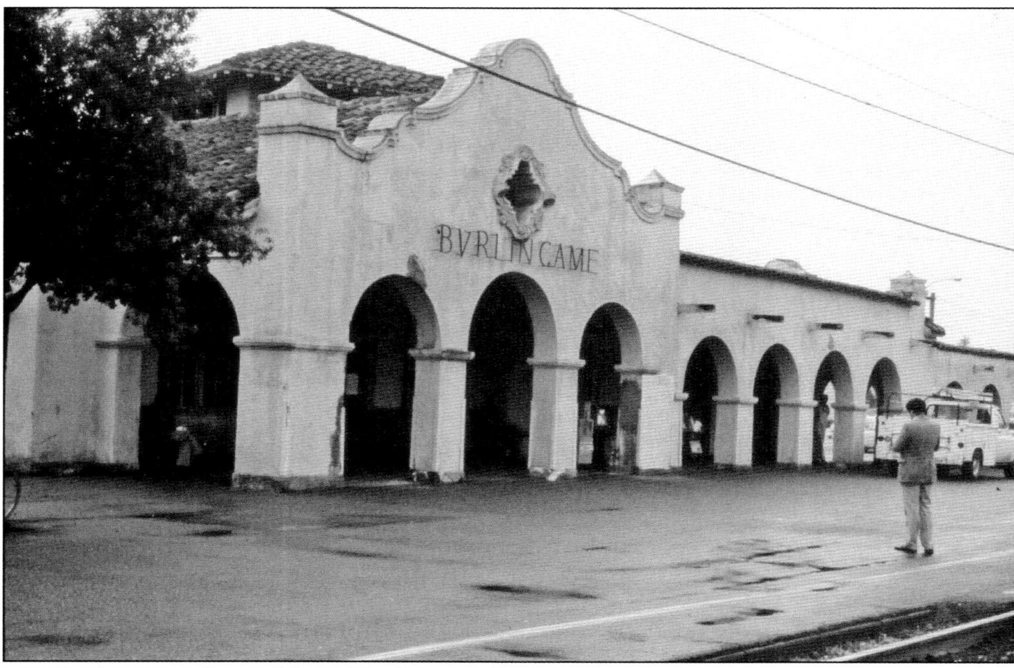


The Burlingame depot, like other historic depots on the railroad, was a victim of deferred maintenance and needed a lot of rehabilitation work. The depot is shown in the early 1980s before the city and the state joined forces for a $300,000 restoration project. (Steve Miller.)

# *Four*

# Caltrain Reinvented

July 1, 1992, ushered in a new era for Caltrain, as the three-county Peninsula Corridor Joint Powers Board (JPB) assumed management of the railroad from Caltrans. For the first time since the 1860s, Southern Pacific no longer operated the trains, with Amtrak (the National Railroad Passenger Corporation) winning the contract. The San Mateo County Transit District led the agency, which includes partners in San Francisco and Santa Clara Counties. Weekday service immediately increased from 54 to 60 trains, and three new stations south of the historic San Jose terminal opened. Initially, the agency completed projects begun by Caltrans, such as installing the first ticket vending machines, while slowly rebuilding and modernizing what the rail services director often called "a fixer-upper railroad." Gradually, track, tunnel, station, and communications system improvement projects set the stage for a rail renaissance and a rebound in ridership. Pivotal changes included the renovation of the San Francisco terminal and the opening of Muni light rail lines across the street. Rail connections in San Jose in 1992, Mountain View in 2000, and Millbrae in 2003 created new linkages. In San Mateo County, 10 highway-rail grade crossing separations made the railroad safer. Though extending the railroad to downtown San Francisco had long been an elusive dream, Caltrain's role as a vital resource grew as development in the South Beach and Mission Bay neighborhoods moved the city's center of gravity closer to the train. Sports fans by the droves discovered that Caltrain is the way to go for baseball games in San Francisco and ice hockey in San Jose. Baby Bullet express trains and Caltrain's welcoming attitude toward bikes on trains established a national reputation for innovation, and the number of weekday trains peaked at 98. A state-of-the art maintenance facility, which opened in San Jose in 2007, provided long overdue space and equipment for keeping the railroad's expanding and modernized fleet on the road. Despite carrying some 12 million riders annually, funding problems persisted and by 2011, Caltrain confronted the most serious challenges to its survival since the late 1970s.

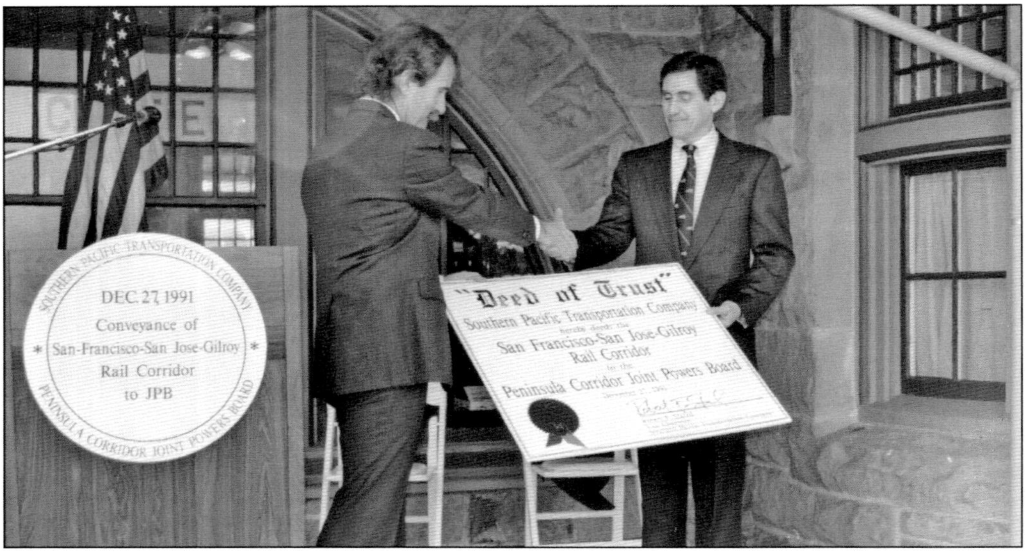


With a giant deed of trust for the "photo op," Peninsula Corridor Joint Powers Board (JPB) chairman Tom Nolan shook hands with Southern Pacific vice chairman Robert F. Starzel on January 15, 1992, to memorialize the sale of the right-of-way. Consisting of partner agencies from San Francisco, San Mateo, and Santa Clara Counties, the JPB acquired 51.4 miles of track from San Francisco to San Jose for almost $220 million and trackage rights to another 25.4 miles to Gilroy for another $4 million. Pictured below, Nolan, SamTrans vice chairman John Asmus and legal staff members sign the right-of-way papers. The San Mateo County Transit District (SamTrans) previously had been designated to administer the rail line on behalf of the three-county agency. That transition occurred six months after the historic purchase of the right-of-way, on July 1, 1992. (Both, SamTrans.)

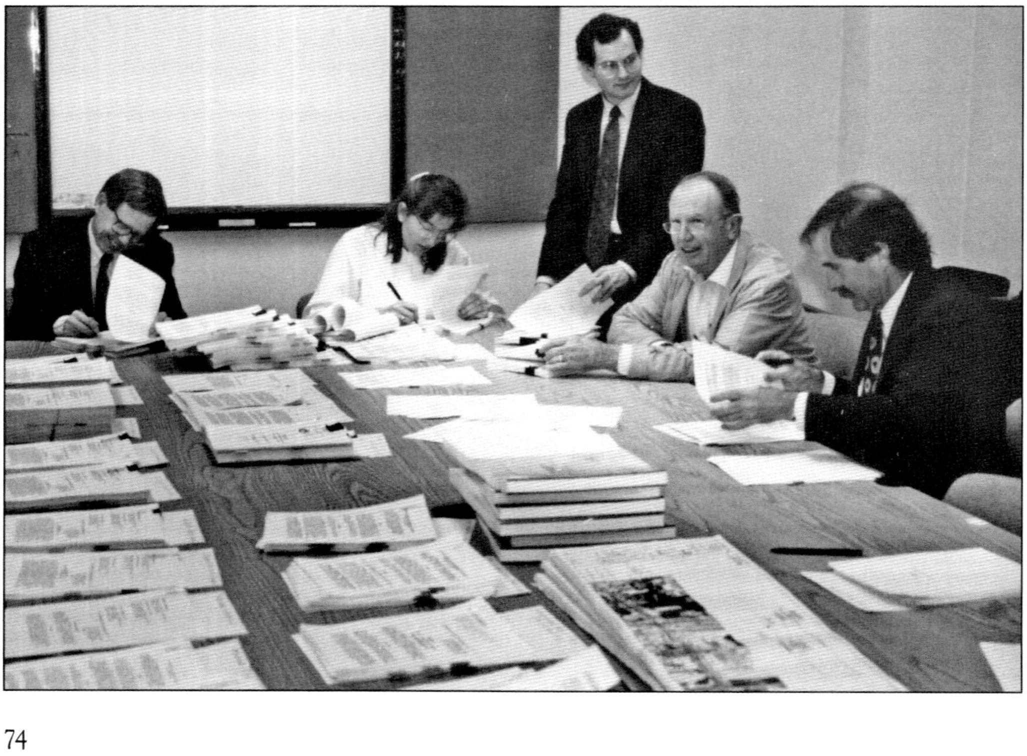

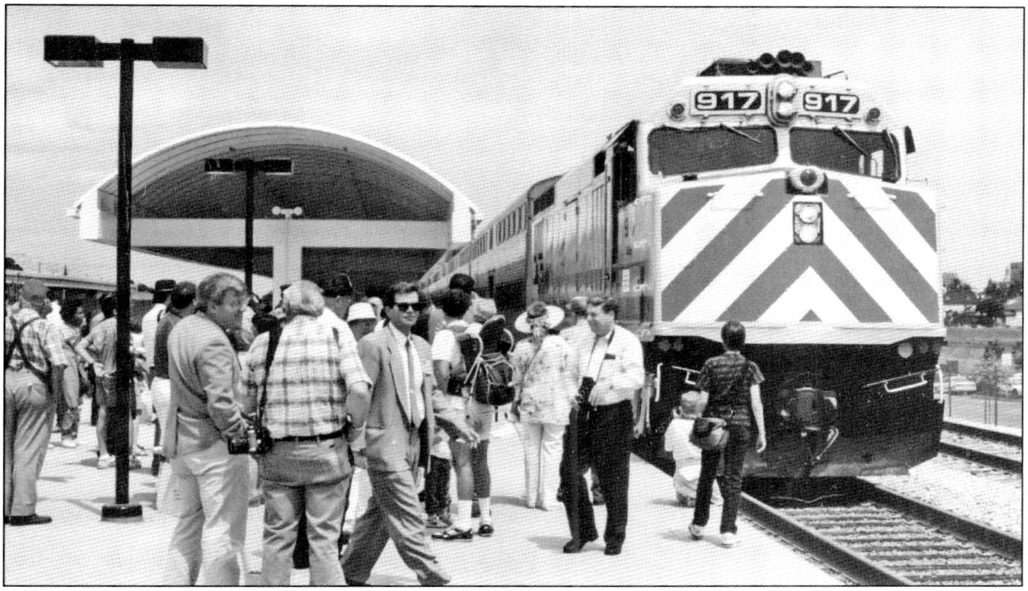


"It's All Coming Together" was the theme of a euphoric daylong celebration on June 27, 1992, which began in San Francisco with whistle-stops at San Carlos, and three of four new stations in Santa Clara County: Tamien, Morgan Hill, and Gilroy. The day marked the operational handoff from SP to the new contractor, Amtrak, as well as the stewardship of the railroad from the State of California to the JPB. The Tamien station provided a first Santa Clara County light rail system connection, and CalTrain service extended to Gilroy, albeit for just four commute-hour trips. Service expanded from 54 to 60 weekday trains, effective July 1. From Dixieland music to a reenacted 19th-century train hold-up, it was a festive day to rival that first inaugural day in 1864. (Both, Richard Mitchell.)

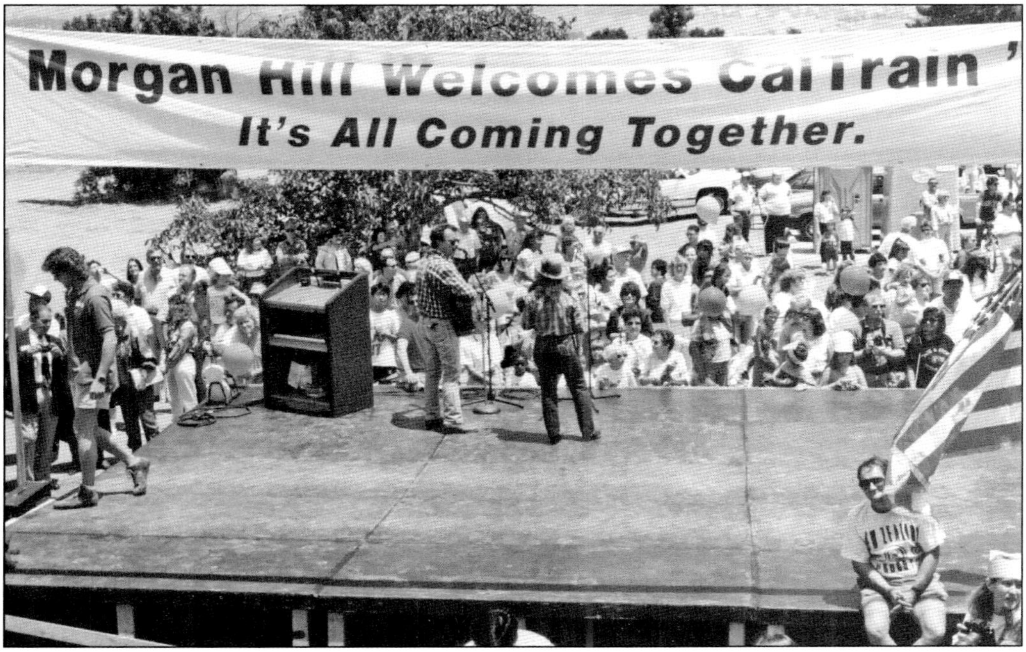

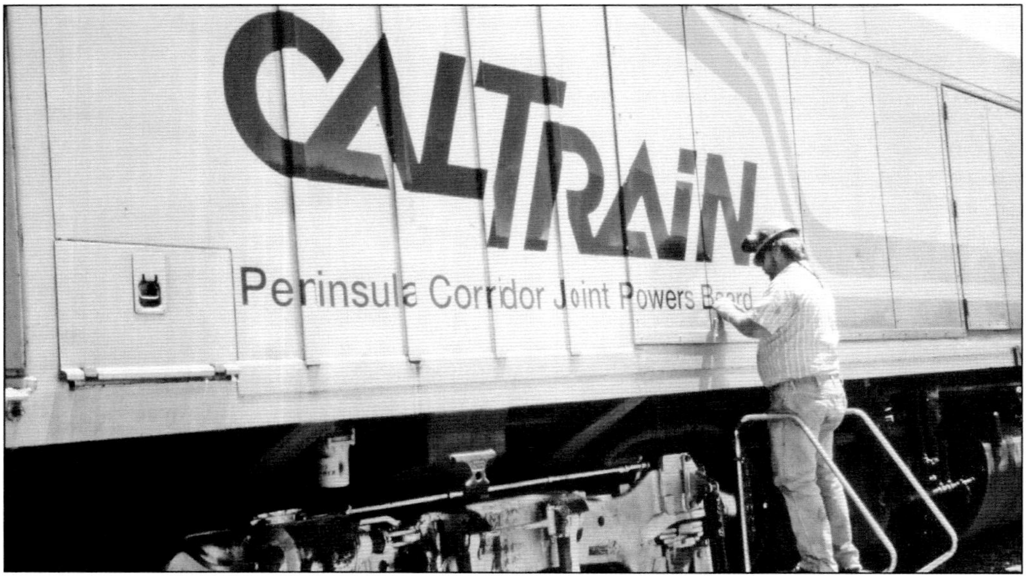


By 1993, crews were replacing the California Department of Transportation's name on locomotives with the "Peninsula Corridor Joint Powers Board." The name "CalTrain" and the teal and green colors remained unchanged until 1997, but marketing manager Gordon Smith believed the logo needed updating to better reflect the upgrades to the railroad. Working with a Salt Lake City–based advertising agency, Caltrain staff mulled changing the name, as well, because people sometimes confused "CalTrain" with "Caltrans." After focus groups and considerable discussion, the name "Caltrain" remained—with a lowercase "t." The new logo, which featured a large red circle and black letters, made its debut June 3. A five-city whistle-stop celebration heralded the change as well as an increase in weekday trains to 66. (Both, Caltrain.)

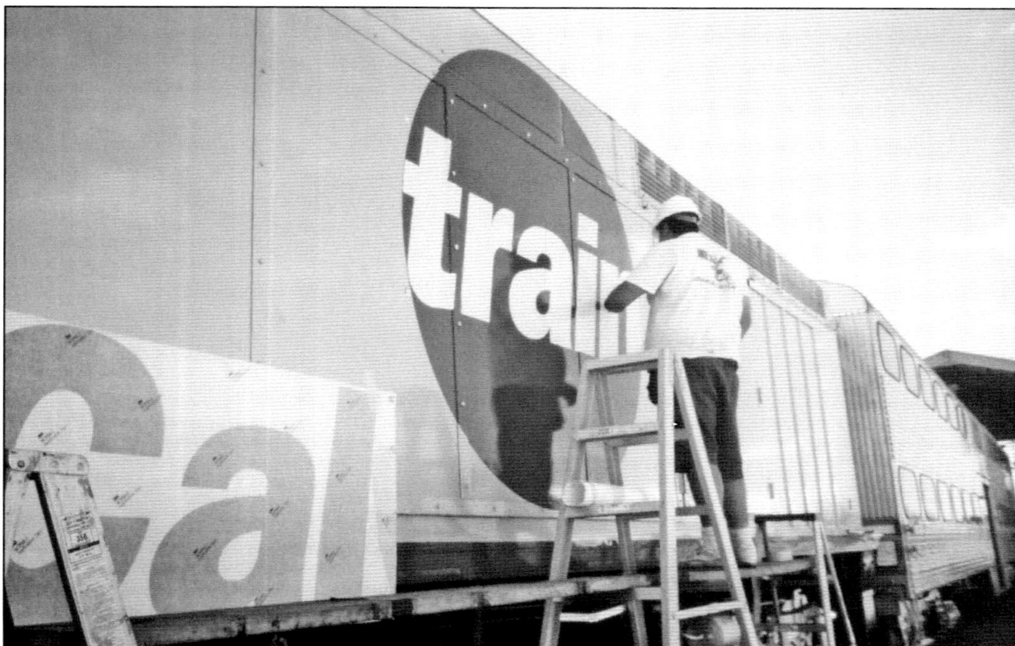

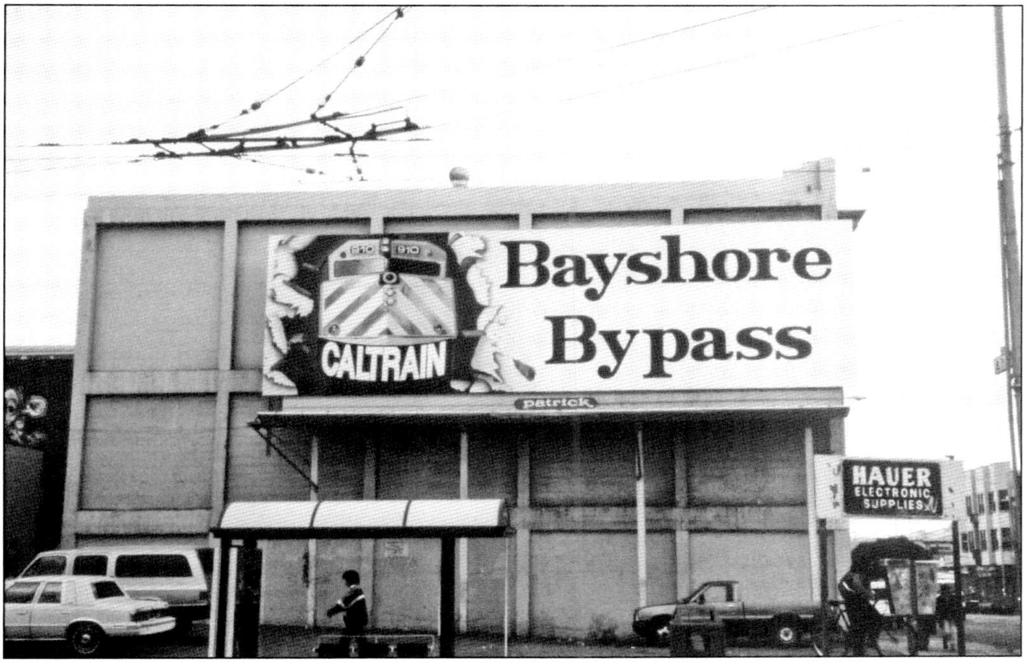


The railroad's number one competition remains the automobile, and this 1993 billboard promoting Caltrain as the way to avoid Bayshore Freeway congestion gave drivers something to think about on their way home. The billboard appeared at Eighth and Mission Streets in San Francisco before moving to ground zero for gridlock—the Bayshore itself. (Caltrain.)

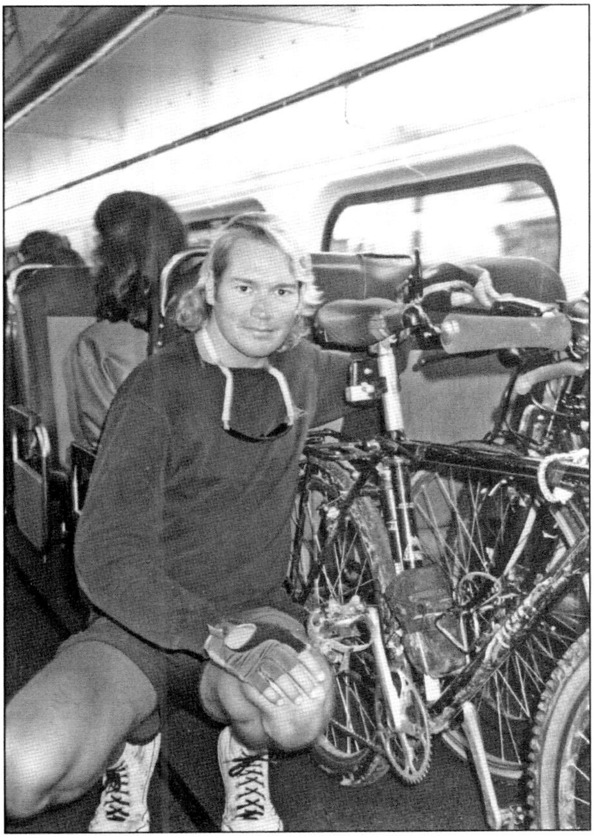

Following through on a Caltrans initiative, Caltrain's bike program began in 1992, limited to about 30 trains. At first cyclists had to park their bikes in the aisle. But bike enthusiast Lawrence "Cap" Thomas came up with an idea—and found funding—to take out seats and install bike racks, allowing trains to carry more bikes. (Caltrain.)

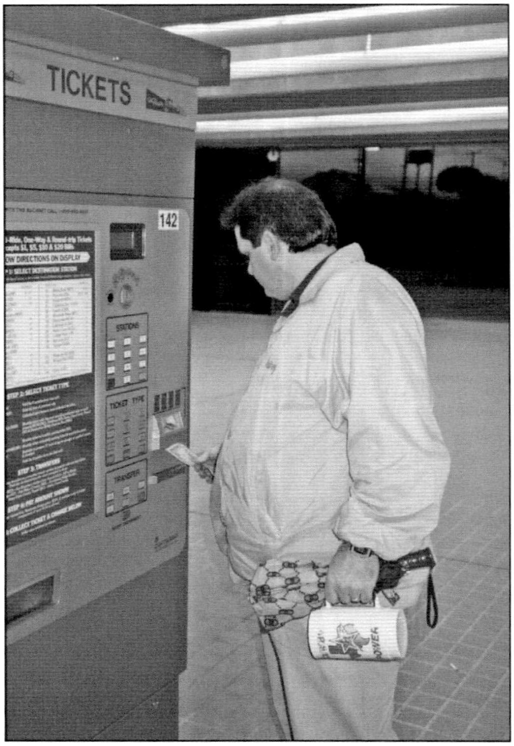


The gradual change in the way Caltrain tickets are sold began in 1993, when the first three ticket vending machines went into service at Tamien station. Caltrans began the project, which was carried forward in later years by the JPB, as vending machines were installed at more stations. An unidentified passenger tries out one of the demonstration models. (Caltrain.)

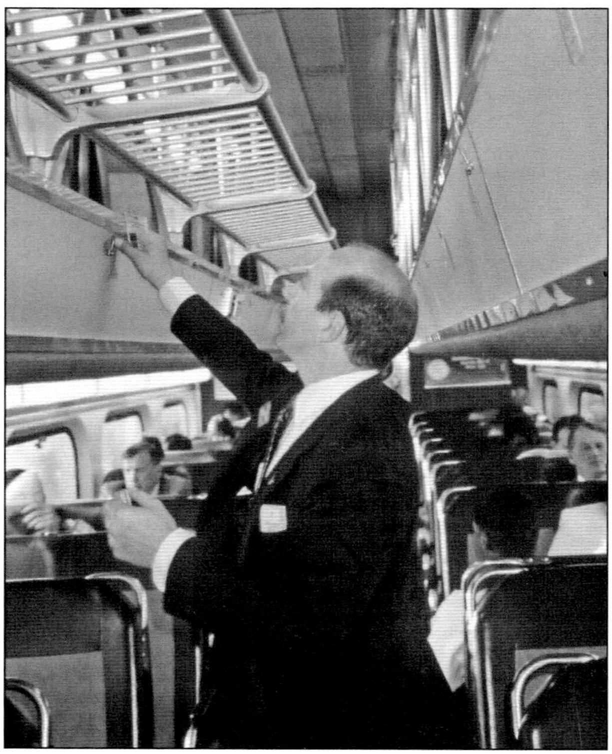

Conductor Jeff Papp attaches a hatcheck above a passenger's seat to indicate that his ticket had been checked. Until Caltrain implemented a Proof-of-Payment system in 2003, conductors still sold tickets on the train, a labor-intensive, costly, and inefficient method of selling tickets. With the implementation of vending machines, patronage at the remaining staffed stations dwindled and, one by one, they closed. (Caltrain.)

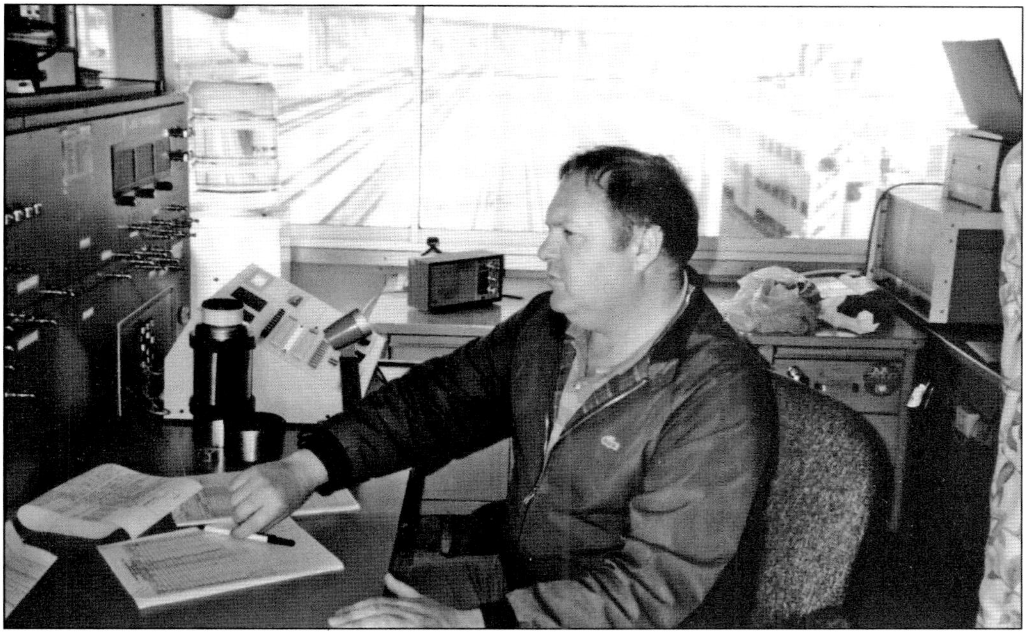

Upon taking control from Caltrans, the JPB continued carrying out long-needed modernization and upgrade plans. Traditional two-story interlocking train control towers at San Francisco, College Park, and Santa Clara were closed in a transition from manual to computerized operation. Train director Bob Kapkin, above, is pictured in 1993 on one of his last days at that job in the San Francisco rail yard. Train movements between South San Francisco and the main terminal had been handled at the San Francisco Tower since 1973. In the summer of 1993, it switched to San Jose Control, where dispatchers at their workstations activated power switches and crossovers remotely. (Both, Caltrain.)

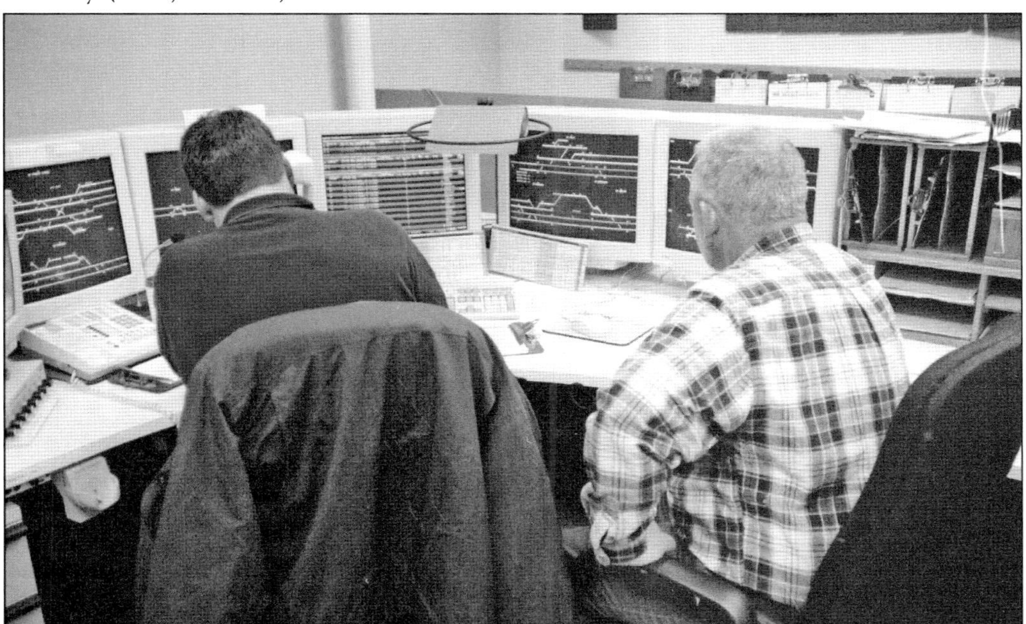

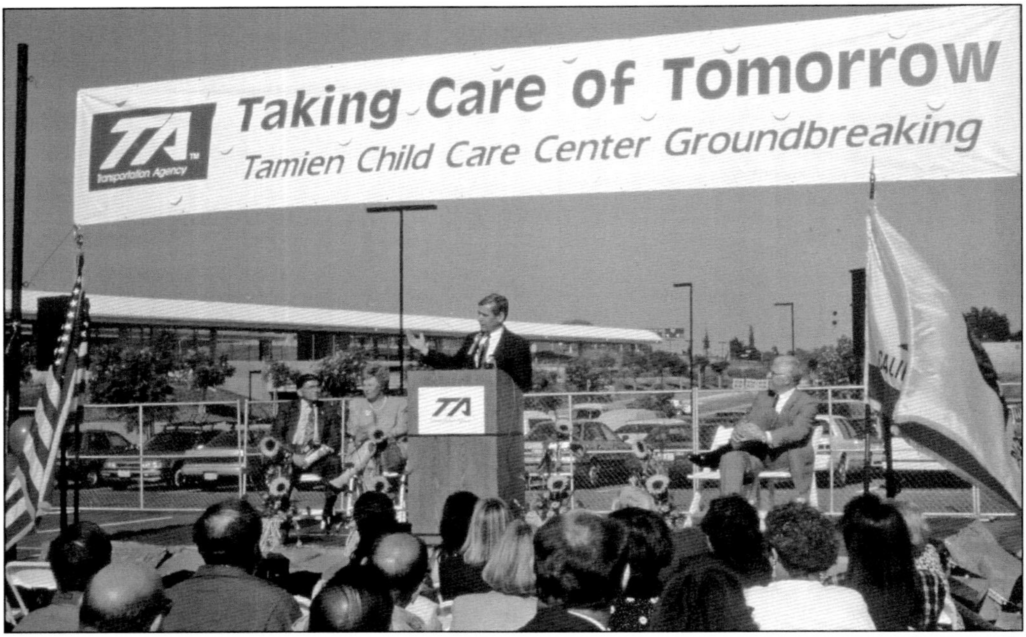


Opened in July 1992, the Tamien station in San Jose's Willow Glen area connected Caltrain with the Santa Clara Valley Transportation Authority's light rail line and buses. Three years later, a childcare center was added. The hope was that this convenient location would increase transit use by commuting parents. (Caltrain.)

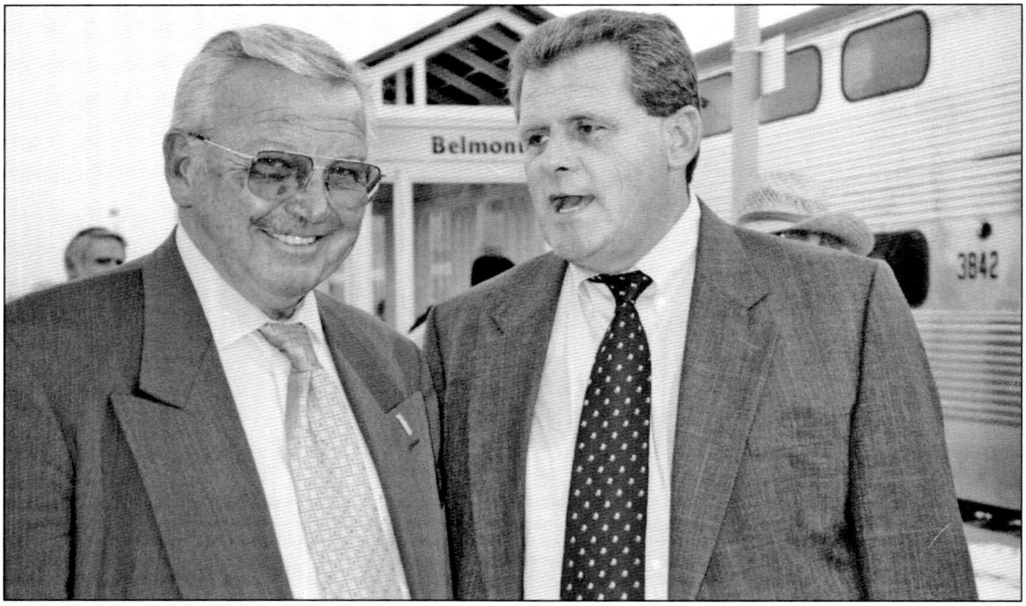


Caltrain's top leadership experienced a changing of the guard in 1999, when Gerald T. Haugh, the first executive director/general manager, retired. Haugh (left) led the San Mateo County Transit District when the JPB took on responsibility for the commuter rail line in 1992. Michael J. Scanlon, who succeeded him at SamTrans and Caltrain, was lured from Florida to head Caltrain and SamTrans. (Caltrain.)

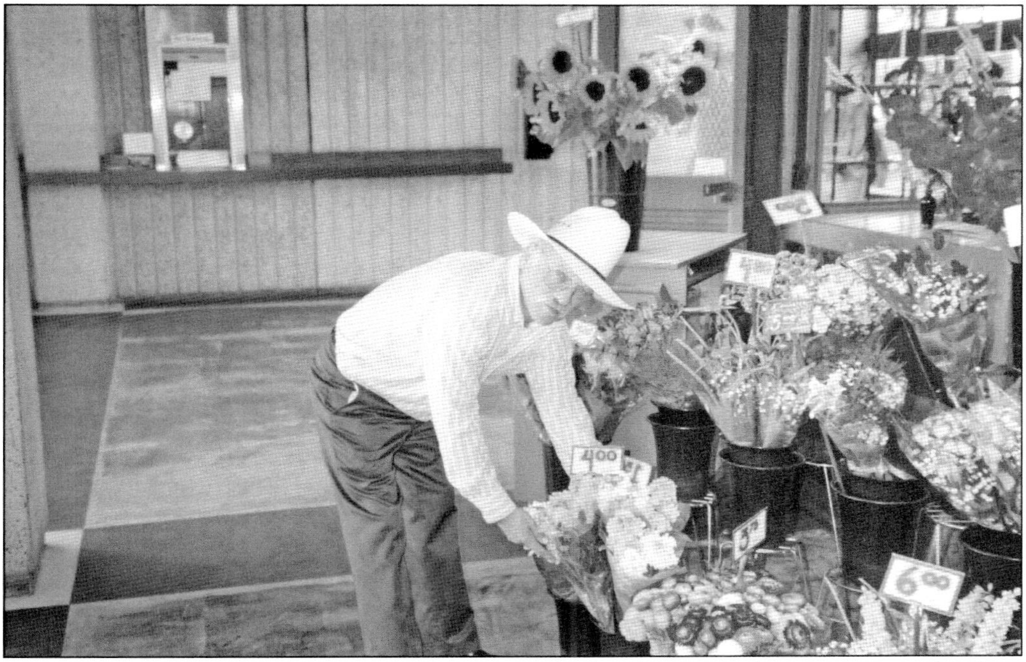

In 1971, Hal Souza opened Bow-K Flowers at SP's Third and Townsend Streets terminal, selling flowers from a cart. In those days, men regularly picked up a bouquet to take home to their wives. When the terminal moved a block south in 1975, Souza moved too. Still in business in 2011, he has been the tenant of all three "landlords"—SP, Caltrans, and its successor, the JPB. (Caltrain.)

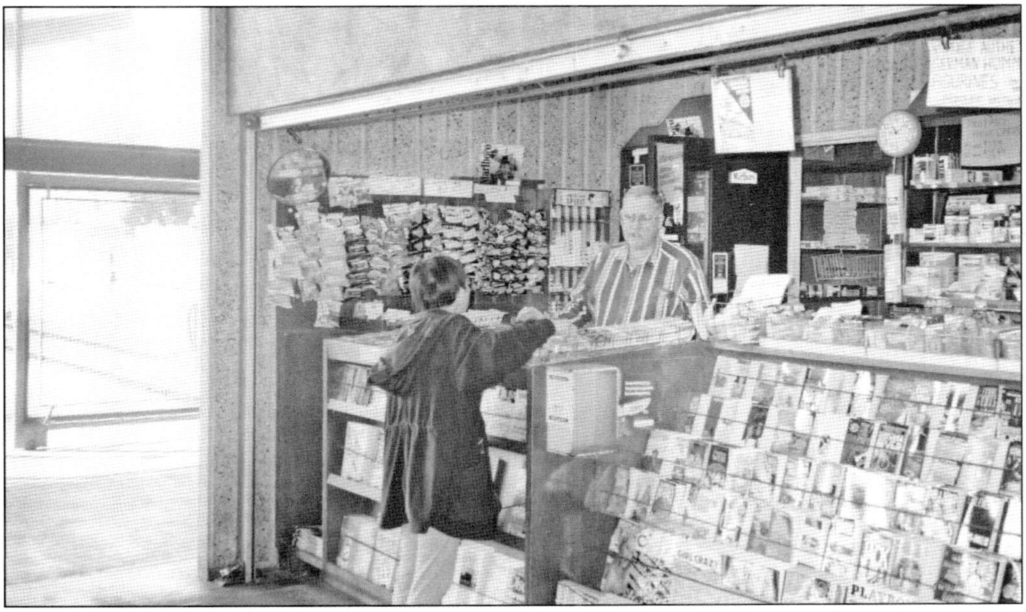

The newsstand, shown in 1997, had been open at the terminals on both Third and Fourth Streets. In 1998, both the Caltrain station and the neighborhood began to change. In January that year, Muni opened the new Embarcadero Line (later the N-Judah), giving riders a long-awaited transit link to the financial district. Remodeling work also began on the train terminal the same year. (Caltrain.)

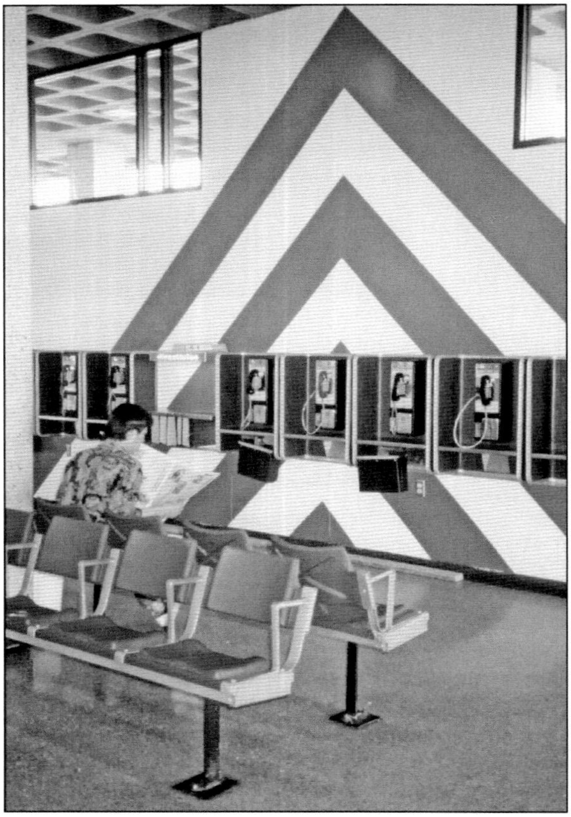

The somewhat dated look of this waiting room with its red chevron stripes would become history because of the $5-million station renovation project. The entire area was gutted. During the construction, most of the concessionaires had to move out and a portable trailer served as the ticket office. At the end of the project, Bow-K Flowers returned in the upgraded concession area. (Caltrain.)

To make way for a widened, glass-enclosed concourse, the existing walkway was demolished and the ends of the platforms were cut back. VBN Architects, who would later design the Millbrae Intermodal BART Station, also reoriented the plaza area to direct pedestrians toward the new E-Line. The former stationmaster's office and waiting room were demolished. (Caltrain.)

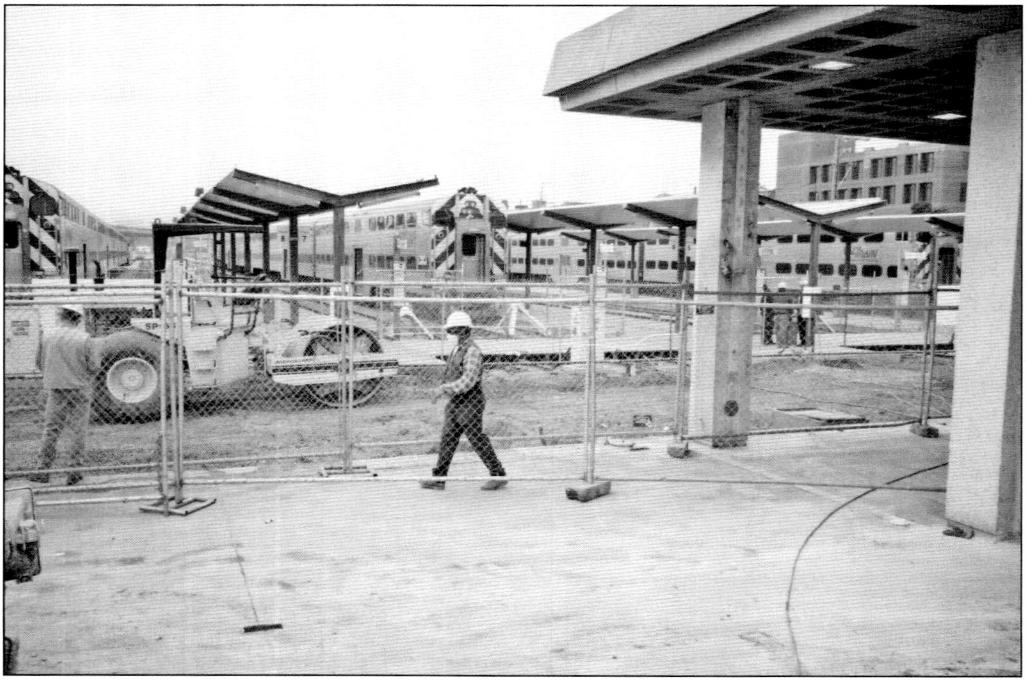

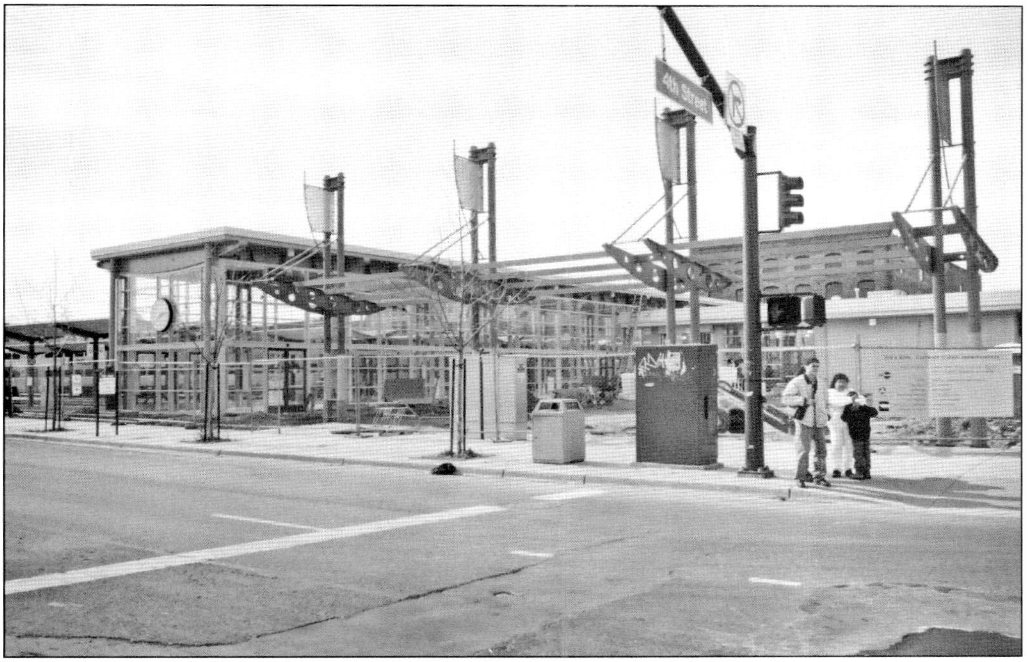


The major part of the San Francisco renovation was completed at the end of 1998 and included the remodeled ticket office, a new waiting room and restrooms and a dramatic concourse, giving an open, spacious feeling to the station. During the December 17 ceremony, a time capsule, to be opened in 75 years, was buried under the plaza. (Caltrain.)

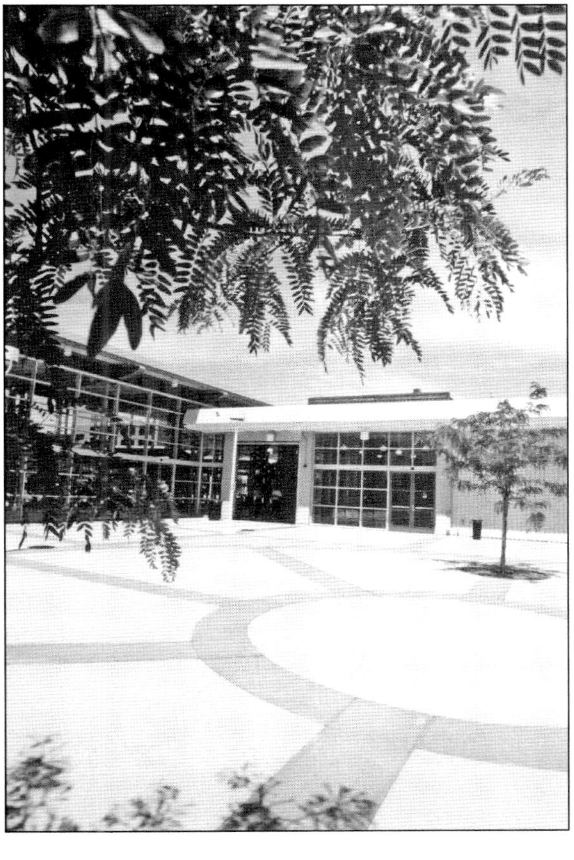

Following work on the interior of the San Francisco terminal, additional construction needed to be done on the perimeter to install new sidewalks, lighting and a canopy on the King Street side of the terminal. The landscaped plaza area presented a much more attractive area for commuters and leisure travelers alike. (Reg McGovern.)

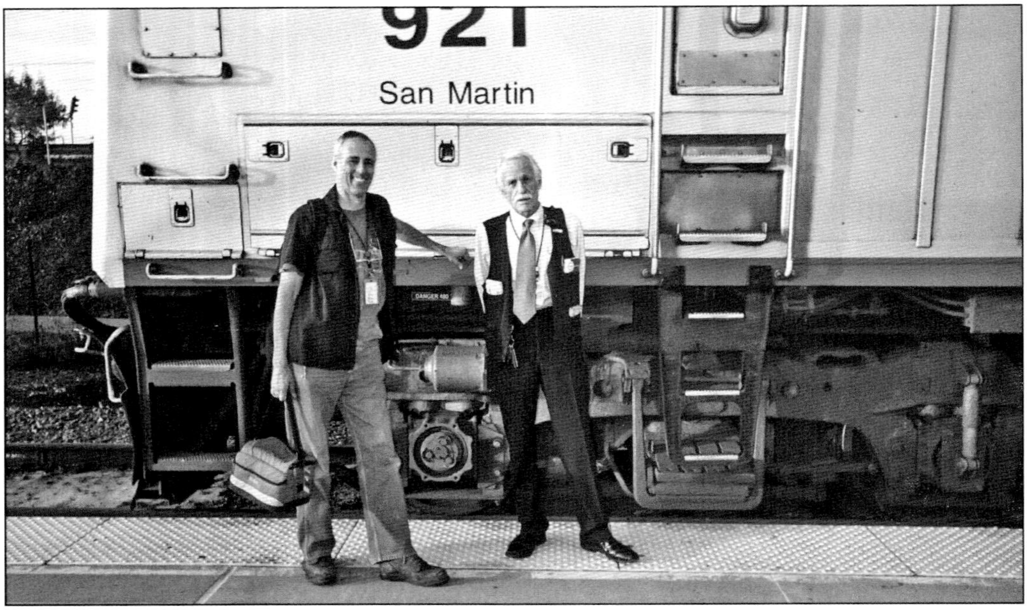


After 34 years as a railroader, on his last day at work in 2006, locomotive engineer Greg Welker (left) said good-bye to conductor Frank Kingman. Employees like Welker, who had begun with Southern Pacific, became Amtrak employees after the National Railroad Passenger Corporation won the first contract as Caltrain's operator in 1992. For 20-plus years, Welker was secretary-treasurer of the Brotherhood of Locomotive Engineers. (Greg Welker collection.)

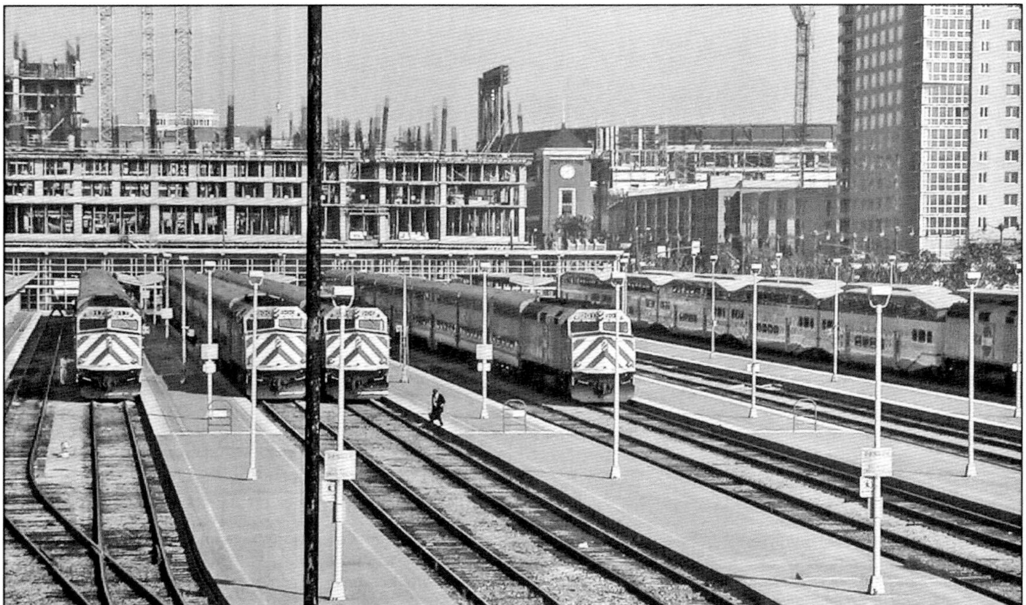

The opening of Pacific Bell Park in 2000 produced a powerful synergy for Caltrain and the entire South Beach neighborhood. The terminal is just two blocks from the ballpark, and baseball fans embraced Caltrain as the way to go to the game. The ballpark in this photograph is barely visible because of the high-rise construction that quickly filled in around it. (Eduardo Gonzales.)

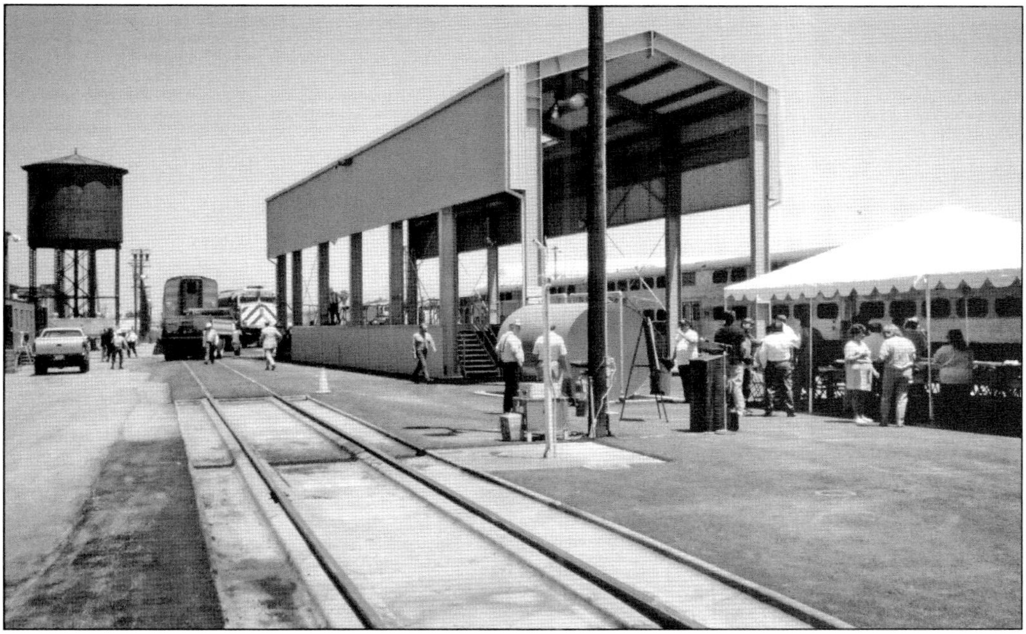

Southern Pacific's longtime Lenzen Avenue maintenance facility and roundhouse was closed because of seismic concerns, but until the $140-million Centralized Equipment Maintenance and Operations Facility opened in 2007, railroad mechanics had to keep trains clean and operating in severely limited conditions. Some major repair and maintenance tasks had to be sent off-site, including to Roseville. A temporary $1.5-million locomotive pit in the San Jose station's yard (above) at least provided a covered area to work for a few years. But until CEMOF opened in 2007, trains were washed the old-fashioned way as this Chuck Fox photograph shows. (Both, Caltrain.)

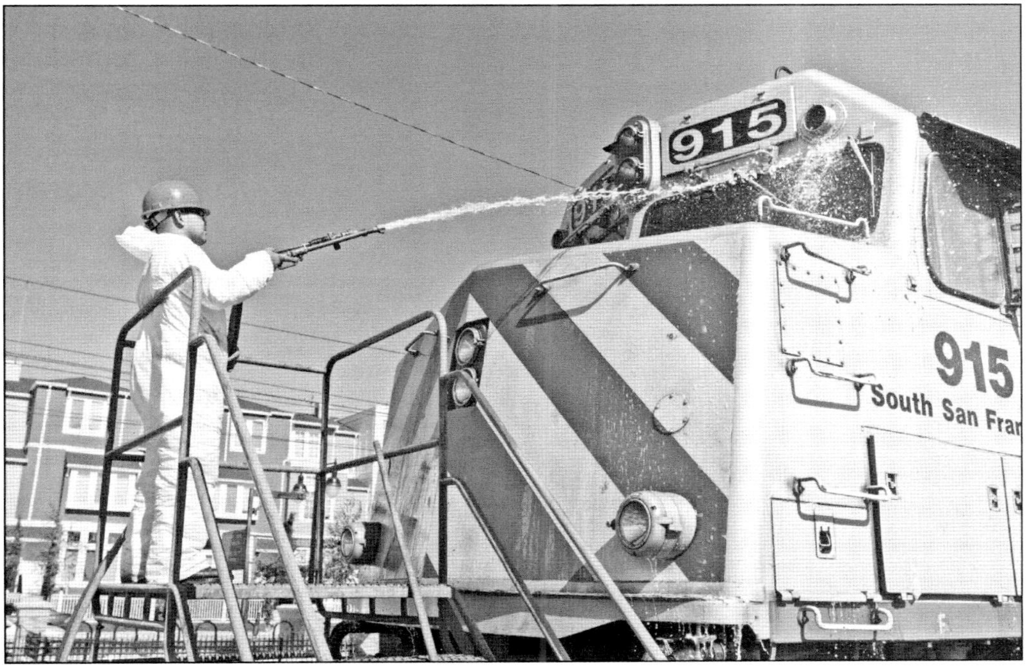

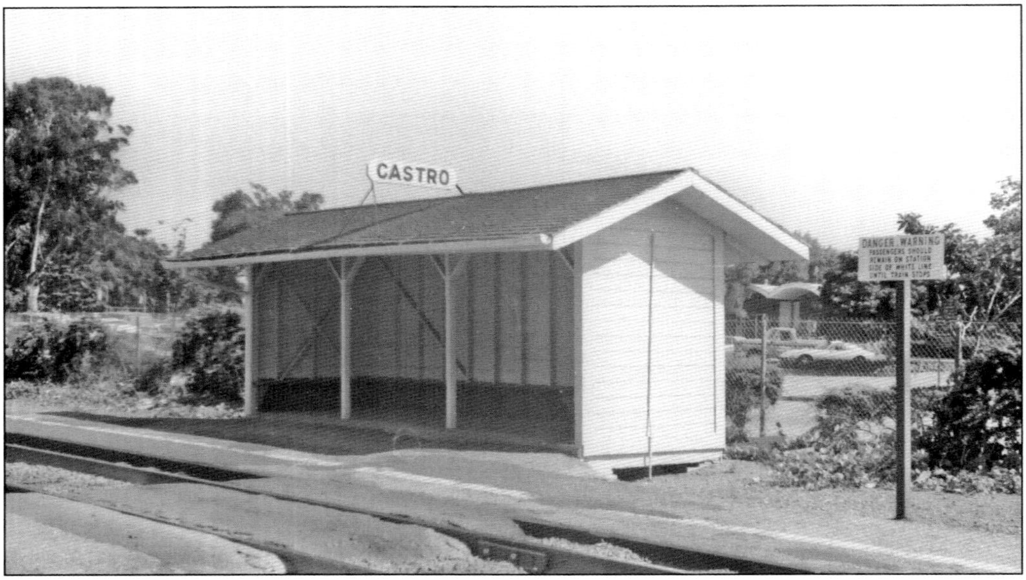


Built in about 1906 on land donated by one of the earliest residents of Mountain View, the shelter shed at Castro station located on Rengstorff Avenue had been a "flag stop" adjacent to the Castro family ranch. Never a busy station, the ridership decline accelerated after the San Antonio station opened just six-tenths of a mile north in 1999. The Castro station closed in February 2000. (Tom Gray.)

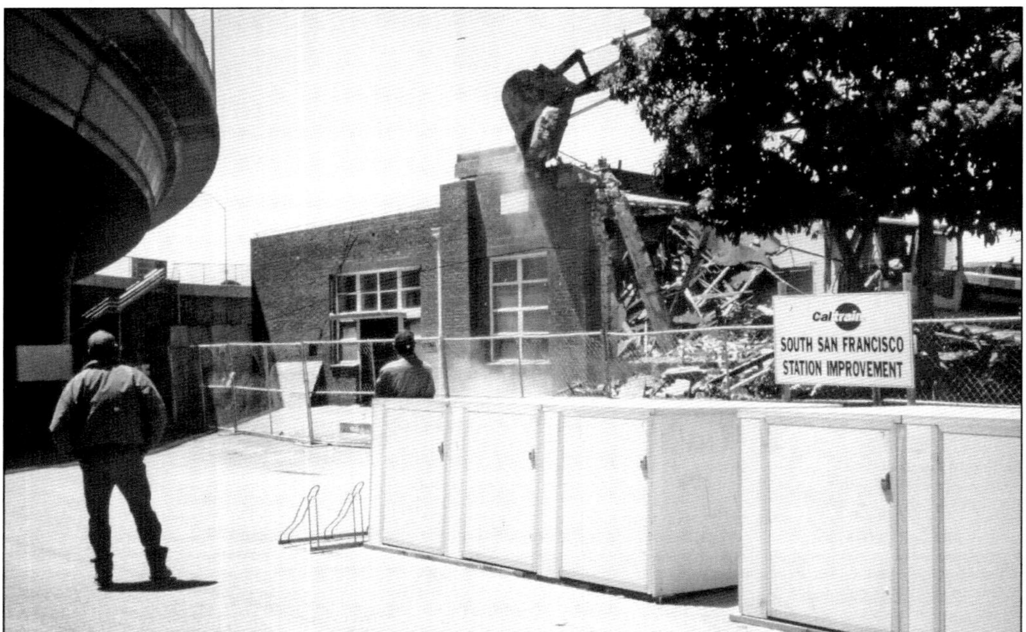


The South San Francisco station was closed in 1989 because it was not busy enough to justify staffing. Caltrain's engineering department staff used some of the space while working on the Ponderosa Project, the first of two major Caltrain construction projects. The building was subsequently declared a seismic risk and razed in 1999. (Caltrain.)

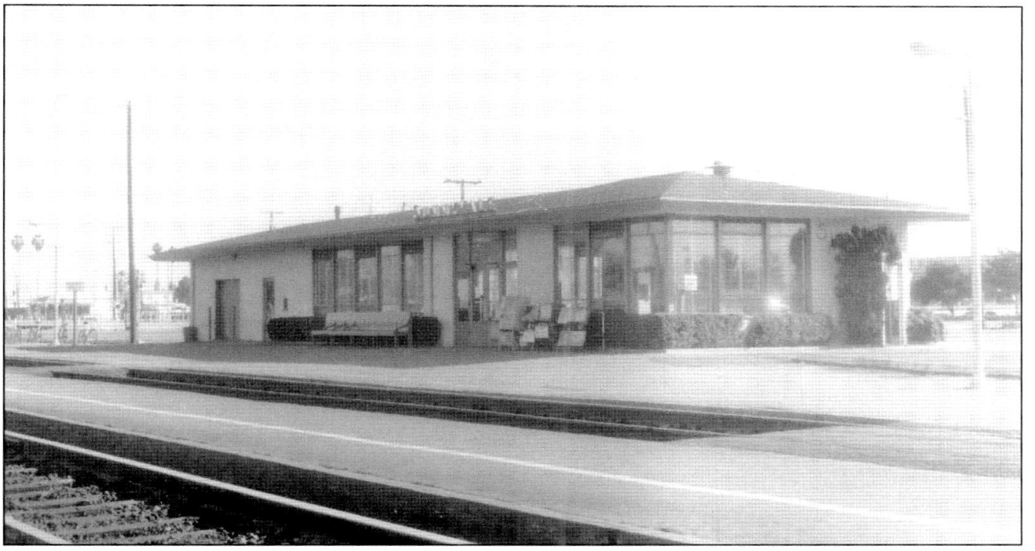

Built across from the farm of Martin Murphy Jr., the original Sunnyvale train stop was called "Murphy's station." Shortly after the turn of the century, a surplus depot from Goleta was relocated to the place by then-called "Sunnyvale." The depot, which had been remodeled, lasted until 1951, when it was damaged by a tornado and condemned. Southern Pacific built this depot, pictured in 1975, to replace it. (Tom Gray.)

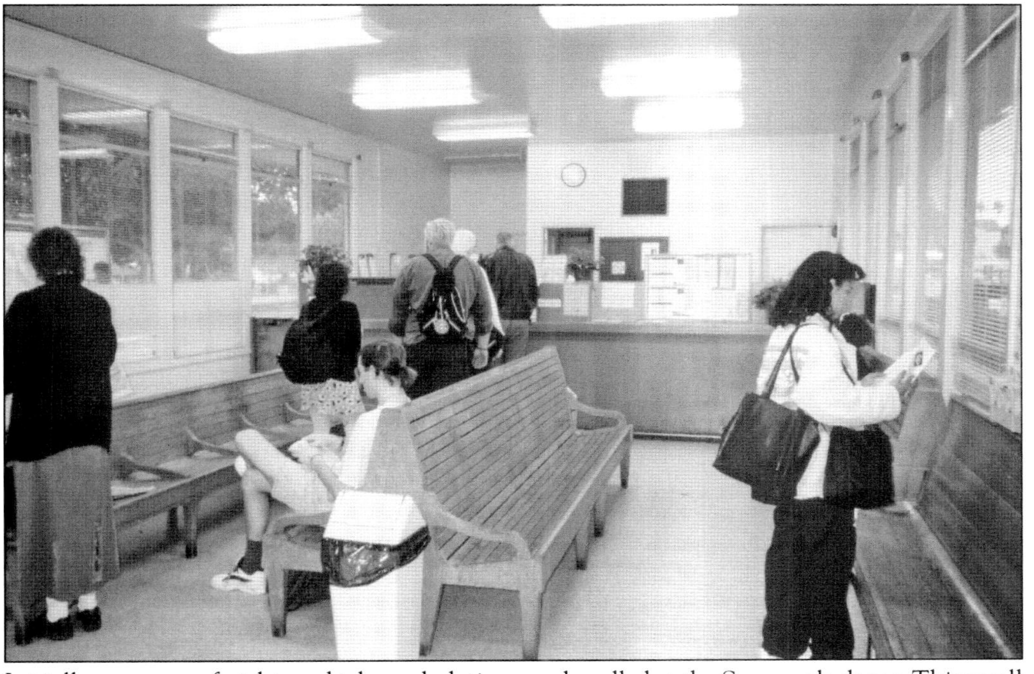

Initially, passenger, freight, and telegraph duties were handled at the Sunnyvale depot. This small passenger waiting room and a snack stand were available for riders waiting for trains. As ticket vending machines were added at more stations, sales at ticket offices like Sunnyvale dwindled. The depot was demolished to make way for an $11.4-million multimodal transit center, which opened in mid-2003. (Caltrain.)

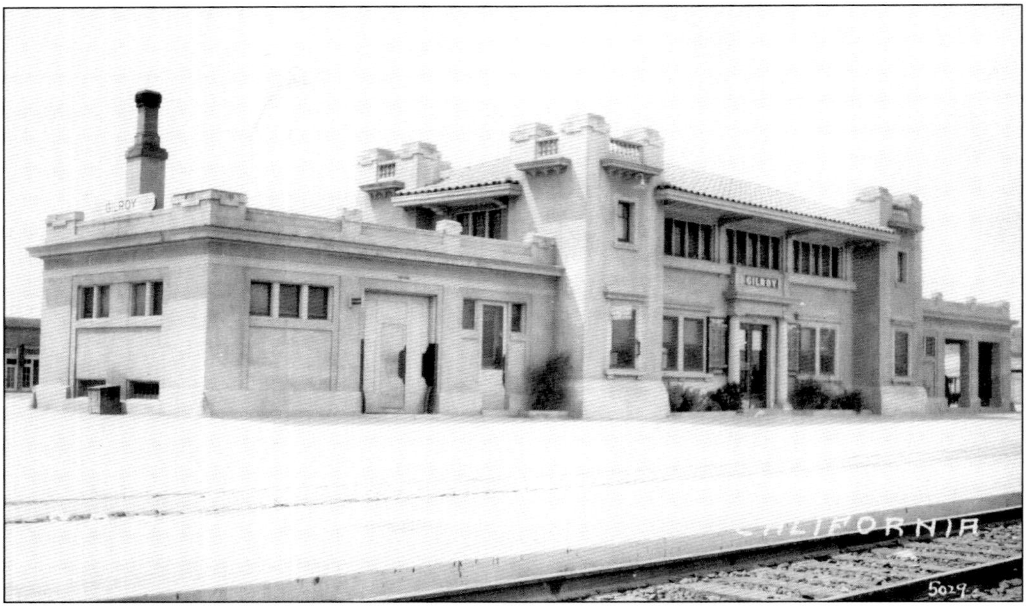

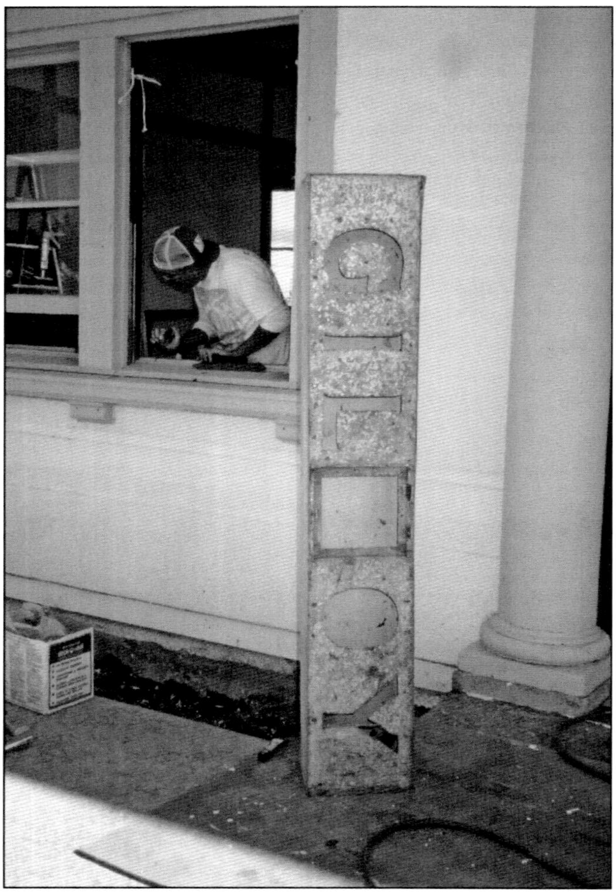

Gilroy's first depot was built in 1869 when the Southern Pacific extended service to the town. Rail activity proceeded to grow and in 1917–1918, after lobbying by the city, the railroad replaced the first depot. The two-story Italian Renaissance–style building included two waiting rooms and a baggage room. Passenger service at Gilroy ended in 1971. The freight agency was closed in 1985. (Arthur Lloyd collection.)

The Gilroy depot had been vacant before it underwent a $1-million restoration in 1998. Built of redwood believed to be from a local mill, the structure itself was in good shape despite its long disuse. An additional $2.8 million-dollar project sponsored by the Santa Clara Valley Transportation Authority added six bus bays and more parking. (Caltrain.)

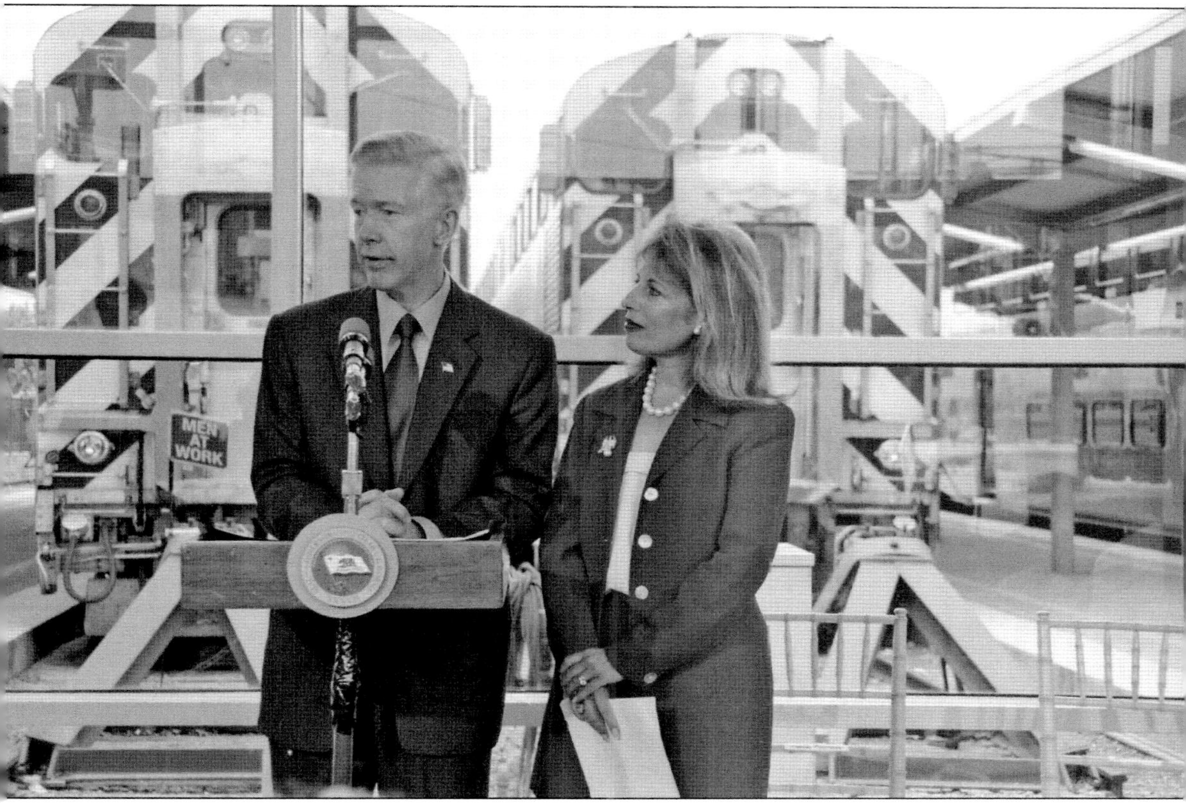


California governor Gray Davis and state senator Jackie Speier spoke at a 2002 ceremony in San Francisco, kicking off two years of construction that set the stage for Baby Bullet express train service. The $127-million CTX project installed passing tracks to enable the Bullets to bypass local trains. They got riders between San Jose and San Francisco in under an hour and were an instant success. Speier was credited with securing state funding for the construction of the necessary infrastructure and purchasing the first rolling stock, as well as for coming up with the name for the Baby Bullet. (Reg McGovern.)

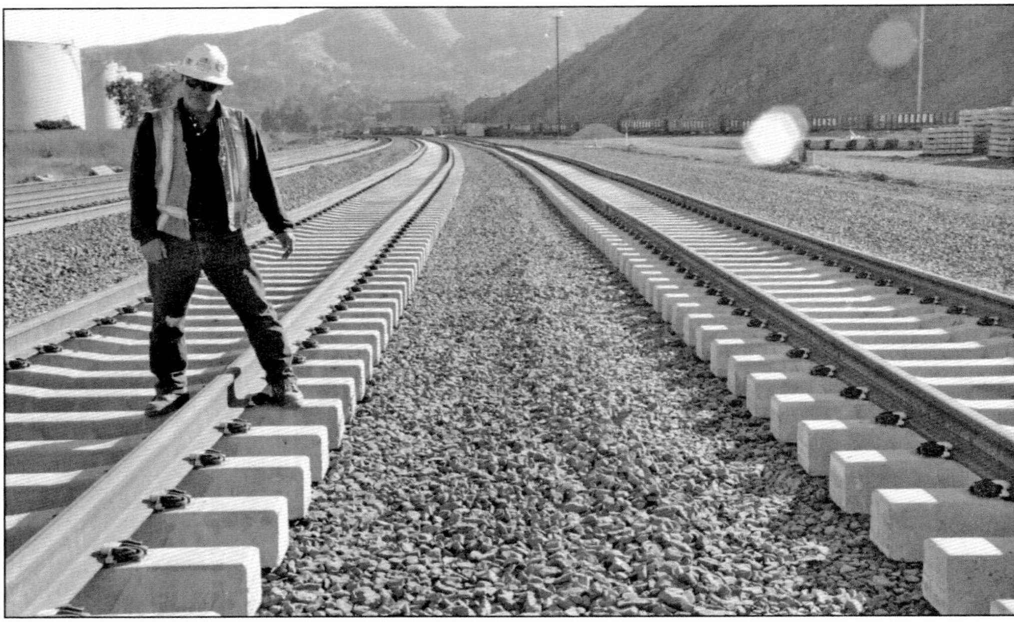

Two new tracks for Baby Bullet service were being constructed in Brisbane near the Bayshore station as part of the CTX project, when this picture was taken in 2003. A second two-track addition occurred in the vicinity of Lawrence station in Sunnyvale. Installation of centralized traffic control was a critical component of this breakthrough for faster service. (Reg McGovern.)

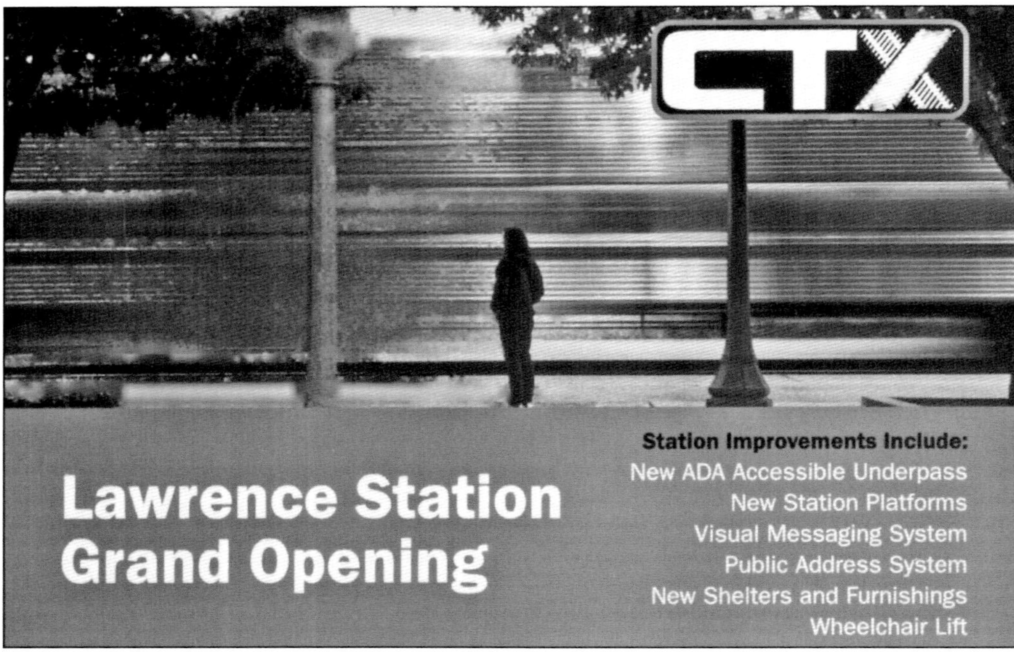


The CTX project brought new amenities to the Lawrence station for passengers, which, prior to that, had been minimal. A new accessible pedestrian underpass allowed riders to cross from one side of the tracks to the other, and new shelters, furnishings, a public address system, and parking were notable enhancements. (Caltrain.)

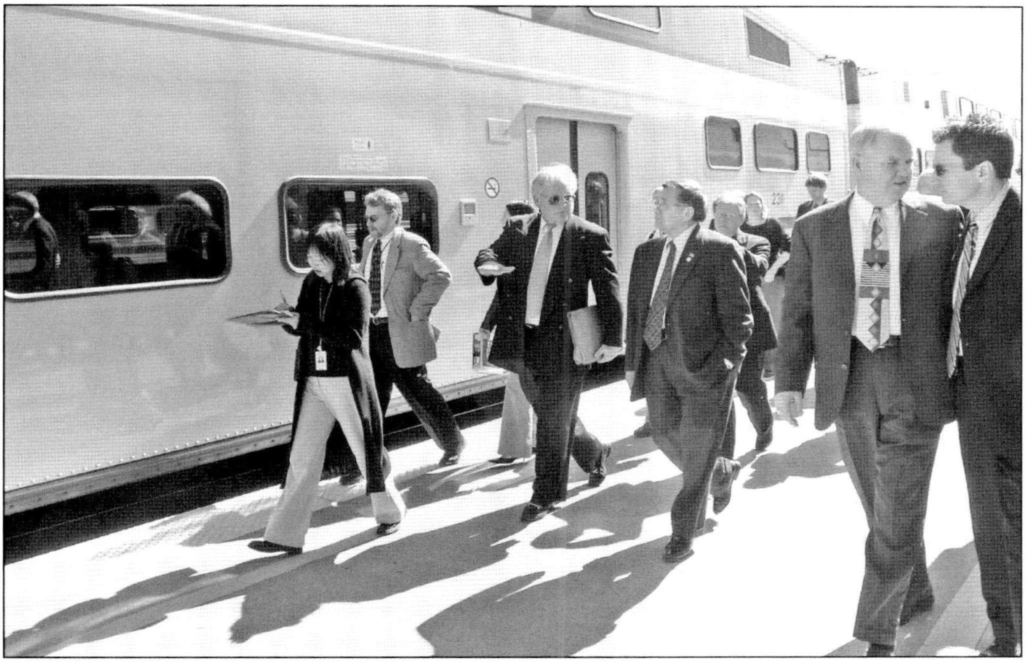

Bob Doty (center, gesturing), who headed Caltrain's Rail Services Department, escorted US Transportation Secretary Norm Mineta during a 2005 visit to San Francisco to see the Baby Bullet success for himself. The first 10 Bullets made their debut in June 2004. Caltrain added 12 more the next year to lure more riders and maximize efficiency by getting more round-trips with the same crews and equipment. (Caltrain.)

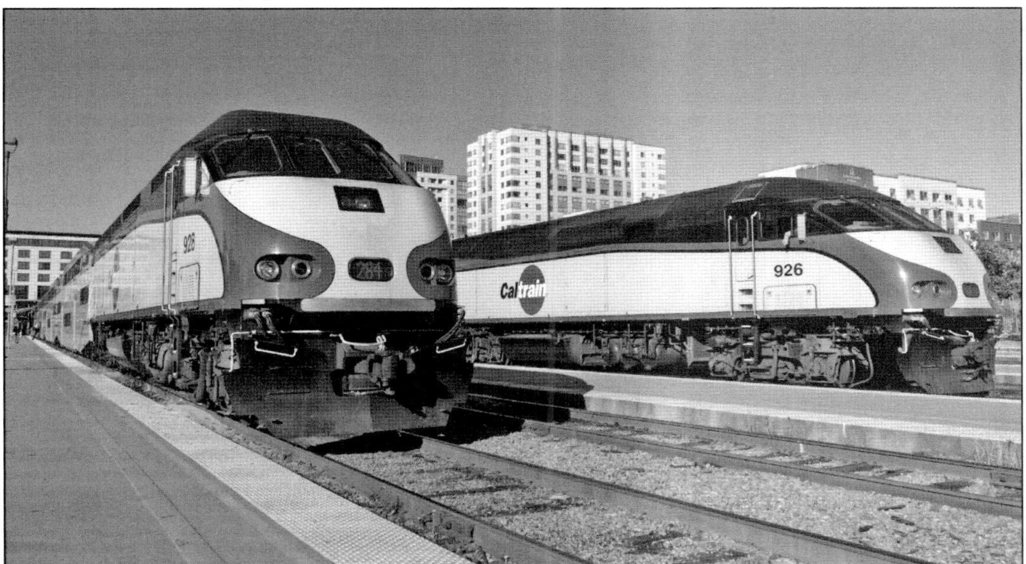


Not only did the Baby Bullets cut travel time for riders, the sleek aerodynamic design of the new locomotives gave Caltrain's image a lift. The trains simply looked modern, as can be seen in this Chuck Fox photograph taken in San Francisco. Caltrain's marketing and promotion campaign capitalized on that new look, advertising Caltrain's "extreme makeover." (Caltrain.)

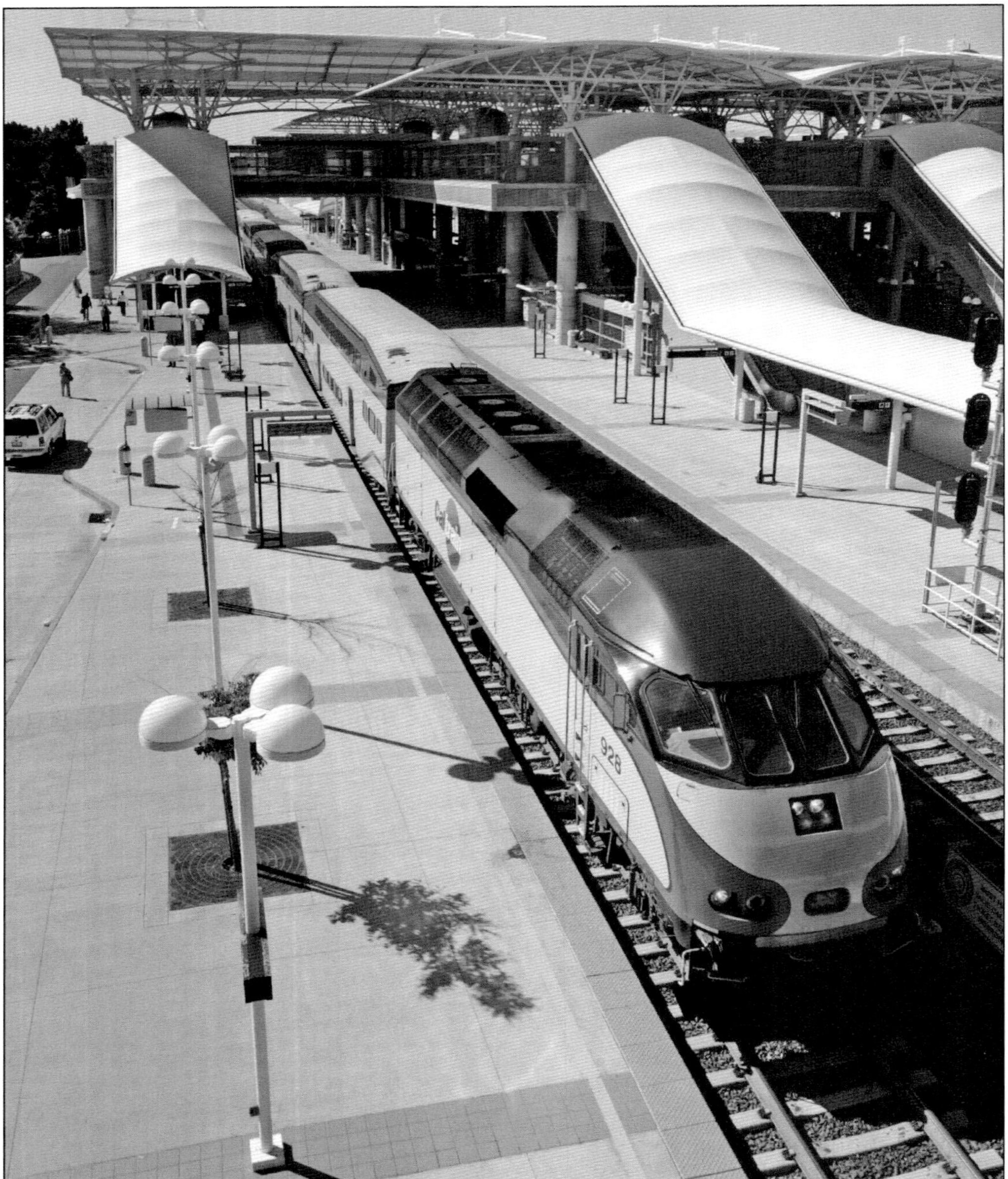

Caltrain and BART connected at Millbrae in the summer of 2003, when the new intermodal station opened. It provided a BART link to San Francisco International Airport, as well as a regional connection for the two rail systems that significantly improved access to Caltrain for residents of the East Bay and beyond. Millbrae, seen in this Chuck Fox photograph, became an increasingly popular Baby Bullet stop. BART passengers could easily transfer to Caltrain and vice-versa, and an expanded area for SamTrans buses and shuttles offered customers even more transit options. In the fiscal year 2008, Caltrain carried nearly 12 million riders, up 8.6 percent from 2007. It was the highest ridership in the railroad's history to date, and the Baby Bullet service was a major factor in this success. Also in 2008, Caltrain added two evening local trains to the schedule, increasing the number of trains to 98, another all-time high. (Caltrain.)

# *Five*

# Community Connections

A railroad is about connections. And throughout its history, the Peninsula Commute Service in ways literal and symbolic has been fundamentally joined with communities and individuals who depend on it. Commuters and students have relied on the train to get to and from work or school, but employers and developers also have recognized the value of the railroad and have deliberately chosen to locate near it. Generations of employees—many of them multiple family members—took pride in their work for the Southern Pacific and for Caltrain, ensuring that passengers got to their destinations safely and on time. A trip on the Peninsula rail line might be the stepping-off point for a trip across country or for soldiers going off to war. The only *Freedom Train* in the nation commemorating Dr. Martin Luther King Jr.'s famed march heads out from San Jose every January. Thousands board Caltrain every May for the Bay to Breakers Race in San Francisco, and special trains have taken fans to the Super Bowl, World Cup Soccer, and the "Big Game" at Stanford University. December 2000 inaugurated a special Caltrain that did not pick up passengers: the first holiday train, carrying Santa and a cast of costumed characters and entertainers, visited stations to present a musical show and collect toy donations for needy children. Dozens of dedicated volunteers and Caltrain employees have outdone themselves in ensuing years to add more lights to a spectacular train that connects thousands of families at their train stations. A roughly 77-mile thread stitches cities together from San Francisco to Gilroy. Train stations and depots occupy a central place in the hearts of these communities—some as historic landmarks—but all as essential to a community's identity. Over the railroad's nearly 150 years, depots have burned down, closed, been rebuilt or remodeled and sometimes moved from one side of the tracks to the other. These train stations have remained more than just a place to board a train or pick someone up. They are an integral part of community identity.

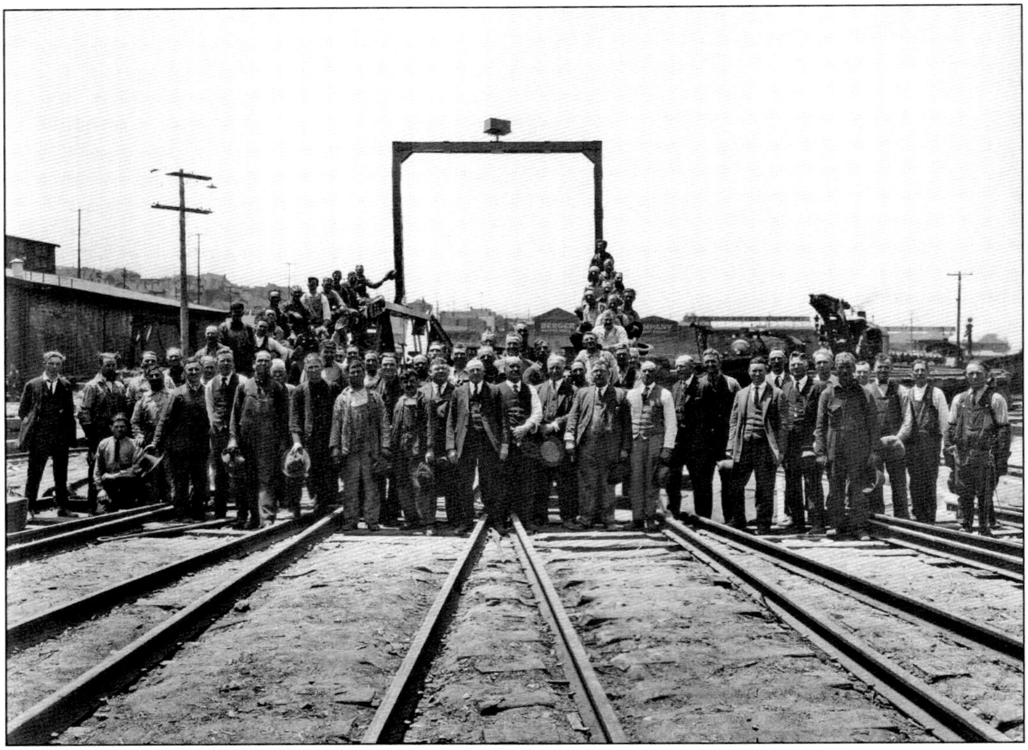

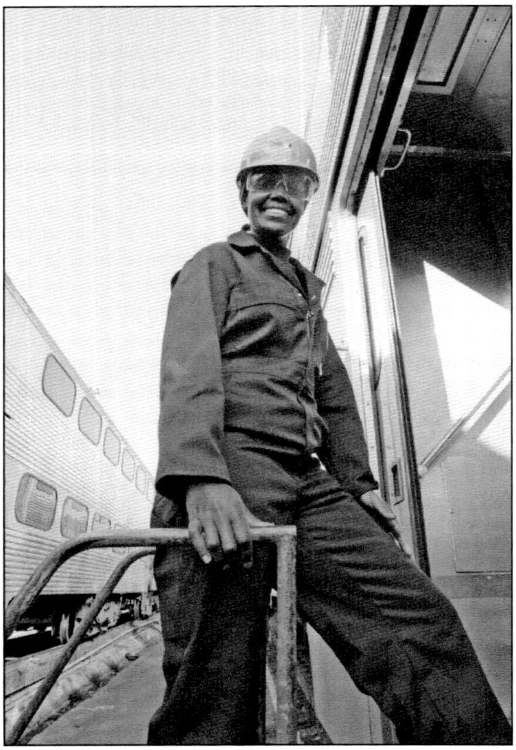

Employees working at Mission Bay pause from their work for this 1924 photograph. During the period that it was open from about 1906 to 1960, the Mission Bay roundhouse and shops serviced steam locomotives used in passenger service from San Francisco to Los Angeles. As steam engines were replaced by diesels requiring less maintenance, activity was reduced. (Courtesy California State Railroad Museum.)

Before being elected to the San Francisco Board of Supervisors in 2000, Sophie Maxwell was an Amtrak electrician at the San Francisco railroad yard. At the time, she was the only woman working in that maintenance yard. As an elected official, Maxwell served for a time as one of San Francisco's three representatives on the nine-member Peninsula Corridor Joint Powers Board (JPB.) (Caltrain.)

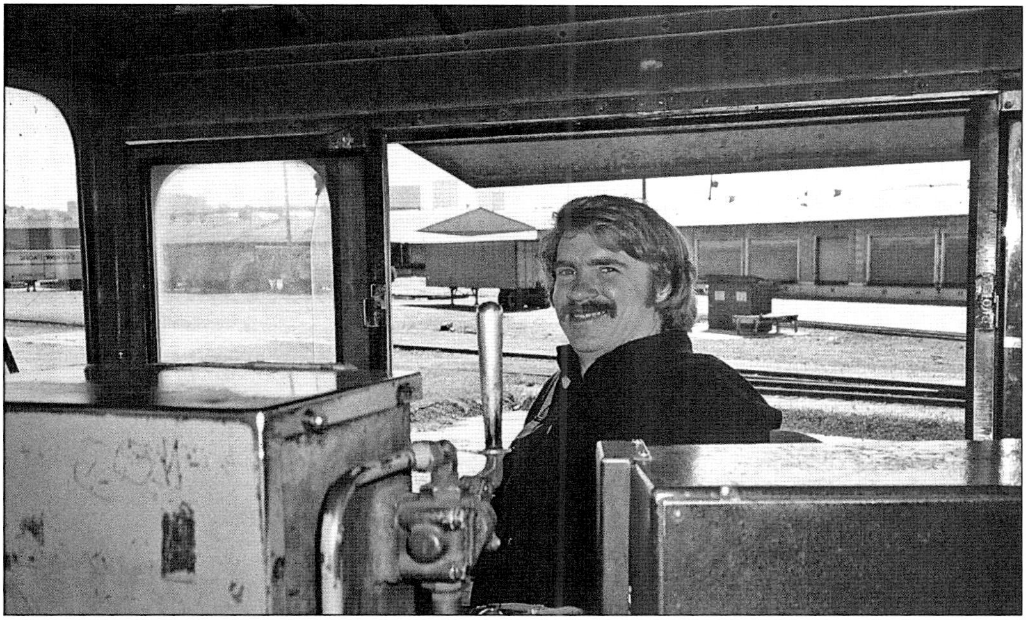

Will Hastings is shown working a "Mission Bay job," switching cars from the Mission Bay railroad yard or spotting cars for nearby industries. Hastings signed on with SP in 1971 and worked his way up to Amtrak's assistant general manager for Caltrain by the time he retired in 2007. The former yard is now the site of San Francisco's giant Mission Bay redevelopment project. (Dana Dillard.)

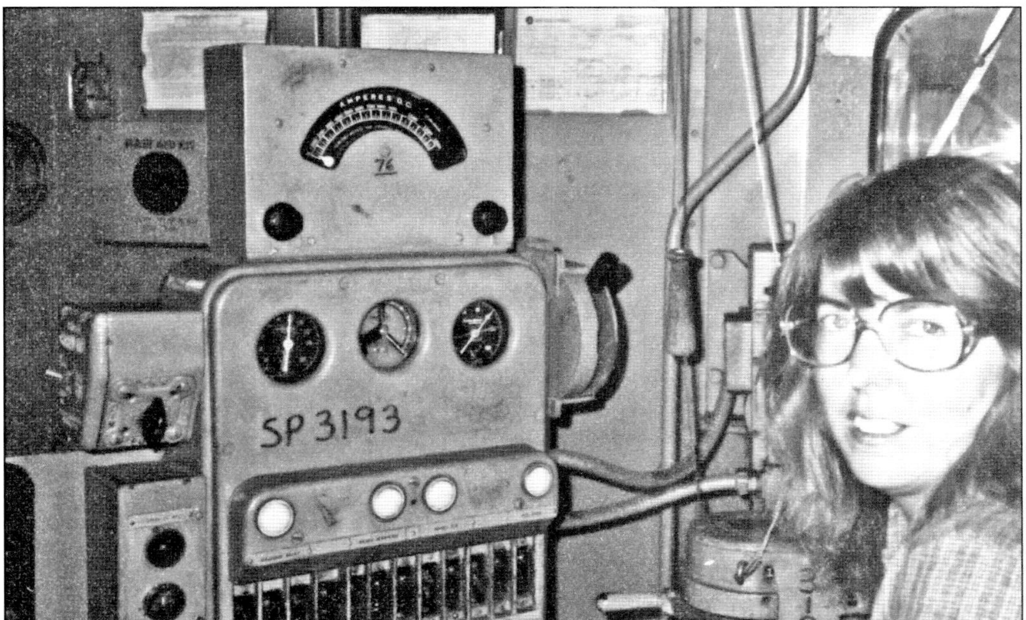


Hired in 1977, Dana Dillard was the first woman locomotive engineer on the Peninsula Commute Service. From clerk to hostler, she advanced into engine service both for Caltrain and the San Francisco Belt Railway, where she moved trains at Pier 96. After a break to work as a real estate appraiser, she returned to Caltrain in 2007 as a conductor. (Dana Dillard collection.)

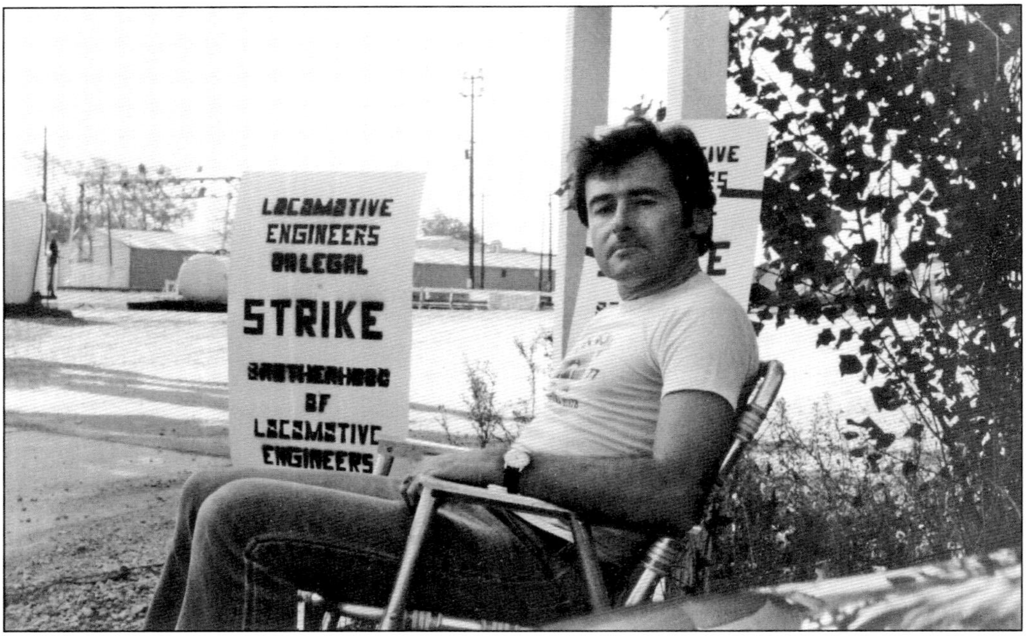


Growing up in Palo Alto, Mike Gondron and his brother Jim used to ride their bikes to the California Avenue station, hollering greetings to the engineers, who would give the young rail fans track bulletins as souvenirs. Mike became a Southern Pacific engineer in 1968. Two years later, Jim was hired too. Mike is pictured here doing picket duty at the San Jose roundhouse in 1982. During their careers as "train handlers," the Gondrons were the only brothers who were Caltrain locomotive engineers. Mike retired from the railroad in 2008, and was there to greet Jim on his last day, in 2010. (Above, Mike Gondron collection; below, Caltrain.)

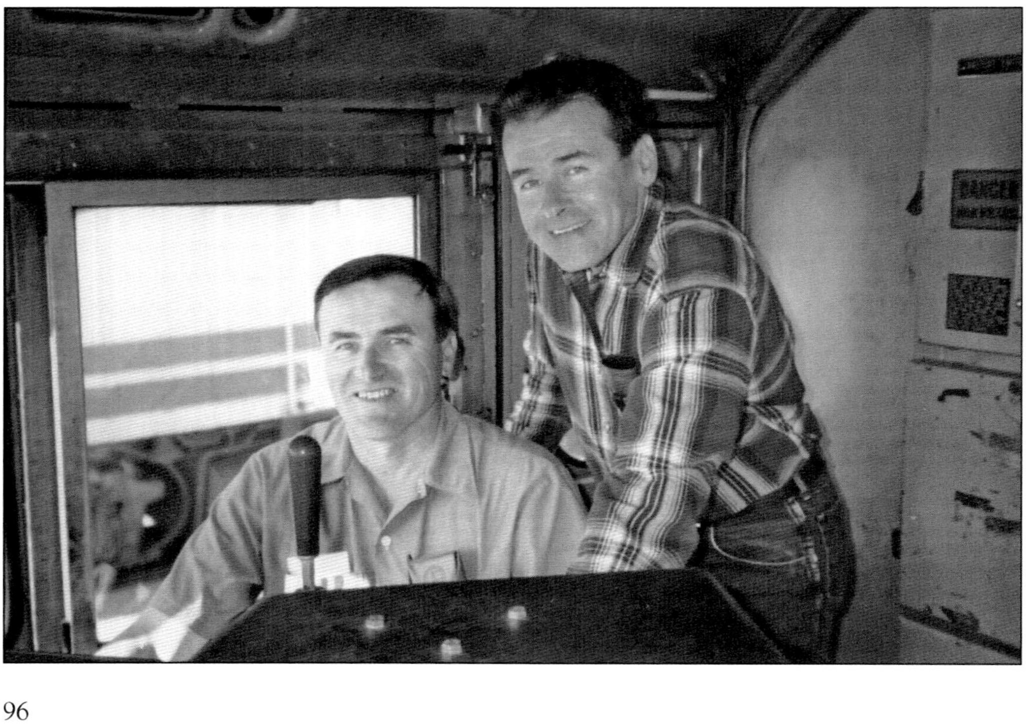

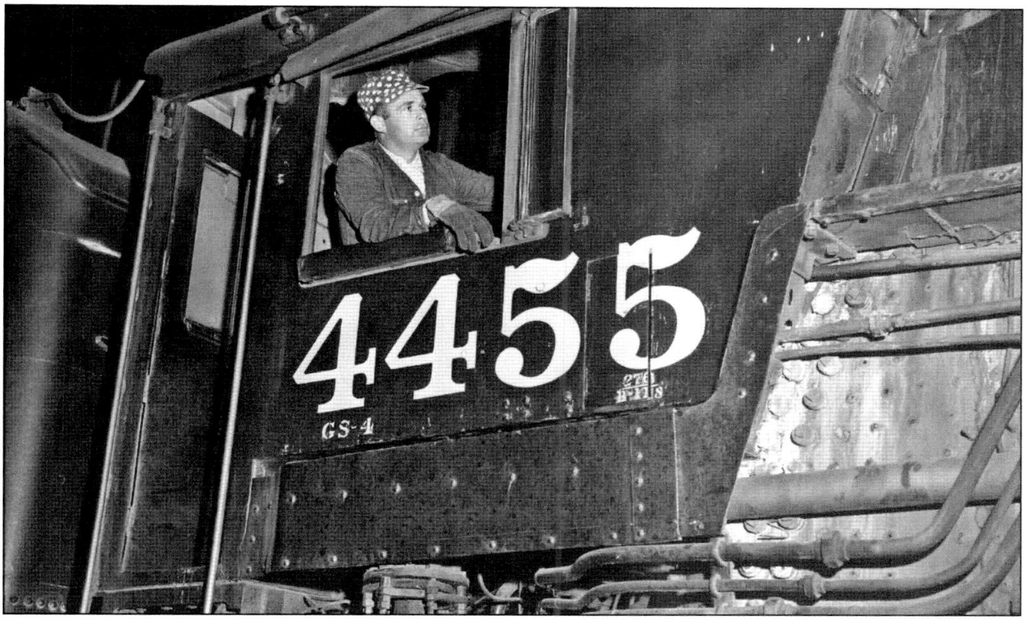


Railroading is a family business; witness the Walter L. Preece family. Following in the footsteps of his father, Walter came aboard SP in 1947. He was promoted to engineer in 1949 and to road foreman of engines on the Peninsula Commutes in 1961. His wife's father, Robert N. Booker, had held the same job in the 1940s and 1950s. Walter, who passed way in 1973 at just 48 years old, produced two more railroaders on the Peninsula Commutes: son Robert Preece, a conductor, and daughter LeeAnn Dickson. Pictured here at the age of 21, Dickson began at SP's Bayshore yard, where rail equipment was repaired. Later, she worked in ticket offices from San Francisco to San Jose. She joined the Federal Railroad Administration in 2000. (Both, LeeAnn Dickson collection.)

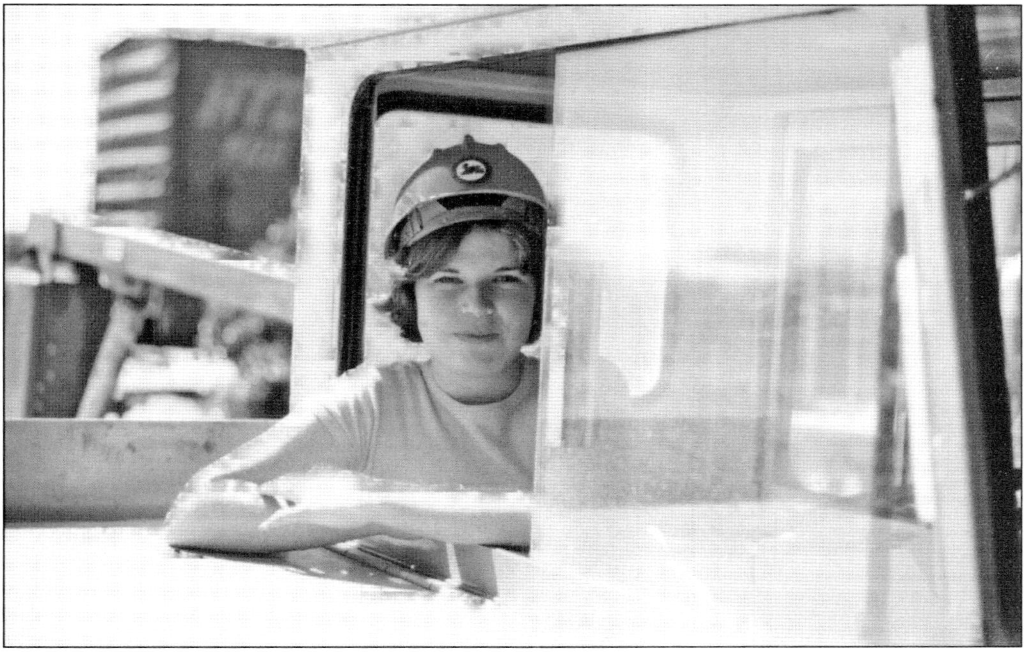

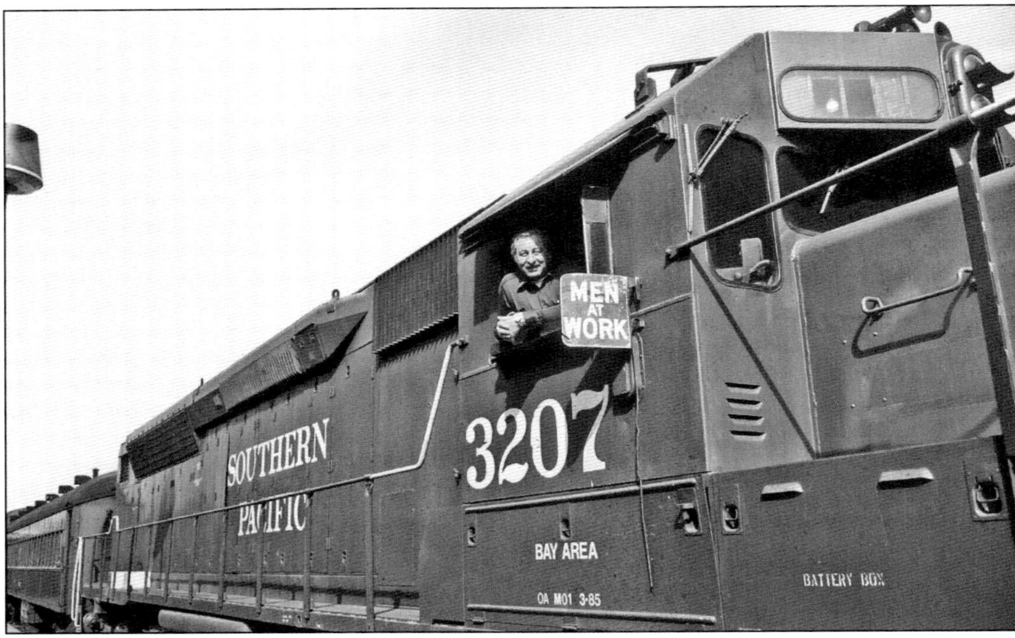


Hired in 1951 as a coach cleaner, Bob Bongiorno found railroading so interesting that he worked his way up to engineer in 1961, earning the name "the Velvet Paw" because of his smooth rides. He maintained his engineer's license even after being promoted to trainmaster and was the only Caltrain engineer still qualified to run a steam engine at the time of his retirement in 2001. (Greg Welker.)

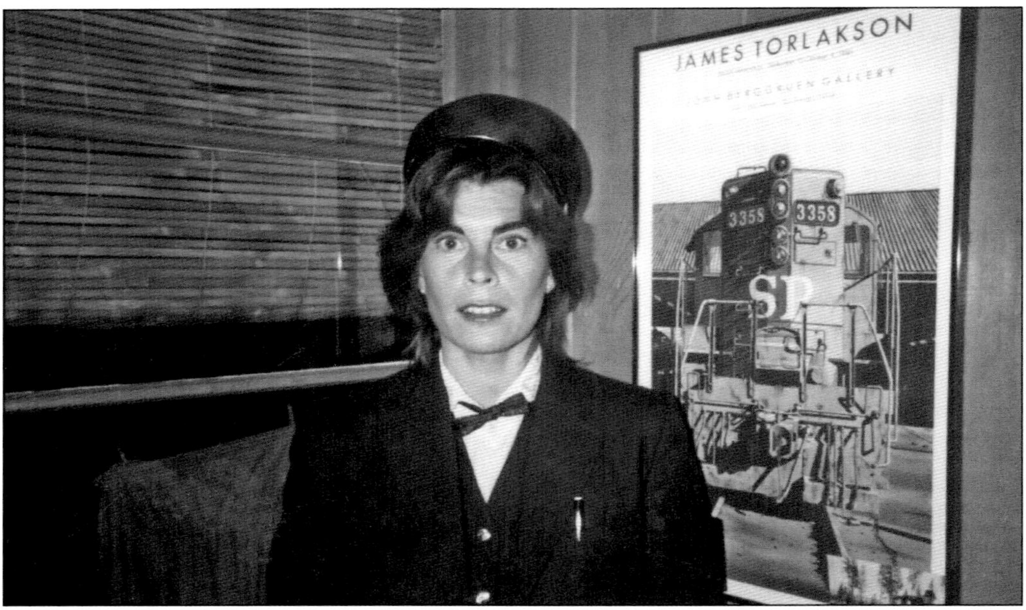


Patty Doolette joined SP during the period in the late 1970s when the railroad began hiring women for nontraditional jobs. Pictured in her uniform, she was the first woman brakeman/conductor working in the Peninsula Commute Service. Doolette said the railroad did not have women's uniforms yet so one had to be made special for her, from the bow tie to the conductor's hat. (Patty Doolette collection.)

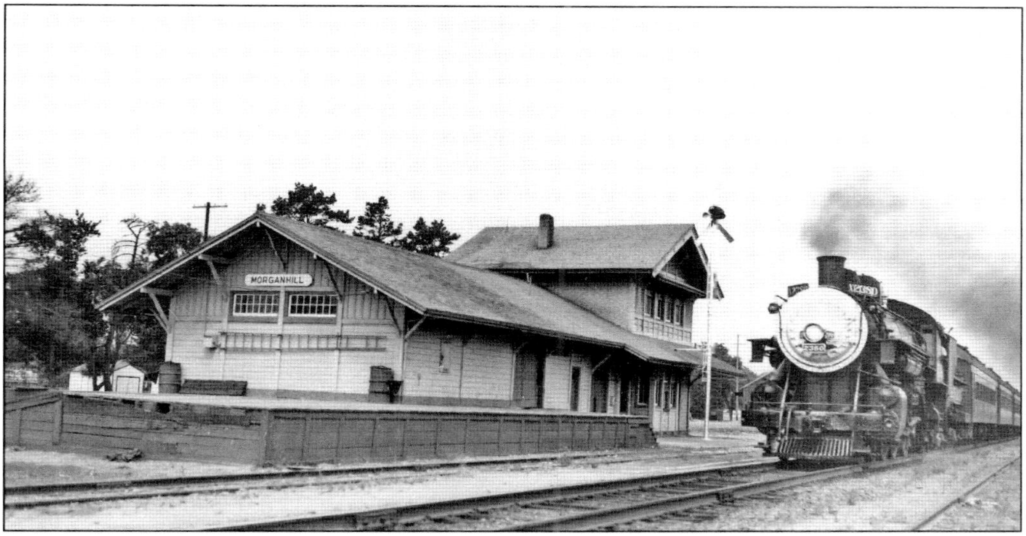


When the SP station was established at Morgan Hill in 1892, the railroad referred to the area as "Huntington." Passengers, however, wanted to stop at "Morgan Hill's Ranch," the vast estate of pioneering couple Diana and Hiram Morgan Hill, and in January 1893, SP changed the name to Morganhill. This passenger and freight depot was retired in 1959. (Courtesy California State Railroad Museum.)

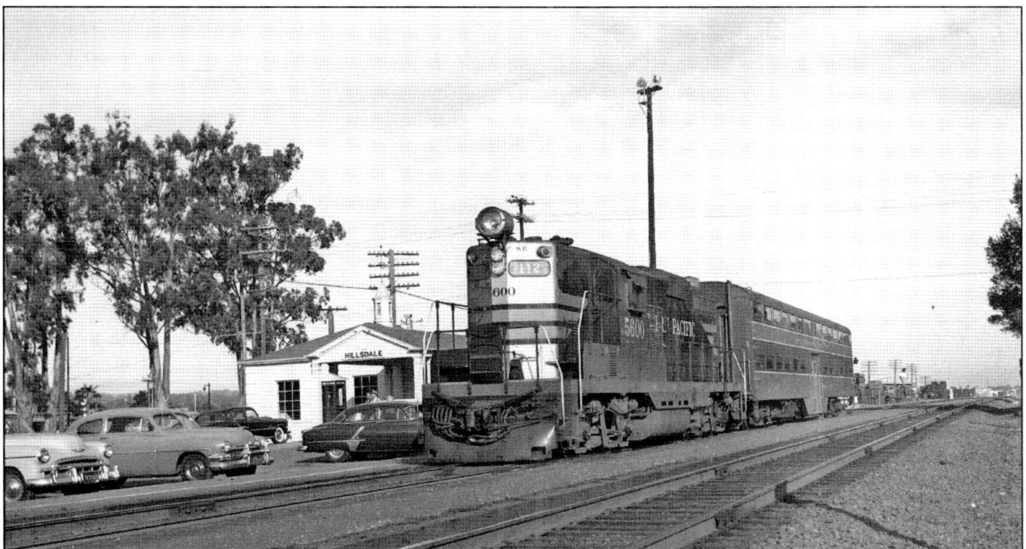


The station was called "Beresford" before developer David Bohannon bought area ranchland for a 5,000-home planned community. He asked neighbors if they objected to renaming their street. When they did not, he then asked SP if he could change the name of the depot—if he built it. Looking forward to the new riders, the railroad agreed, and "Hillsdale Station" was dedicated in August 1941. (Arthur Lloyd collection.)

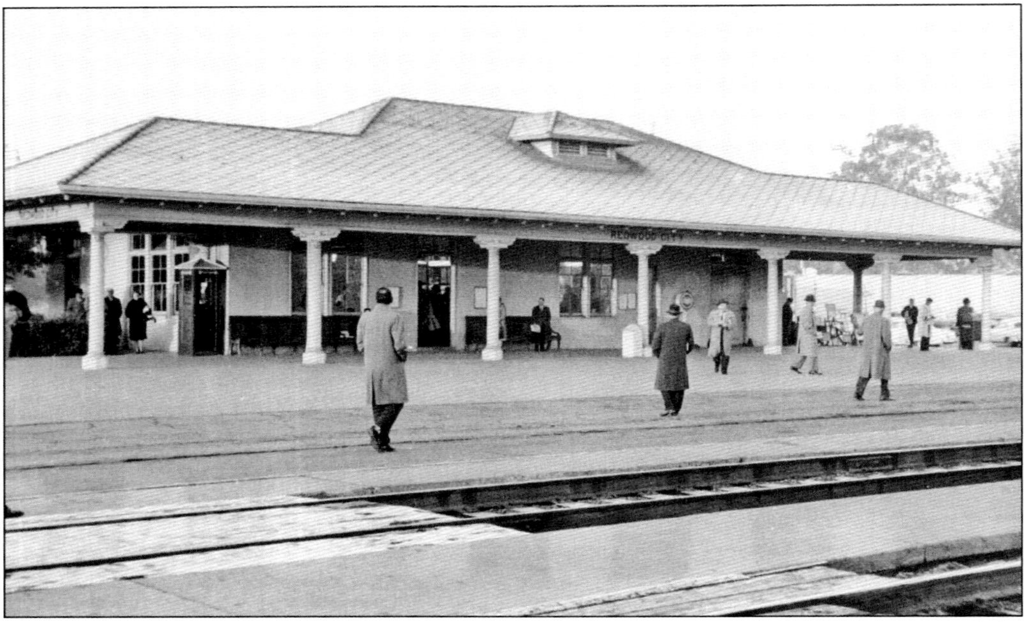


Redwood City has seen a succession of depots. The first one was located on the east side of the tracks, but it was replaced by the one pictured, which was constructed in 1901–1902. It featured a colonnade of seven columns supporting a 14-foot-wide arcade. An arsonist damaged it in 1979, and then SP razed it. (Reg McGovern.)

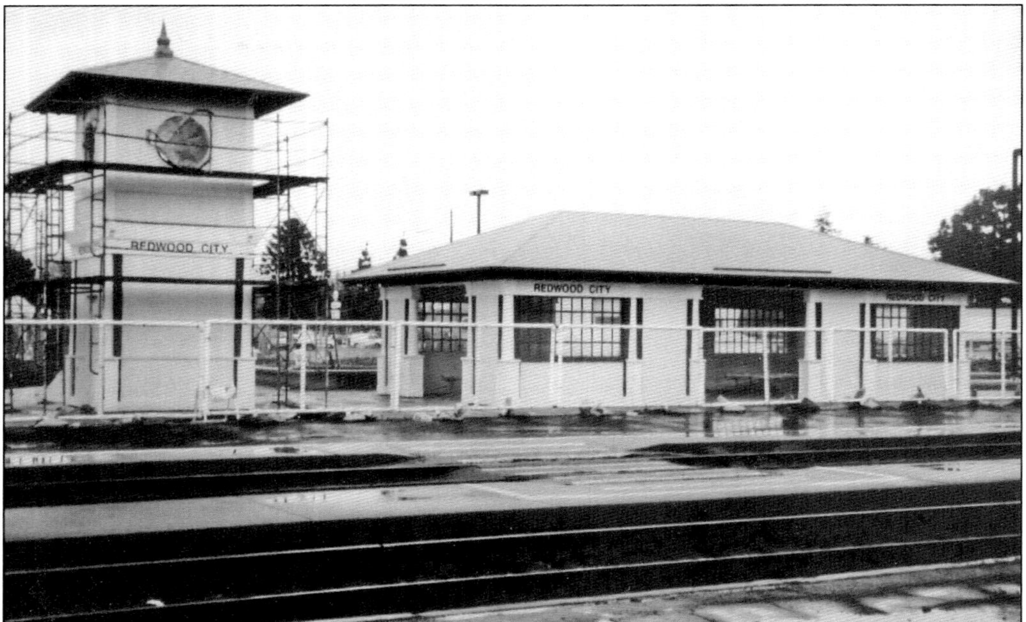


Built in conjunction with the development of the Sequoia station retail center, the current passenger shelter, shown here when it was under construction, mimics the architecture of the old depot. The Redwood City Transit Center, serving Caltrain, SamTrans buses, and shuttles, was "introduced" with a community celebration in July 1995. (Reg McGovern.)

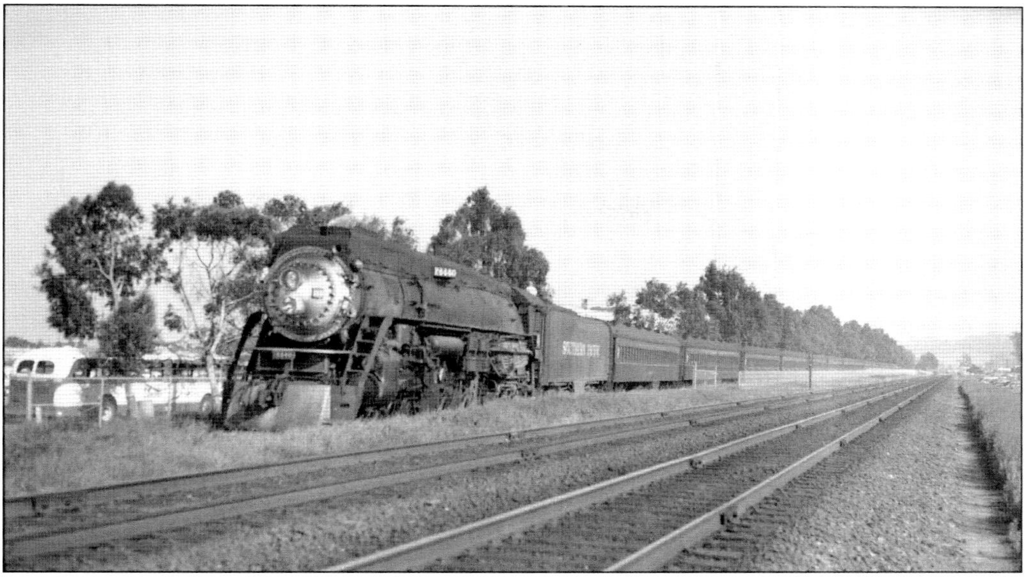

A Bay Meadows Special sits on the siding next to the racecourse in this undated photograph. One train per day ran in the racing season, nonstop from San Francisco. The engine continued to the Redwood City wye to be turned and brought back to get positioned for the return trip. When the races ended, the train was loaded up and returned nonstop. (Arthur Lloyd collection.)

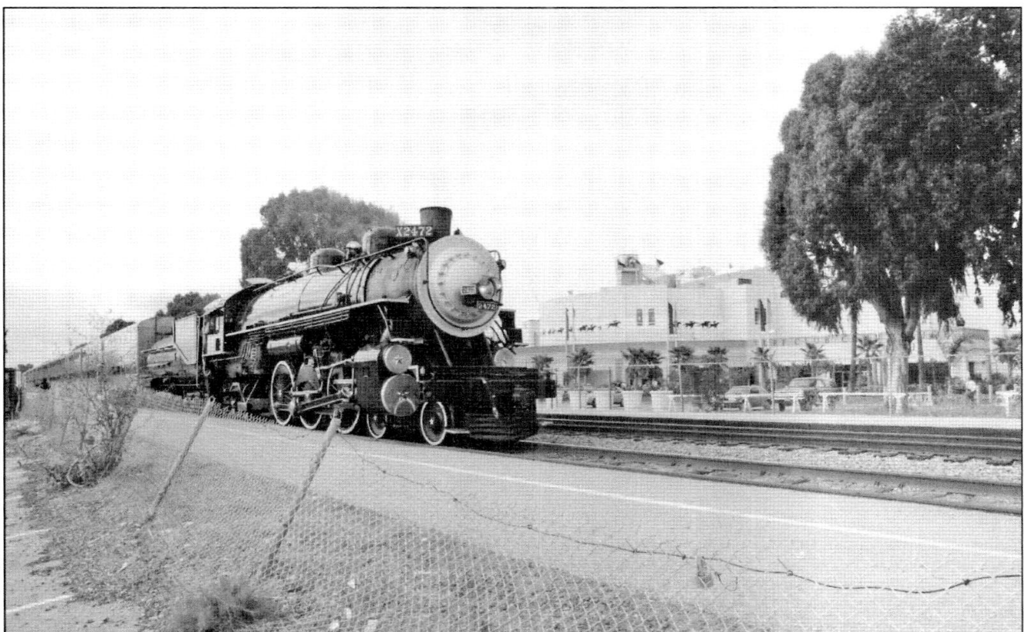


Golden Gate Railroad Museum volunteers restored former SP 2472, working at the San Mateo County fairgrounds next to Bay Meadows Racecourse. In 1996, when SamTrans hosted the American Public Transit Association's Commuter Rail Conference, the 2472 made a "triumphal return," dropping off visiting transportation professionals for a reception. Number 2472 relocated its home to Niles Canyon in 2007. (Reg McGovern.)

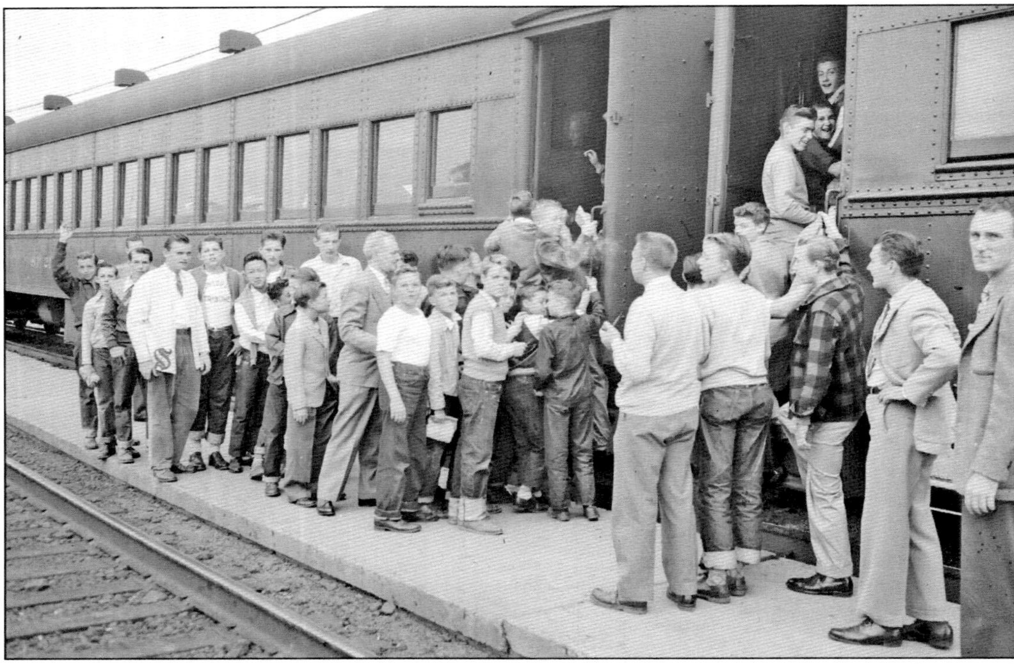

Getting to ride a train has long been a thrill ride for generations of kids. This 1948 photograph of *Redwood City Tribune* carriers and district managers is an example, as the young men boarded for a ride to the San Mateo County Fiesta in observance of Newspaper Day. More than 101,000 people attended the fiesta at the fairgrounds near Bay Meadows station. (Reg McGovern.)

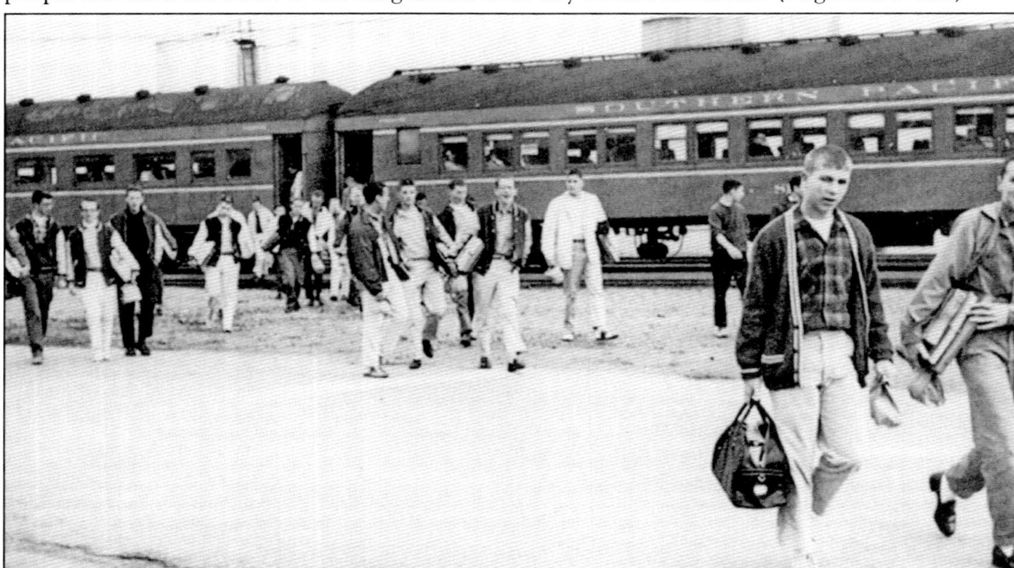

For generations, the Peninsula Commute Service has served as the "yellow school bus" for students at schools such as Bellarmine College Preparatory, on the former site of the College of the Pacific. Trains stop at a small wooden shelter a short walk from the San Jose school. Bellarmine students, faculty, and alumni have proven to be loyal—and vocal—about maintaining passenger service to the station. (Bellarmine.)

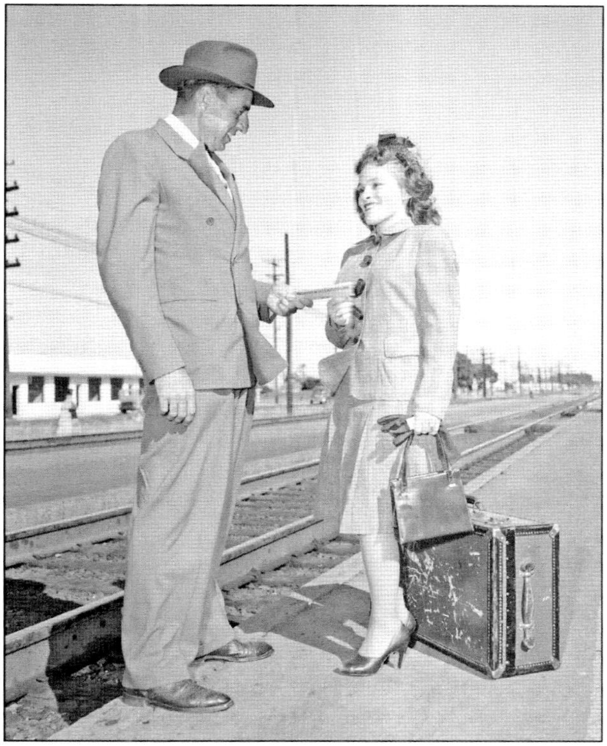

The Southern Pacific corridor also connected local residents to faraway destinations. Fresh from reigning as queen of the 1947 San Carlos Fourth of July celebration, Paulette Rinck headed out from the station for a vacation in Catalina, which was one of her prizes. Seeing her off was chamber representative Marion French. (Reg McGovern.)

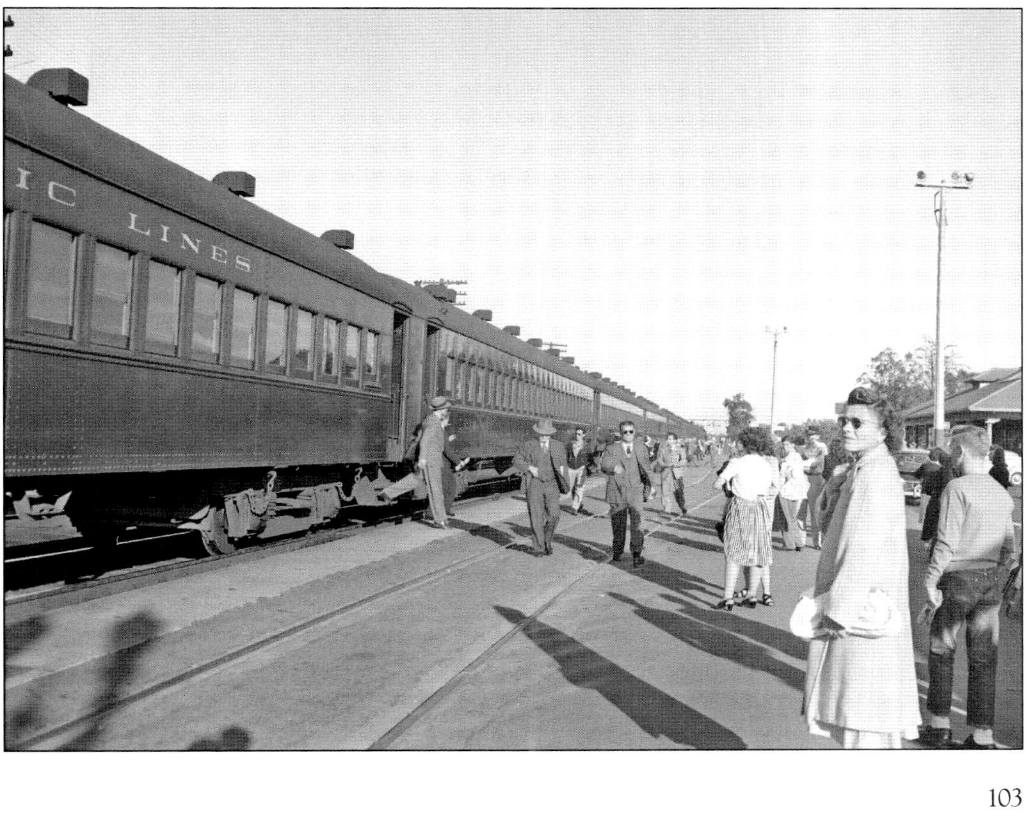


Before the 1960s propelled women into the workforce in droves, the typical SP commuter was a man traveling into San Francisco in the morning and returning home at night, where stay-at-home wives had dinner waiting for them. Three-piece suits and hats were also typical attire in the post-World War II era. (Reg McGovern.)

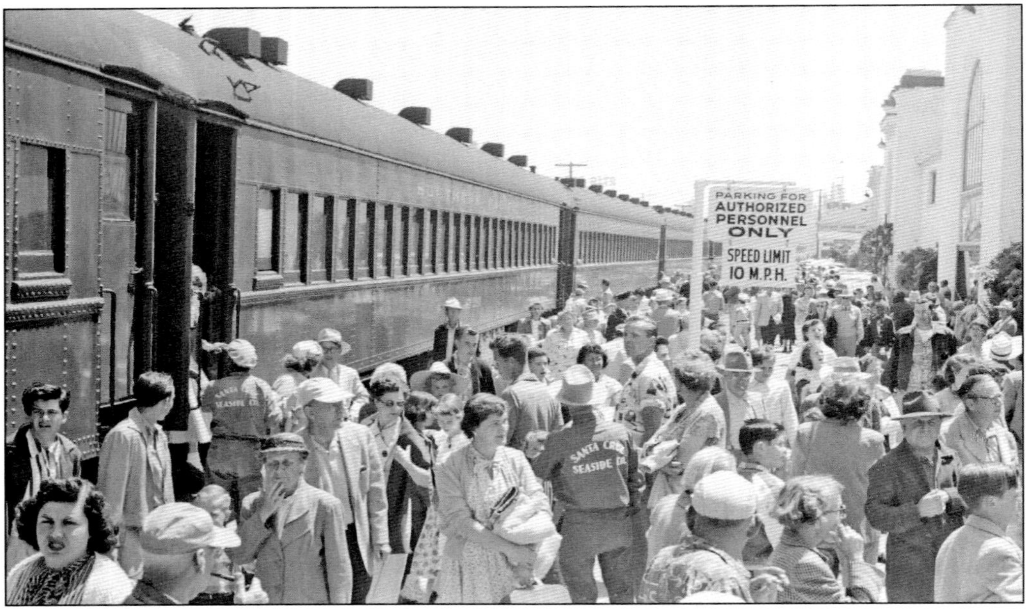


Southern Pacific Suntan Special trains to Santa Cruz brought thousands of riders from the San Francisco Bay Area to the coastside for weekend fun. This June 1953 picture shows crowds disembarking outside the boardwalk, where Santa Cruz Seaside employees were waiting to show them the way to the Giant Dipper and other attractions. Begun in 1927, the Suntan Specials initially ran from San Jose via the Los Gatos branch line until 1932, when the origin moved to San Francisco. The trains proved so popular that two locomotives were required. Operating over various trackage to the coast, the Suntans were canceled during World War II but resumed in 1947. The Suntan Specials ceased in 1959. (Above, Reg McGovern; below, Arthur Lloyd collection.)

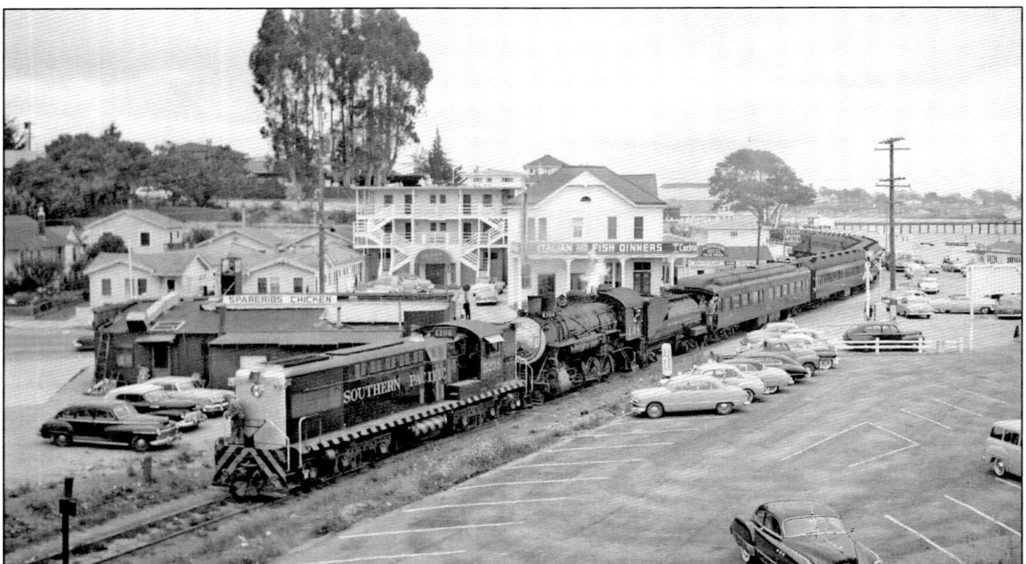

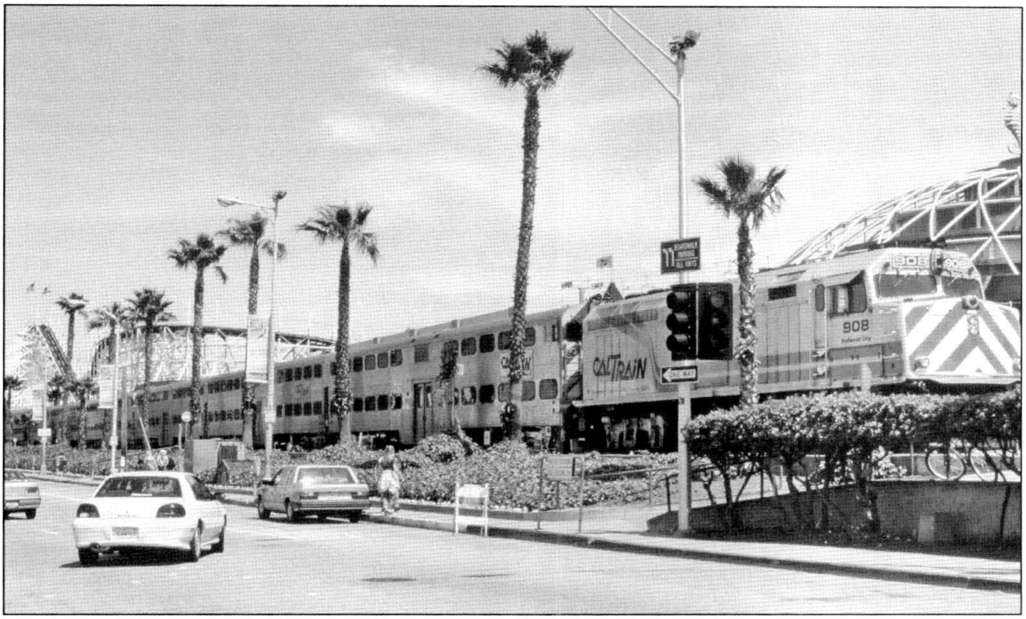


The *Suntan Special* made a return trip to the Santa Cruz Boardwalk on May 18, 1996, in an attempt to demonstrate the energy-saving and other benefits of rail travel. Caltrain operated two passenger trains for the demonstration trip using Caltrain equipment, which carried more than 1,000 dignitaries and rail fans to the beach. (Caltrain.)

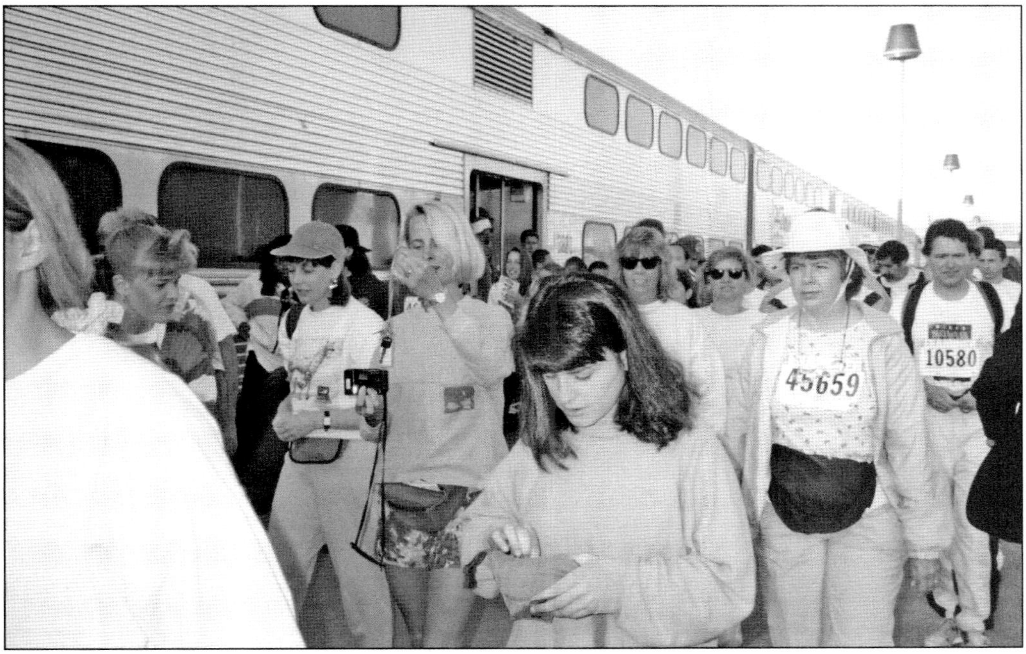


An early morning May ride to San Francisco is a hardy tradition for Bay to Breakers Race participants. Whether in costume or standard runners' wear, countless thousands like this 1999 trainload have been able to get to the starting line for the run from the bay to the ocean without having to worry about driving. (Caltrain.)

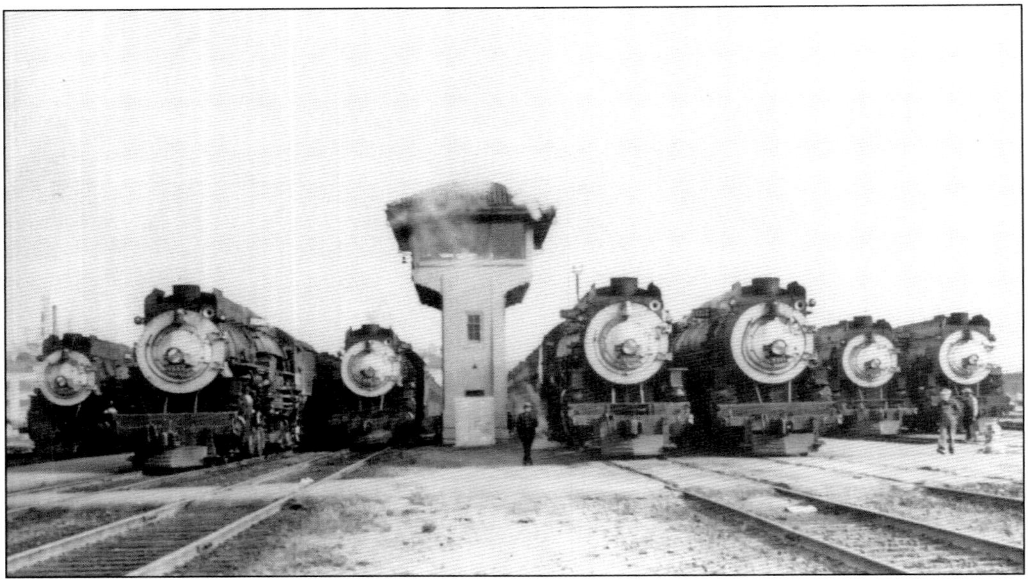

In the pre-freeway era, special football trains marshaled at the San Francisco station hauled huge crowds to the Stadium station in Palo Alto for games. The top photograph by Fred Stindt shows steam engines, taken in 1955, chomping at the bit ready to roll, one after the other, while the 1930 photograph below shows passengers detraining for the annual Big Game battle between the Stanford Indians and the University of California's Golden Bears. Fans walked past the area that is now the Town and Country Shopping Center to reach the stadium, just as they do today, albeit in much smaller numbers. (Above, Tom Gray collection; below, Henry Bender collection.)

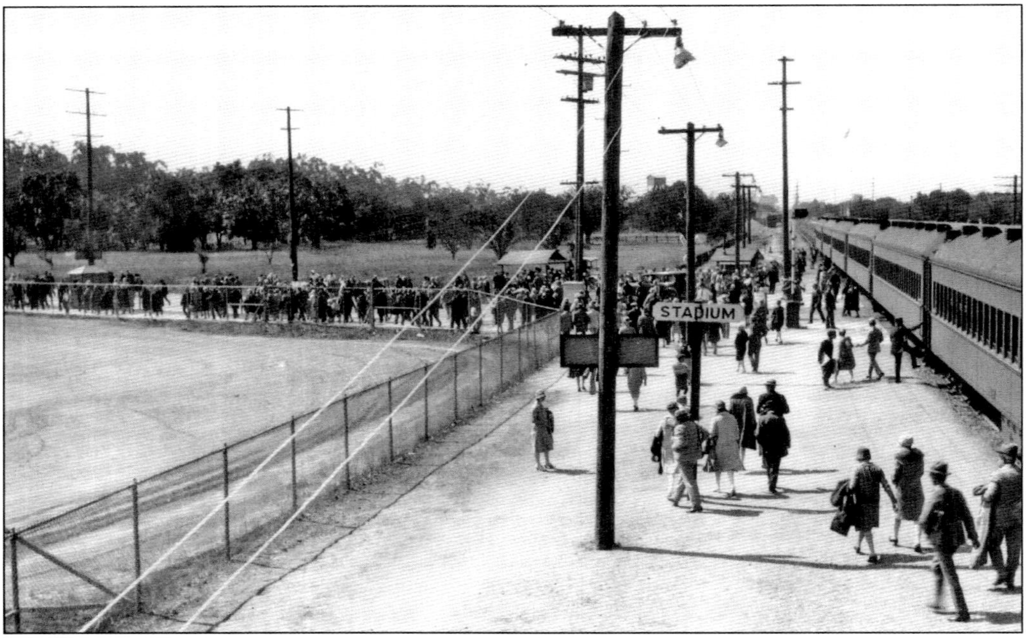

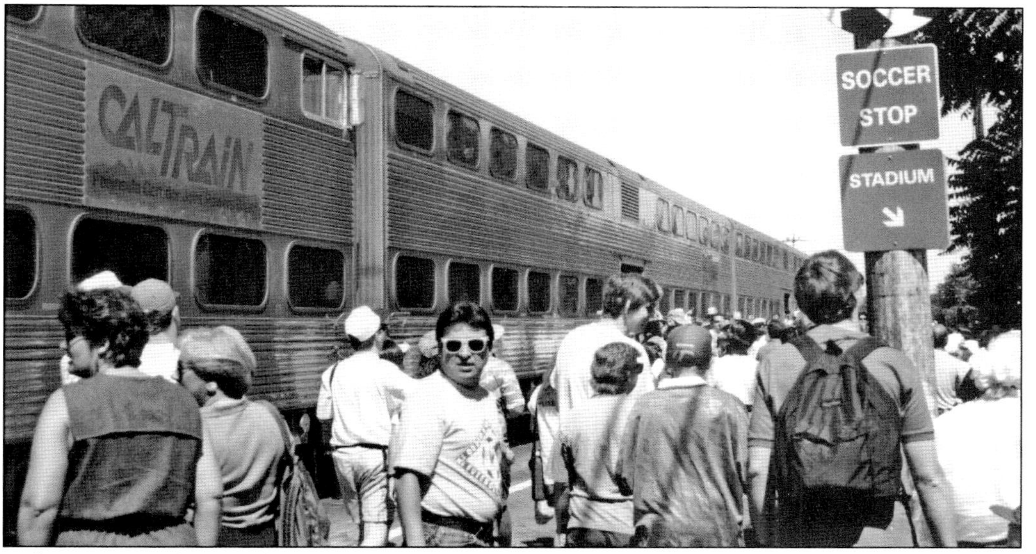


Caltrain carried more than 174,000 riders to and from World Cup soccer games at Stanford Stadium in summer 1994—about 20 percent of those attending. Accommodating vast crowds of visitors from around the world put rail employees to the test, and staff hustled to round up rail equipment to meet the demand. Even former SP Harriman cars came out of mothballs in the herculean effort. (Caltrain.)

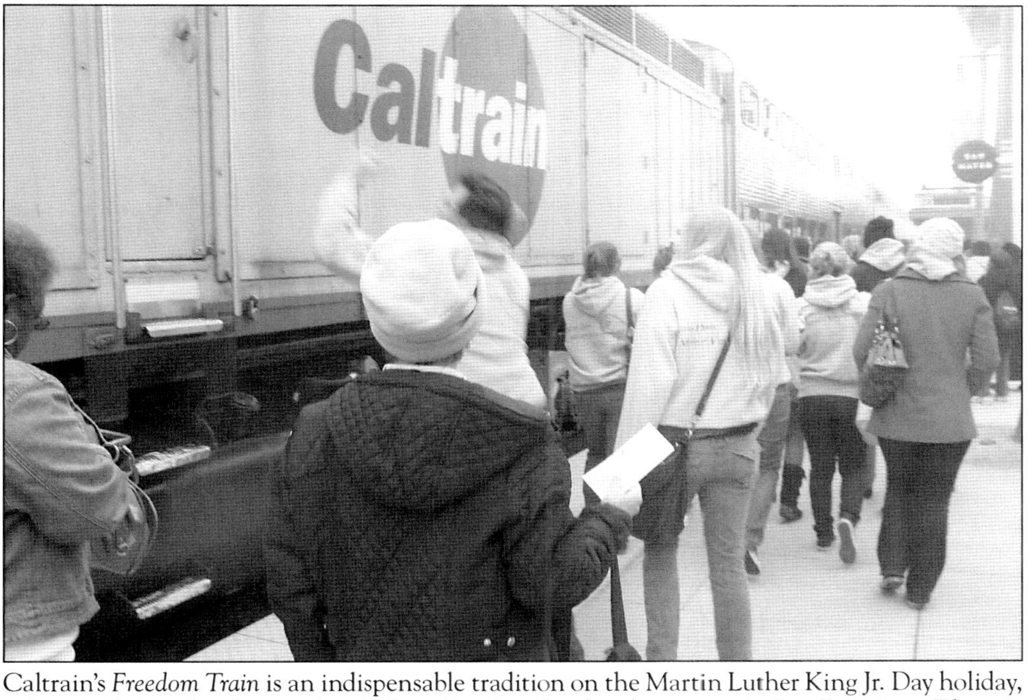


Caltrain's *Freedom Train* is an indispensable tradition on the Martin Luther King Jr. Day holiday, as hundreds board a chartered train from San Jose for the observance in San Francisco. The trip between the two cities is about the same distance as the famed Selma march (51 miles), adding to the symbolism of the ride. Shown picking up passengers at San Mateo, the 2011 train was the 26th event. (Reg McGovern.)

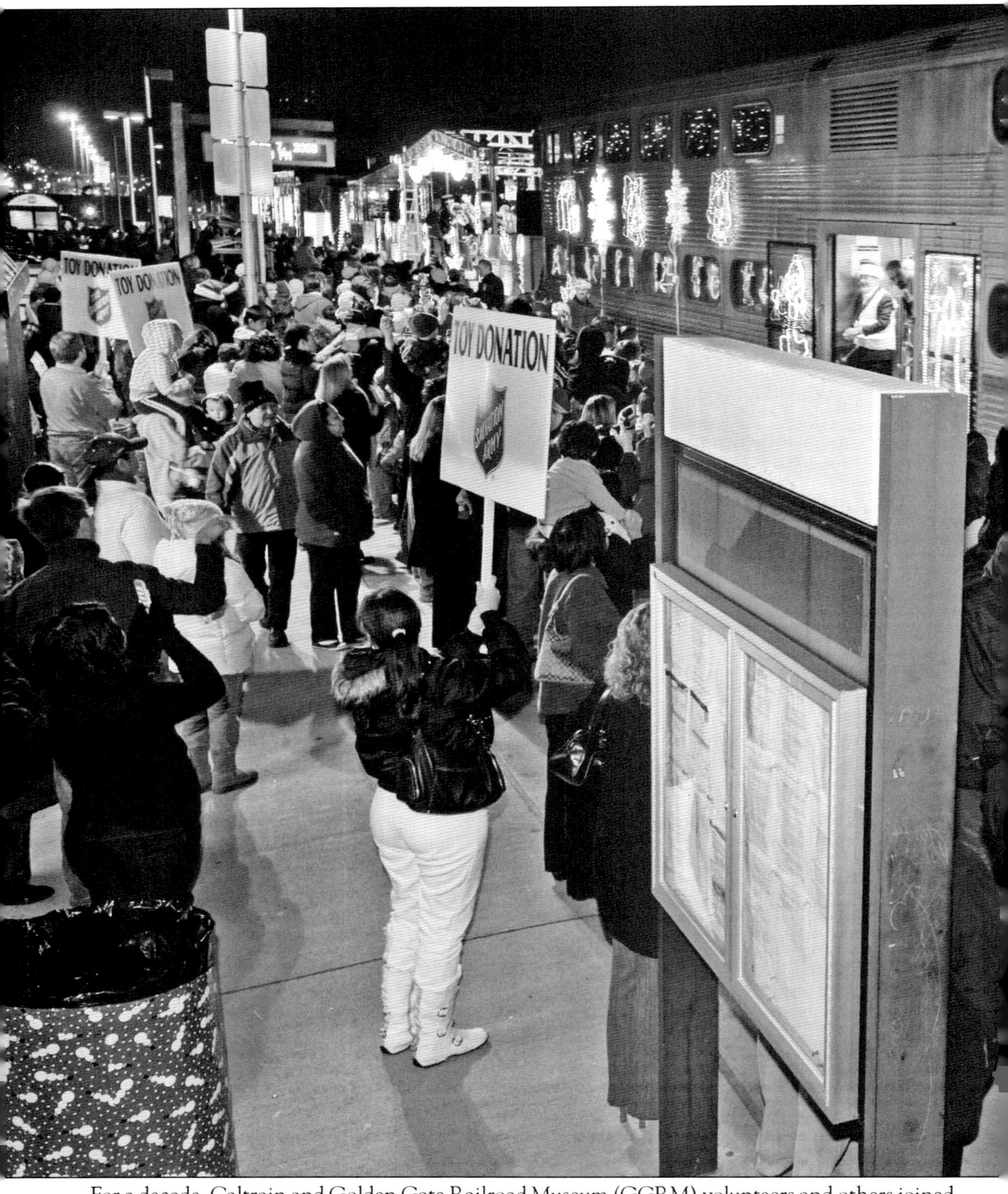


For a decade, Caltrain and Golden Gate Railroad Museum (GGRM) volunteers and others joined in presenting a spectacularly decorated holiday train, shown in the Chuck Fox photographs on these pages and page 110, as a benefit for the US Marines's Toys for Tots program and the Salvation Army. The train visited nine stations over the first weekend in December, presenting

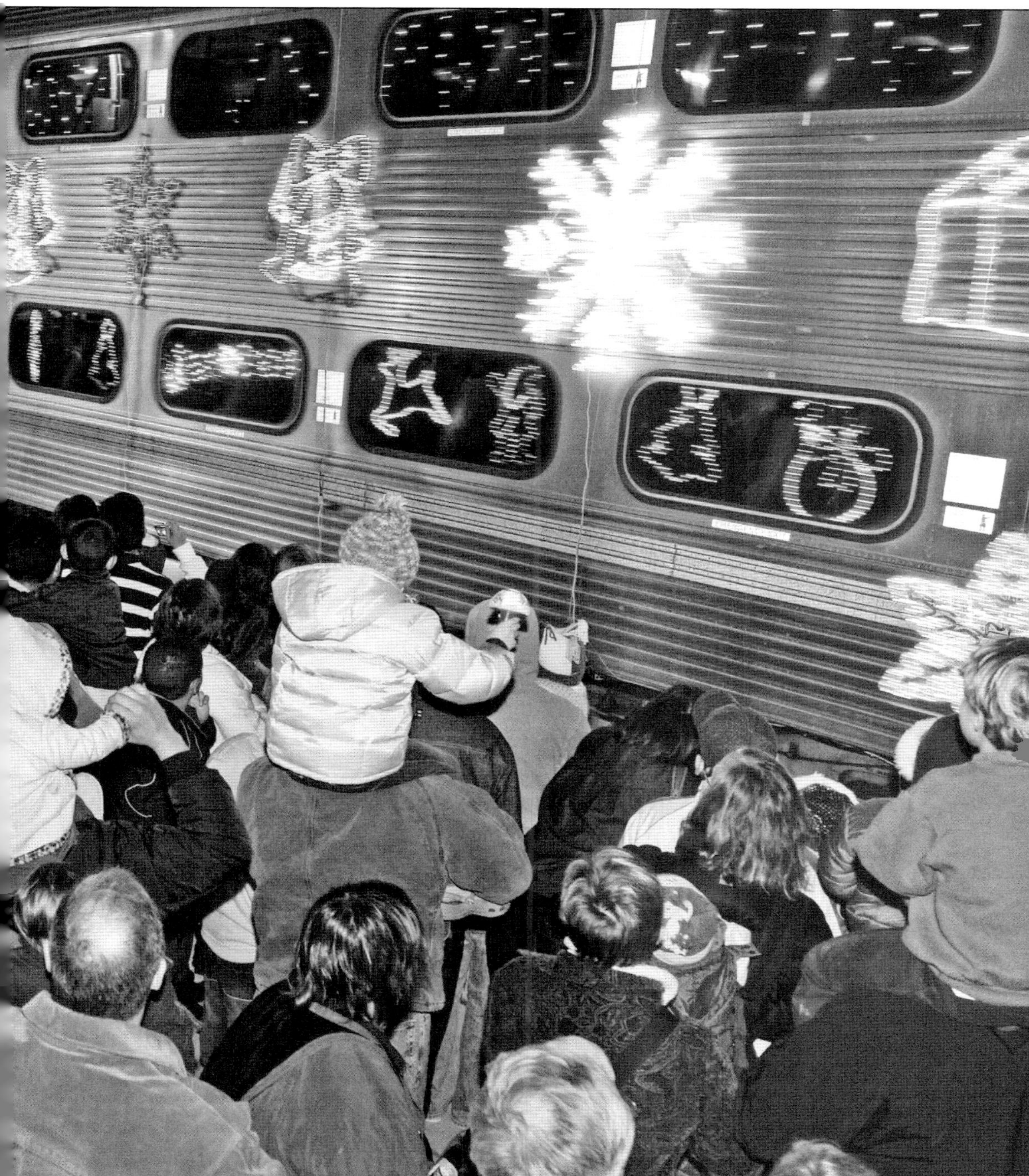

a show featuring live music and bringing Santa Claus to greet kids and pose for photographs. Over 10 years, the event generated more than 43,000 toy donations for the two charities. Faced with growing budget problems, Caltrain management did not hold the event in 2010 or 2011 but plans to bring it back in 2012. (Caltrain.)

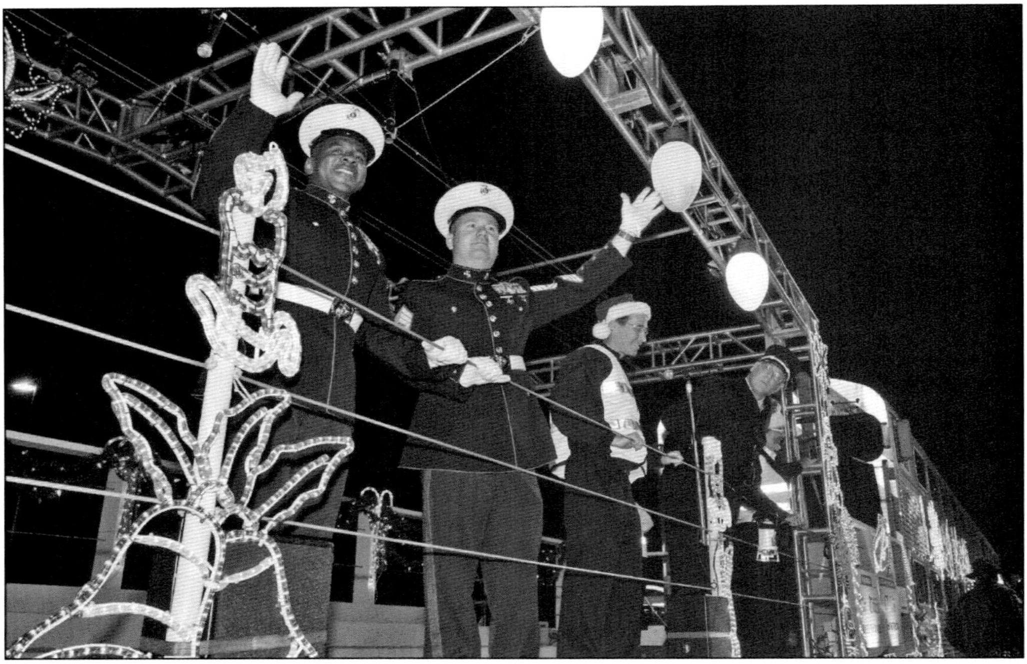

Caltrain and SamTrans staff, Marines, and GGRM volunteers led by San Mateo resident Ross Peterson (right) labored every year on weekends decorating the train with thousands of lights for the much-anticipated rail extravaganza. Also on the stage car, from left to right, are an unidentified Marine, Gy. Sgt. Tim Anthamatten, and volunteer Derry Kabcenell. (Caltrain.)

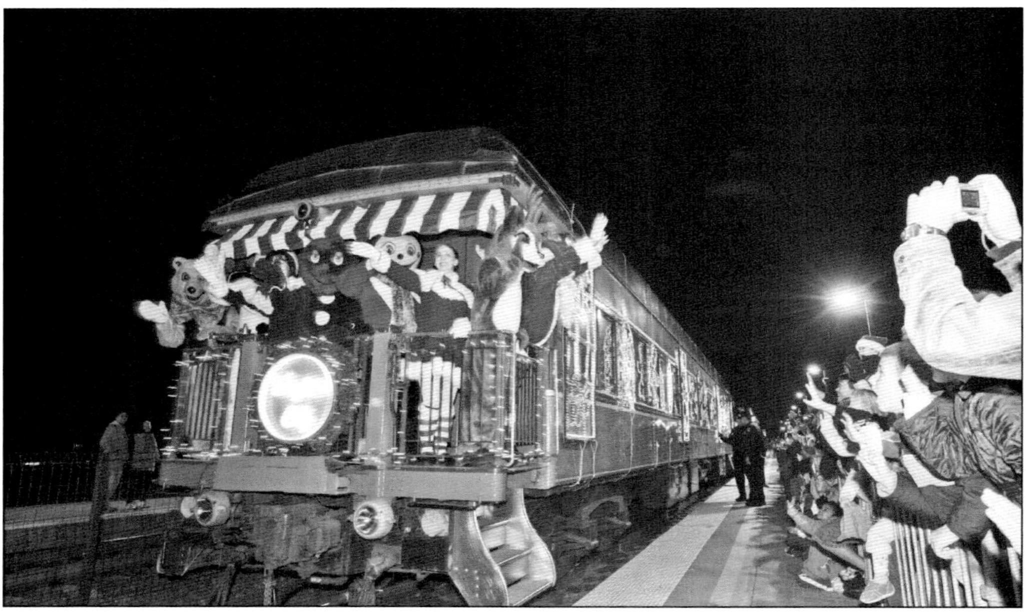

Convinced that Santa Claus needed to ride in style, Wade Pellizzer of Redwood City offered the *Virginia City* as part of the holiday train. The costumed characters can be seen on the platform waving good-bye as the holiday train moves on. Another private car owner, Dave Jansson, made the *Yosemite Falls*, a restored Pullman car, available as well. (Caltrain.)

# *Six*

# THE MAGNIFICENT SEVEN

Seven Caltrain depots are recognized in the National Register of Historic Places—quite a distinction for a rail line with 32 stations. The depots and respective dates of listing are: Millbrae and Burlingame (both 1978), San Carlos (1984), Menlo Park (1974), Palo Alto (1996), Santa Clara (1985), and San Jose Diridon (1993). Though only the latter still has a ticket office, this eclectic mix of depots has fulfilled a variety of functions, from providing offices for chambers of commerce, to becoming destinations in their own right. The Millbrae Train Museum offers tours of the venerable depot and the *Civic Center* rail car. Renovated in 1994, the Diridon station added *The Way to San Jose* transportation exhibit in 2010. A museum opened in Burlingame in 2008. The chambers of commerce have located their offices at Burlingame and Menlo Park for many years. Model railroaders welcome rail fans of all ages to watch trains run inside a former baggage/express house at Menlo Park. San Carlos's Depot Café, in that landmark depot, is itself a local institution. At Palo Alto, a bicycle storage facility and a café cater to 21st-century riders. The South Bay Historical Railroad Society (SBHRS) has its displays in Caltrain's oldest depot, Santa Clara. A remarkable group of rail enthusiasts came forward to rescue the dilapidated treasure in 1985, in the early years of Caltrans's management of SP service. The SBHRS was allowed to contribute time and labor in lieu of rent. The result of this ongoing partnership has been the complete rehabilitation of the building, which today houses elaborate model railroad layouts, a huge collection of rail artifacts and photographs, and an extensive railroad library. The SBHRS occupies an oversight role to ensure that the historic character of Caltrain's National Register depots is maintained, and member Lorie Garcia is the designated covenant representative. For their work, the organization won the governor's Historic Preservation Award in 1996, the only preservation award presented by the State of California to recognize such efforts. Garcia received the same award in 2010.

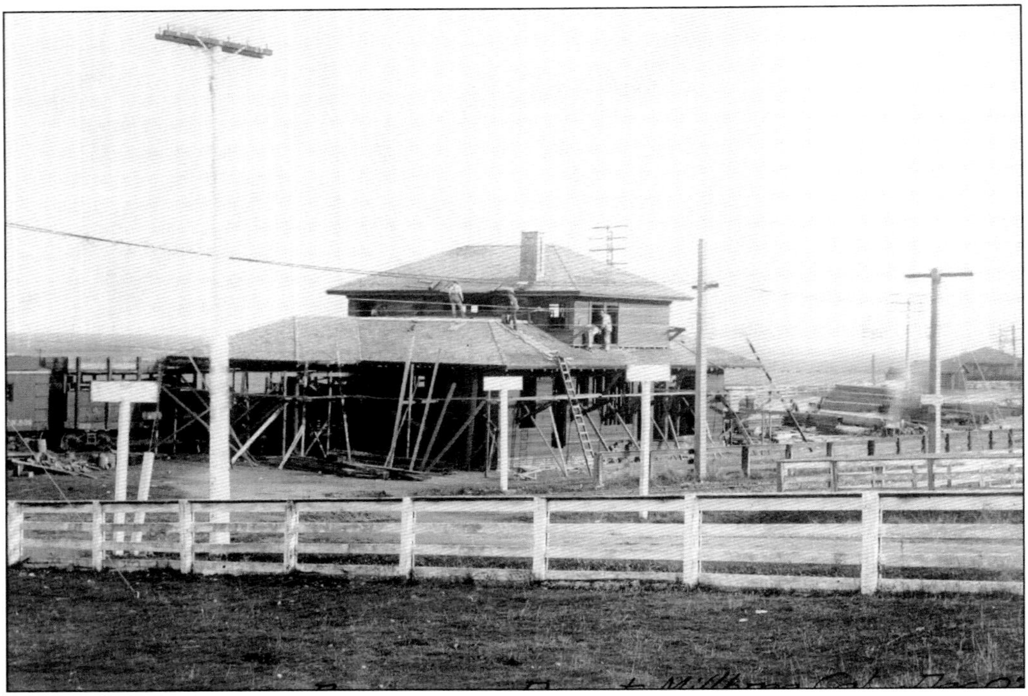

The first Millbrae depot was on land deeded by Darius Mills and was completed in 1864. It burned in 1890, and it was first replaced that year. In 1907, that building also burned in 1907. This photograph shows the present depot under construction during the same year. The *Redwood City Democrat* pronounced it larger and more attractive than the one it replaced. (Henry Bender collection.)

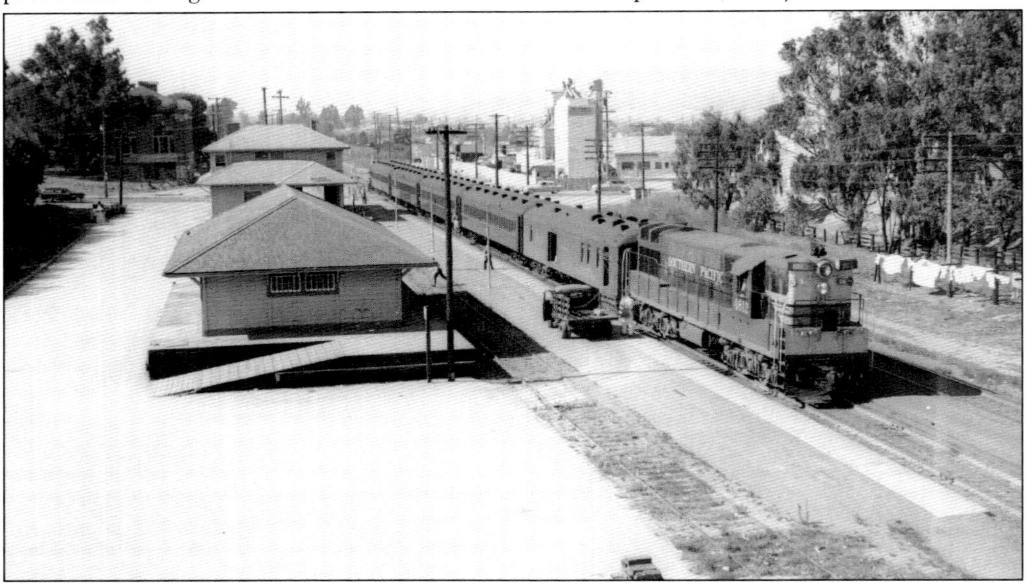

SP No. 4812, a Fairbanks-Morse model H-24-66, pulls across Millbrae Avenue and into the depot in this 1952 Will Whittaker photograph. The former freight depot, which was built in 1924 and was retired in 1966, is in the foreground. The Millbrae depot was moved 200 feet south in 1980 to make room to build an overpass at Millbrae Avenue. (Tom Gray collection.)

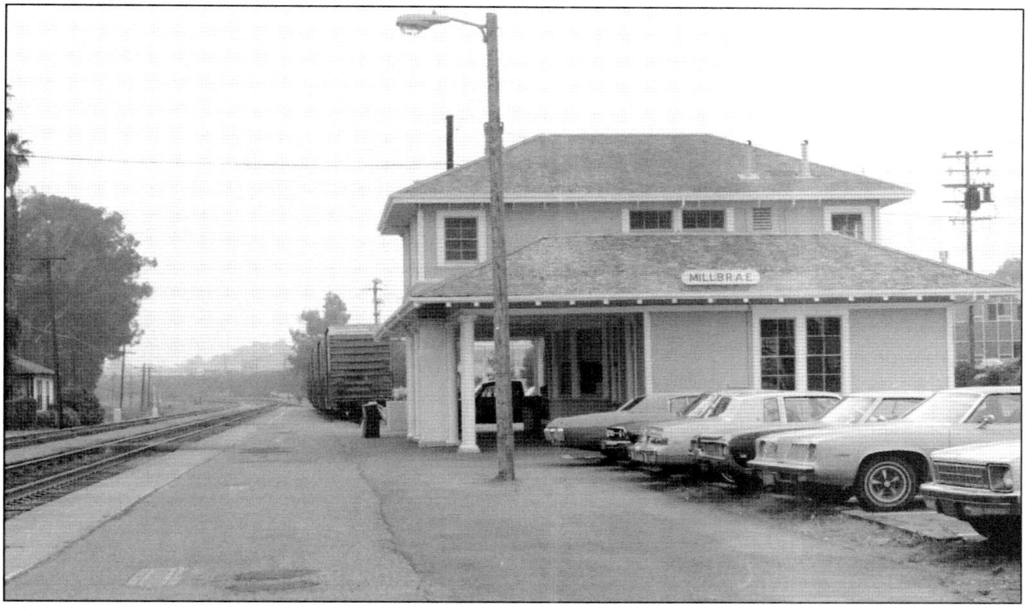


The Millbrae depot is the only two-story example of a Southern Pacific Colonnade–style depot and is the last two-story depot on the Peninsula. It had an office, waiting room, and baggage room, and the living quarters for the station agent were upstairs. With the opening of a BART/Caltrain station at Millbrae, the landmark depot was not needed for train operations. (Bill Kepner.)

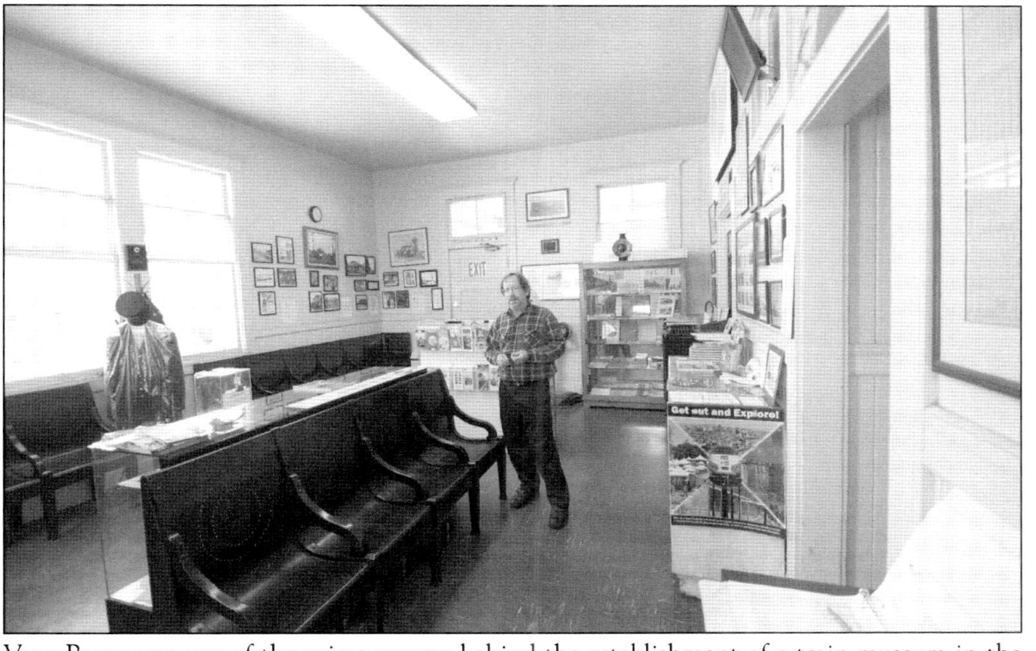


Vern Bruce was one of the prime movers behind the establishment of a train museum in the former depot, and the Millbrae Train Museum opened in 2004. Visitors can view railroad artifacts, photographs, maps, and equipment. The deluxe sleeping car, the *Civic Center*, is also available for tours. The 1941 Pullman-Standard car has four double bedrooms, four compartments, and two drawing rooms. (Janet McGovern.)

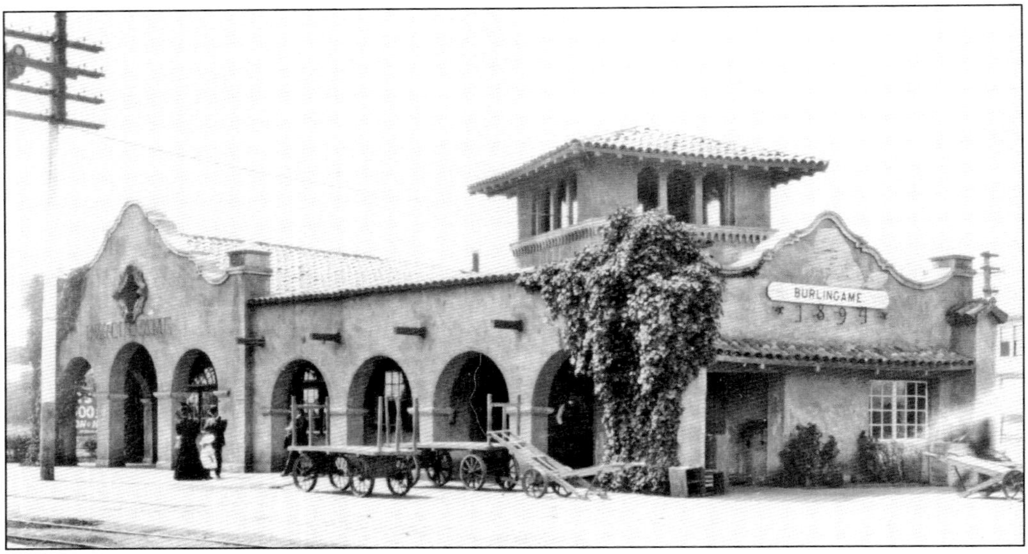


The Burlingame depot was the first Mission Revival–style depot in the United States and is the oldest remaining example of that architectural style. Completed in 1894, it was constructed of redwood with an adobe exterior and roof tiles formed by Mission Indians. Until the 1950s, an agent lived in an apartment on the southern end of the depot, where the chamber of commerce has been since 1977. (Tom Gray collection.)

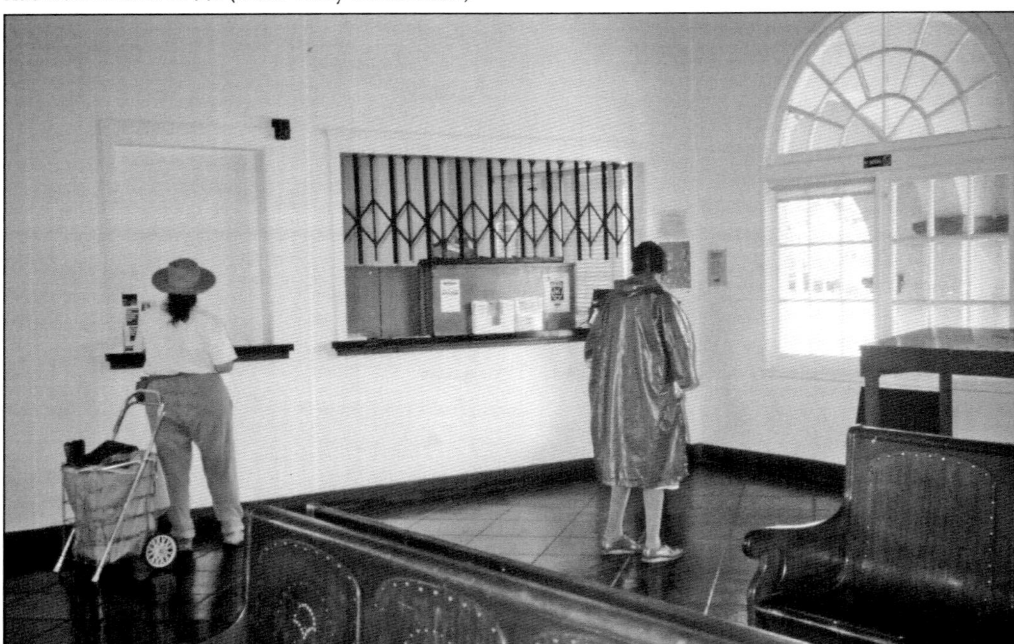

The ticket office at Burlingame was staffed by an agent until 2004. After the depot closed, the Burlingame-Hillsborough Historical Society approached Caltrain about creating a museum in the building. It opened in 2008. The train station underwent a $13-million upgrade project, which began in 2007 and included the removal of the center platform and reconfiguration for outside boarding of trains. (Caltrain.)

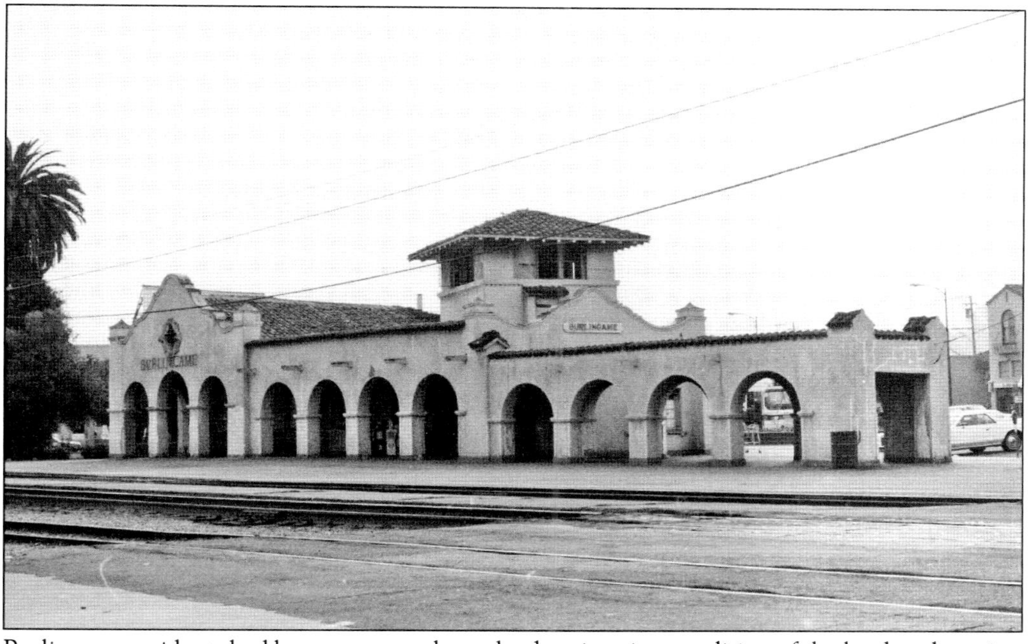

Burlingame residents had become upset about the deteriorating condition of the landmark station and in 1983 formed a Save Our Station committee to raise funds and advocate for an accurate restoration. Fortuitously, the city and Caltrans saw value in the rehabilitation project because its condition proved to be far worse and more expensive than envisioned, at $300,000. The station was rededicated in June 1986. In 1994, the whole city turned out for a festive celebration of the depot's centennial, with speeches and entertainment befitting the occasion. The Golden Gate Railroad Museum's restored locomotive SP No. 2472 made a special appearance for tours. (Above, Bill Kepner; below, Caltrain.)

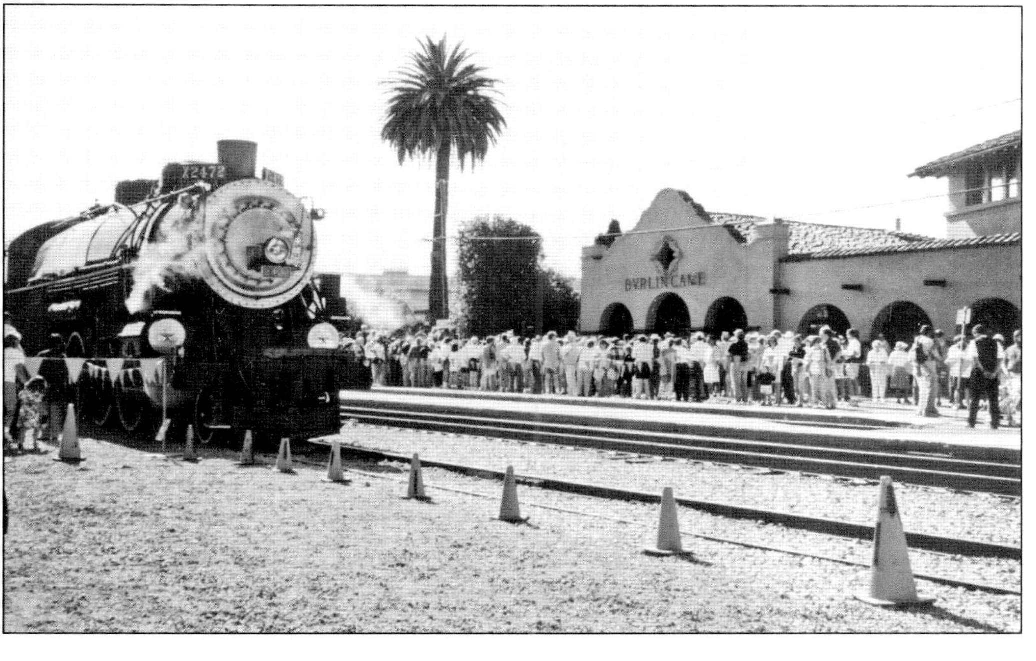

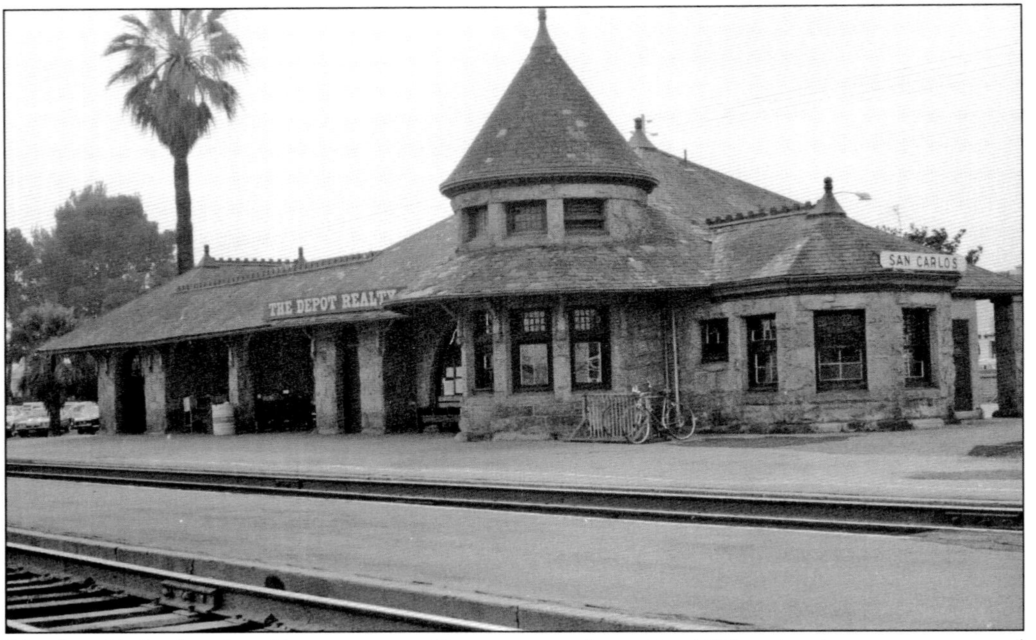


The San Carlos Land and Improvement Company was formed in 1887 to develop a new town and sell lots. Land for a train station was granted by Nathaniel Brittan, and in 1888, this stone masonry depot was constructed, of sandstone donated by Leland Stanford and quarried in the Almaden Valley near San Jose. The depot's style is Richardson Romanesque Revival. (Bill Kepner.)

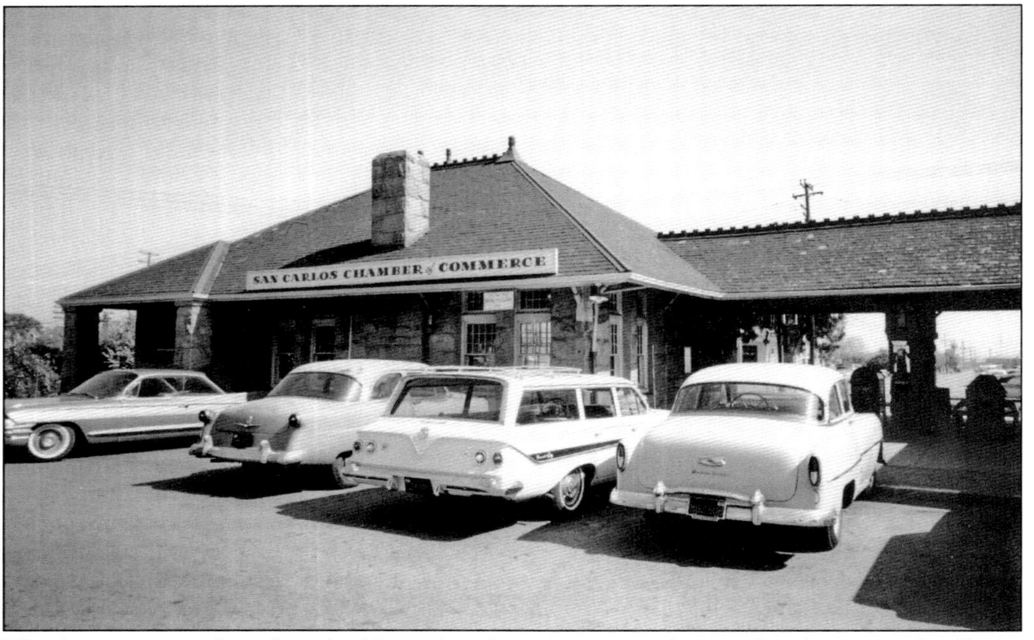


The depot is a complex of two buildings that share a common slate roof, with a covered walkway connecting them. A notable feature of the depot is a diagonal bay on the north corner and a round, two-story tower on the east side. SP closed the ticket office in 1960 and leased the depot to a real estate firm. (Reg McGovern.)

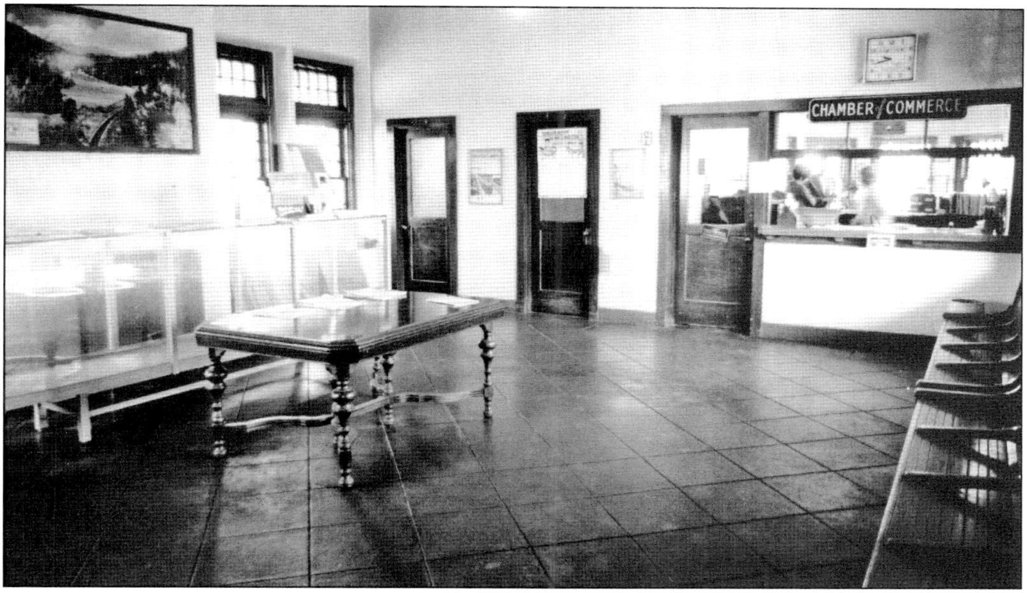


This photograph and the previous one were taken in April 1964, when the chamber of commerce occupied the San Carlos depot. Since 1983, Mary Abolmoluki has operated the Depot Café, serving an all-American menu. She prides herself on creating a homey atmosphere, decorating nearly every wall surface with railroad photographs. (Reg McGovern.)

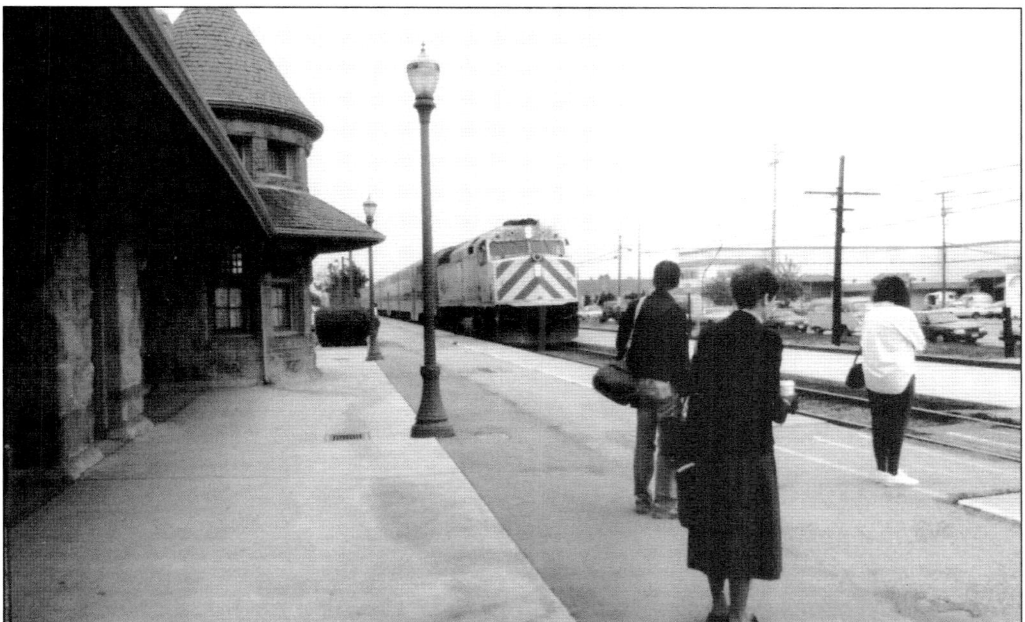

In 1982, the San Carlos depot was the first the state purchased for restoration. Caltrans reroofed it with slate and repainted the depot to match the original colors. Entertainment and speeches marked the 1988 centennial celebration of the local landmark, which was once a post office, church, and library. When the railroad tracks were grade-separated at Holly Street in 1999, great care was taken to preserve the depot. (Caltrain.)

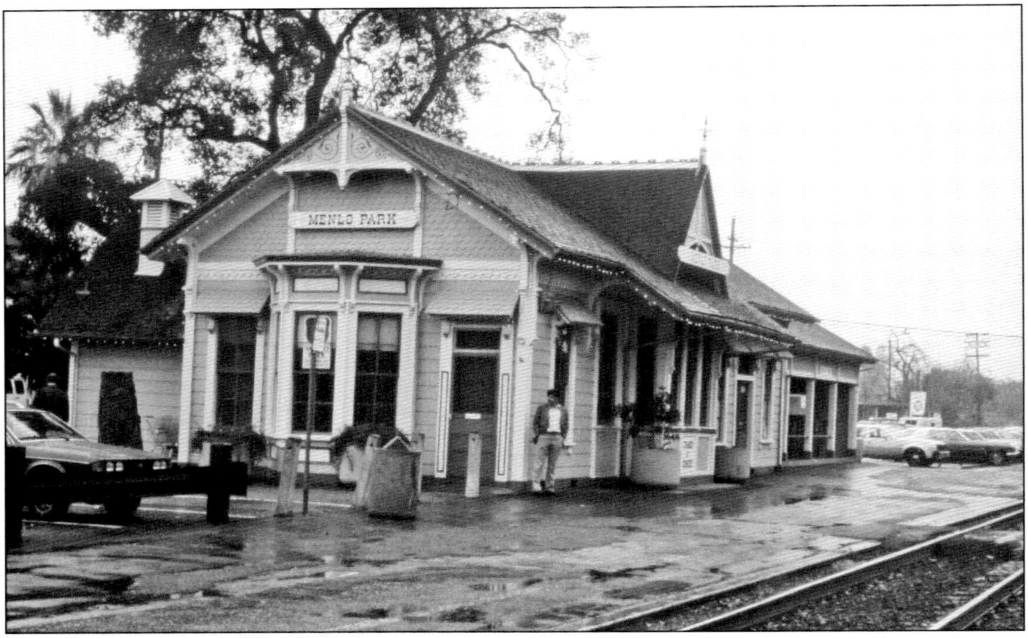


Built in 1867, the Menlo Park depot is the second oldest on the Peninsula line and has a distinct charm. Originally in the "Picturesque Cottage" style, it was remodeled in 1890 in preparation for the opening of Stanford University the next year. The Victorian trim and shingles ornamenting the gables were added then. (Steve Miller.)

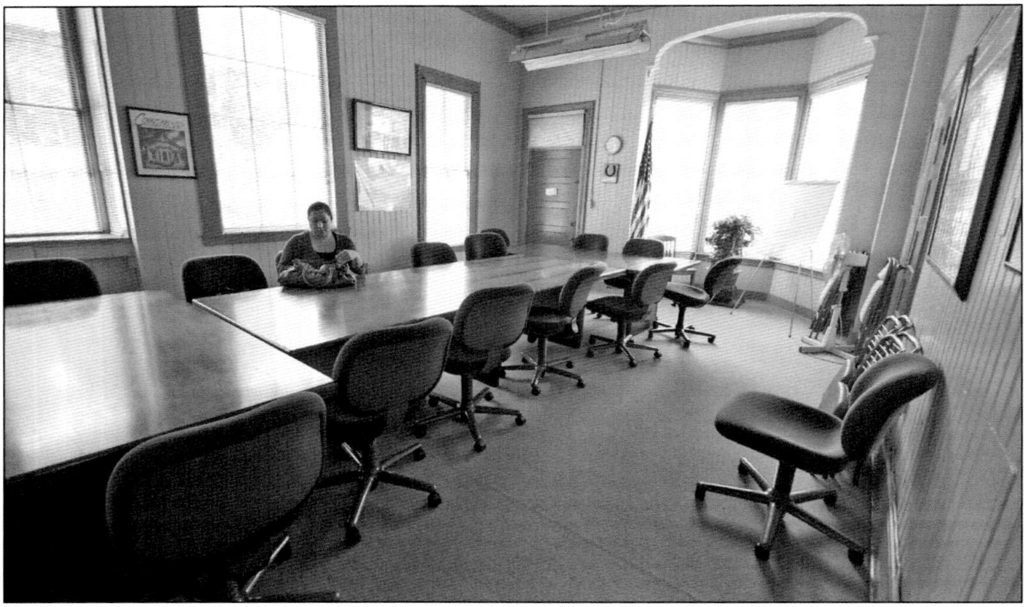

The Menlo Park Chamber of Commerce has had its office in the depot since 1960. The room shown in this picture was the ladies' waiting room of the 1867 depot, with a general waiting room on the north and the station master's office between them. In 1987, Caltrans completed a $500,000 rehabilitation project. Landscaping, a new clock tower and fountain, an enclosed bicycle storage area, and parking were provided. (Reg McGovern.)

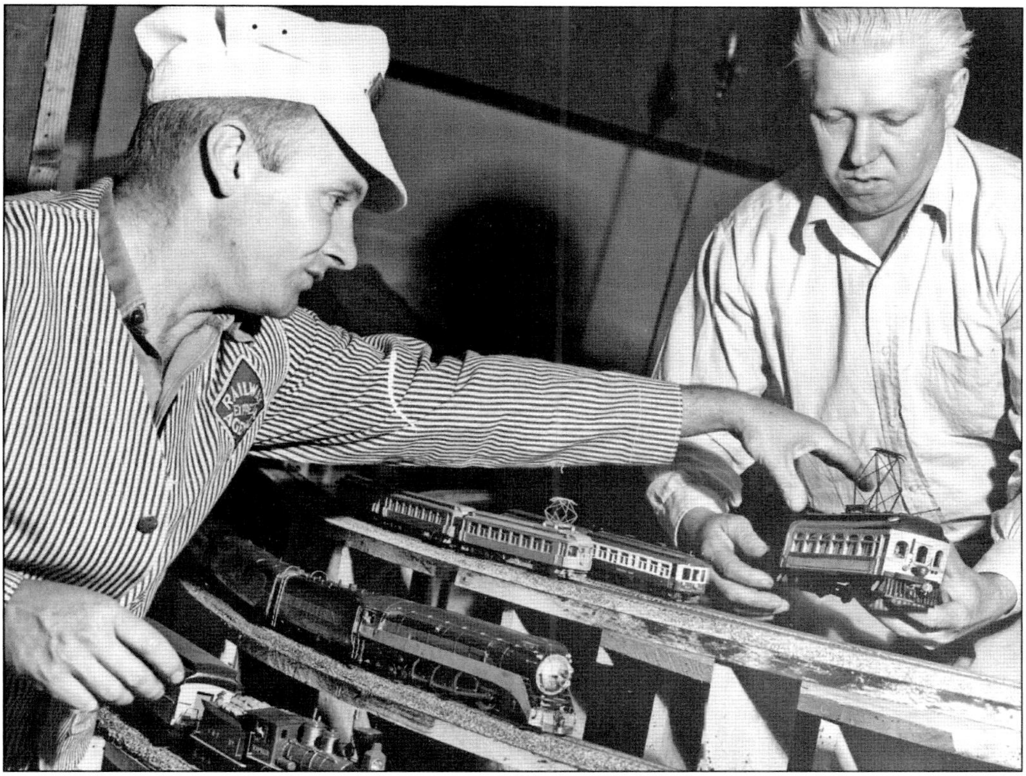

The West Bay Model Railroad Association was organized in 1947 by Jerry White, a Redwood City machinist who made model trains for a living. The group's elaborate layouts were set up inside a small redwood baggage house southeast of the SP depot in Menlo Park. Other early members included railroad employees, as well as pure aficionados who enjoyed getting together on Wednesday night, "play night." These 1950s photographs show members Joe Moore (above, left) and Henry Sprague checking out an interurban car. In the photograph at right, Silas Mattingly carefully places his model *California Zephyr* on one of the multiple tracks. The West Bay group still enjoys inviting visitors to watch the model trains run. (Both, Reg McGovern.)

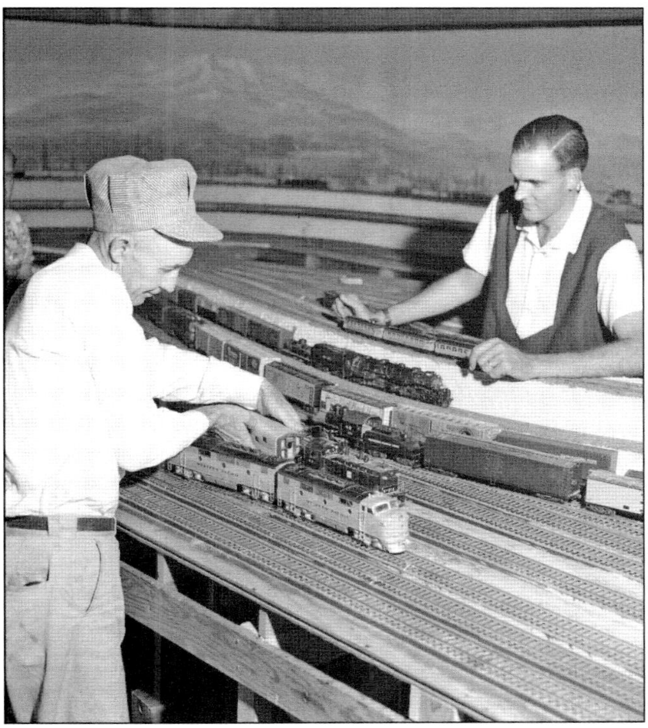

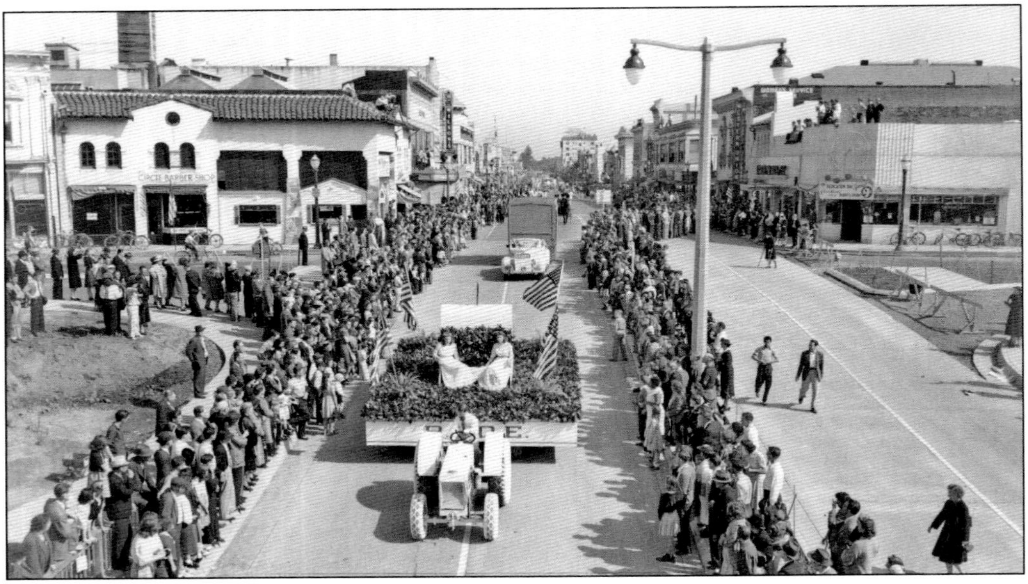

An elaborate ceremony heralded the March 8, 1941, opening of Palo Alto's University Avenue depot. The main line track and depot had to be relocated because of the construction of the underpass. The event was linked to the 50th anniversary of the founding of Stanford University by Leland Stanford, one of the leaders behind the transcontinental railroad. The reinforced concrete depot had 1,325-foot platforms and a subway passageway to reach the northbound track. The depot is an example of Streamlined Moderne architecture, a form using materials appropriate to the Machine Age. (Both, Henry Bender collection.)

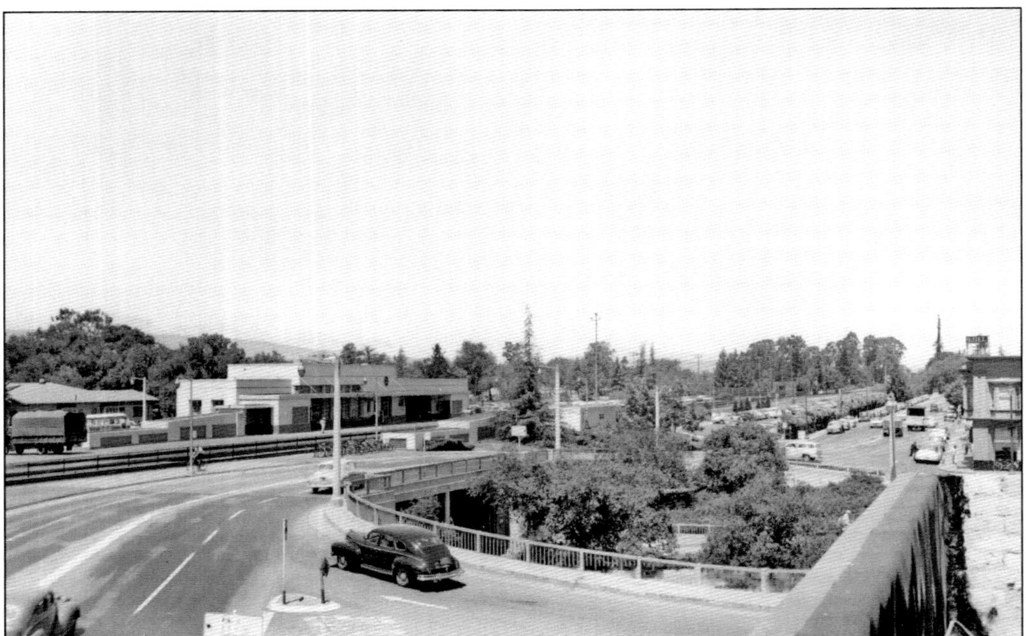

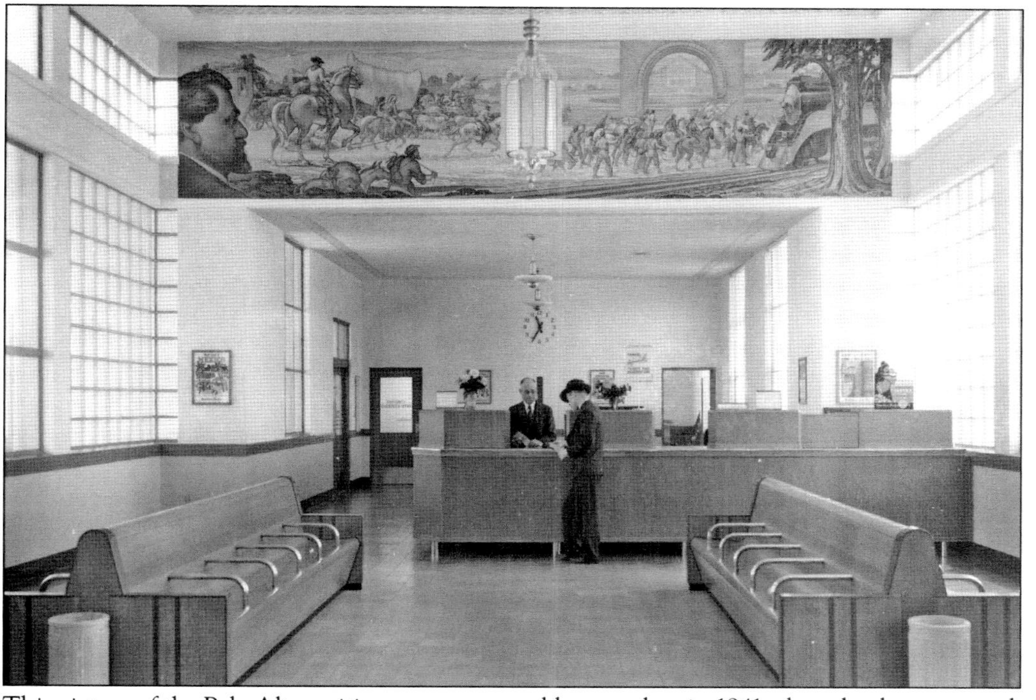

This picture of the Palo Alto waiting room presumably was taken in 1941 when the depot opened. The 26-foot-long mural above the ticket counter by painter John MacQuarrie portrays the changing story of California transportation, from stagecoaches to Streamliners. MacQuarrie also painted a mural at the San Jose terminal. (Henry Bender collection.)

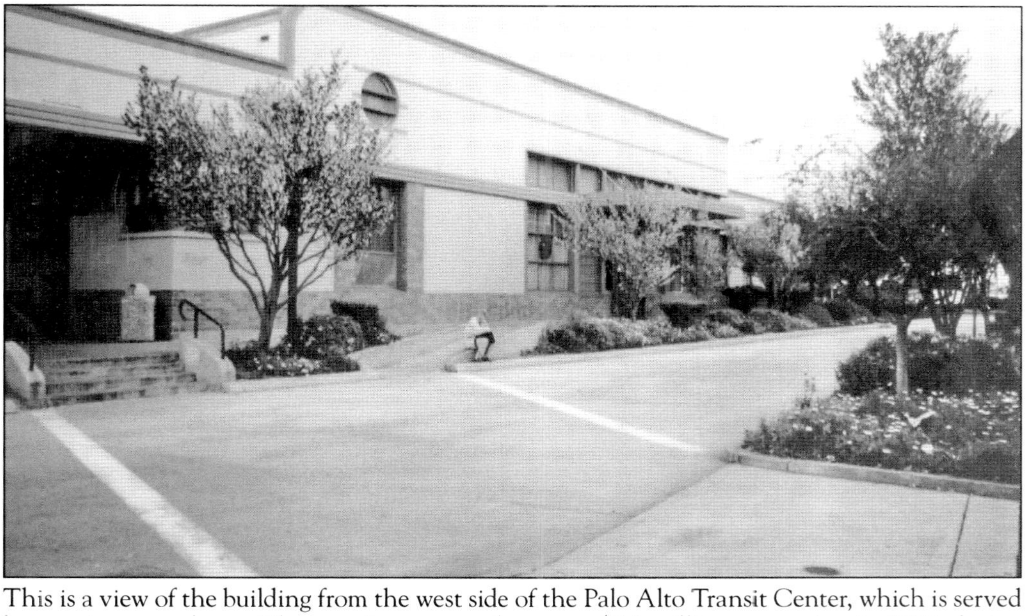

This is a view of the building from the west side of the Palo Alto Transit Center, which is served by transit agency buses. The transit center underwent a $7.5-million renovation in 2006, during which the depot floors, bathrooms, and lighting fixtures were restored or repaired. A Bikestation where cyclists can park their bikes is in the former baggage room next to the depot. (Caltrain.)

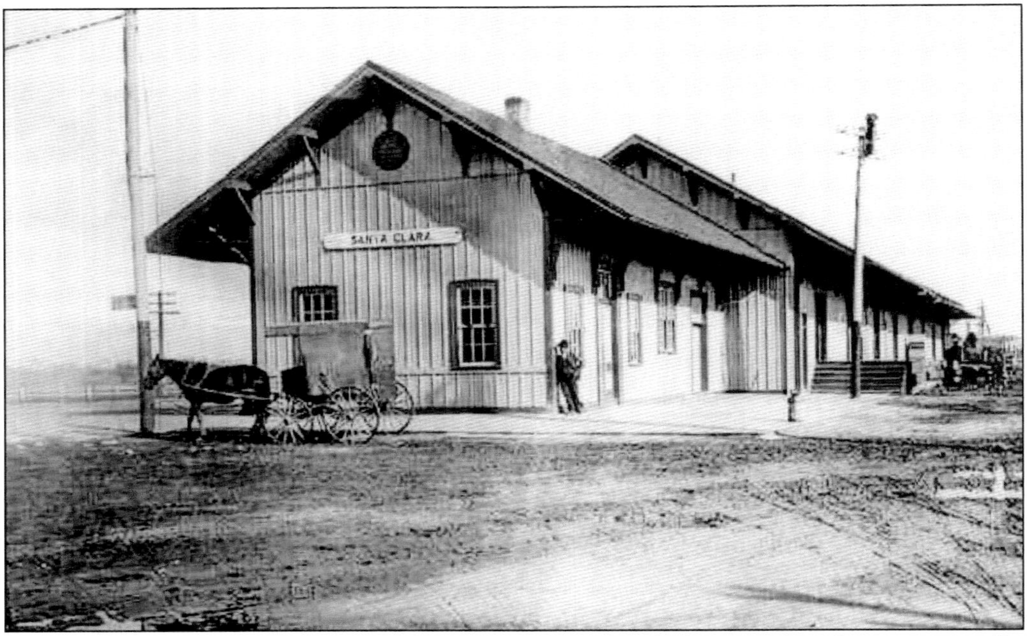


Work on the Santa Clara depot started in 1863 and it opened Christmas Eve that year. Initially, the passenger portion of the depot stood on the opposite side of the tracks but it was moved in 1877 to the present location on the west side of the tracks and joined to the freight shed. This photograph was taken in 1912. (SBHRS.)

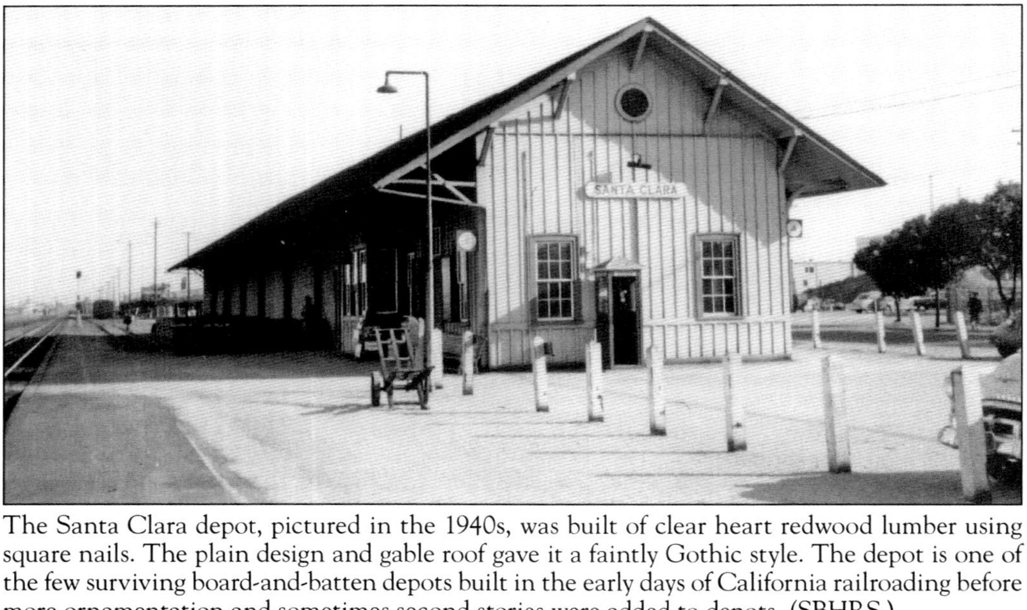


The Santa Clara depot, pictured in the 1940s, was built of clear heart redwood lumber using square nails. The plain design and gable roof gave it a faintly Gothic style. The depot is one of the few surviving board-and-batten depots built in the early days of California railroading before more ornamentation and sometimes second stories were added to depots. (SBHRS.)

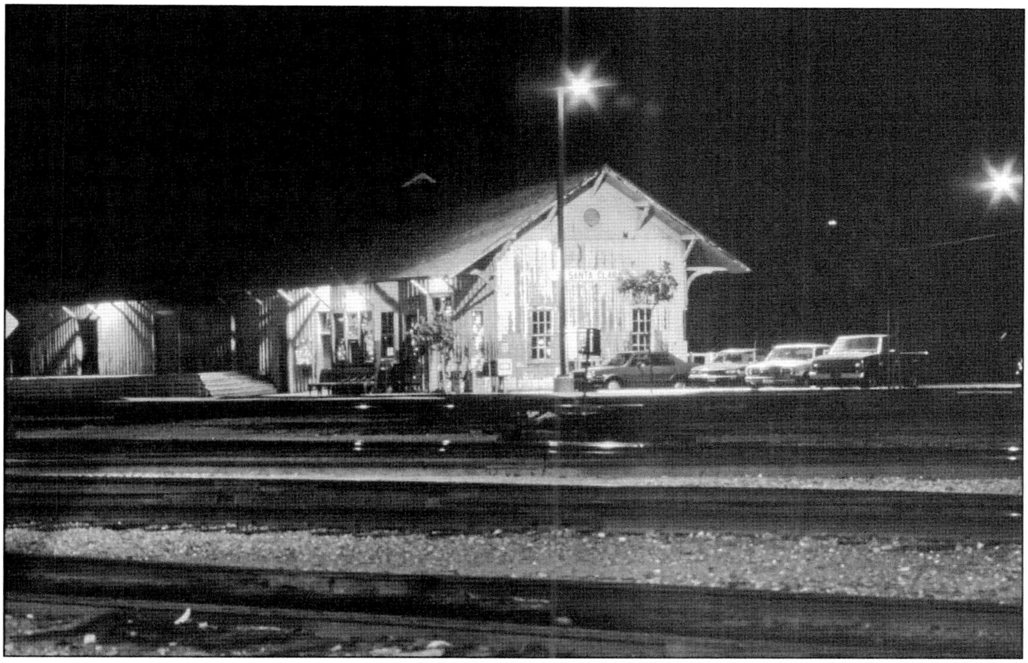

The Santa Clara depot, seen in 1982, had fallen into a state of disrepair before Caltrans acquired it from the Southern Pacific in 1983. Originally a deep reddish-brown, the building had been repainted light green and pink; not only had it faded, but it obviously needed repainting. In 1985, the South Bay Historical Railroad Society approached Caltrans and entered into a lease agreement to rehabilitate the depot. (Bill Kepner.)

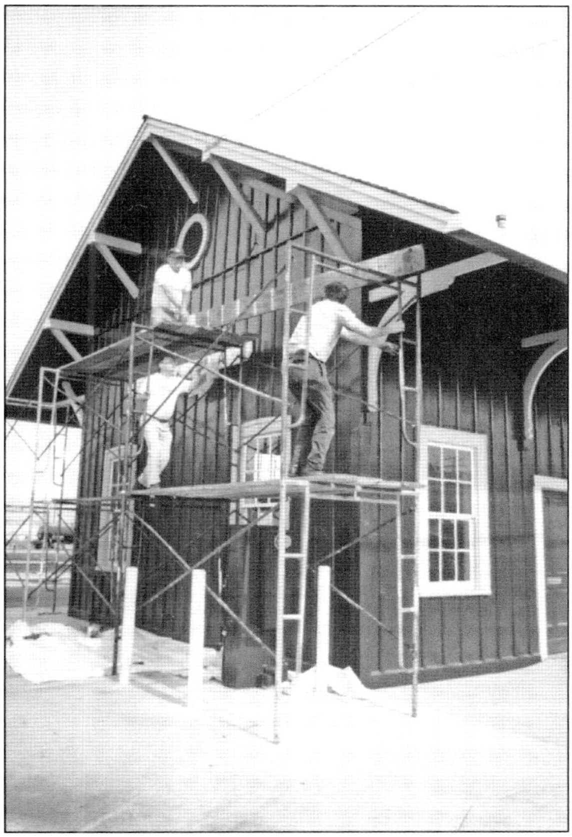

With city grants totaling $32,000 and community support, SBHRS members invested some 50,000 hours of labor over seven-and-a-half years to restore the depot. The work involved replacement of 30 percent of the dock supports, the dock deck, and inside floors. Freight doors were repaired and the depot was fumigated, reroofed, and painted. Repair and upkeep continues; witness this 1996 repainting work. (Caltrain.)

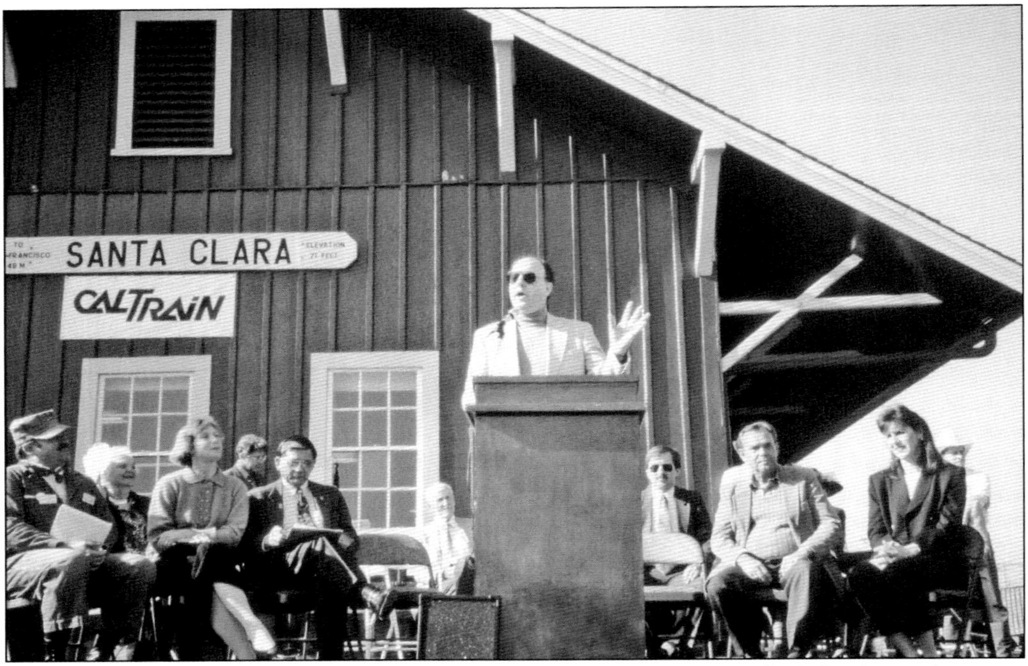


Jerry Kirzner, the JPB's first rail services director, spoke at Santa Clara at a January 15–16, 1994, event celebrating the 130th anniversary of the depot and of the railroad, which got its start as the San Francisco & San Jose Railroad. More than 10,000 attended and toured the depot. The Golden Gate Railroad Museum's steam locomotive No. 2472 added to the festivities. (Caltrain.)

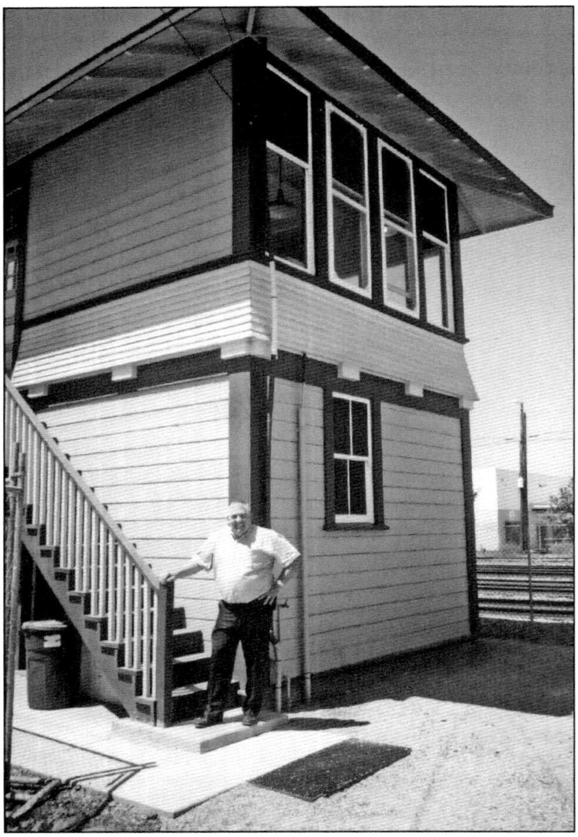

In addition to the depot, the SBHRS has restored the two-story interlocking tower, which was built in 1926 and was used to safely route trains. The tower operator pulled levers to "lock in" a route for trains, using a 48-lever interlocking machine that controlled 18 signals and 10 switches. Photographed in 2002, Chuck Catania managed the restoration. (Caltrain.)

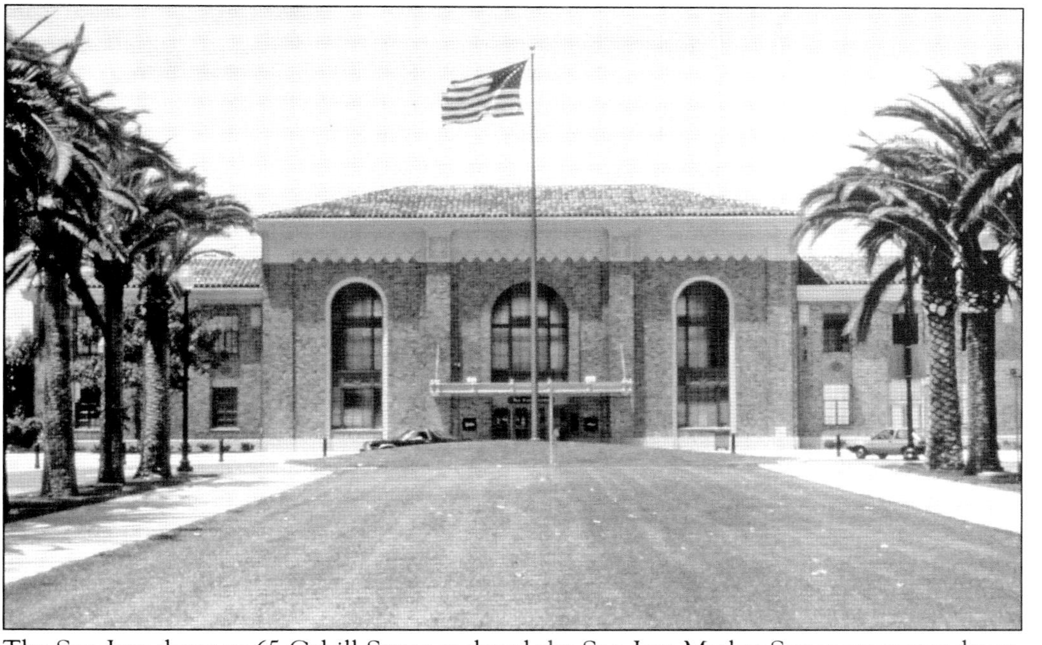

The San Jose depot at 65 Cahill Street replaced the San Jose Market Street passenger depot, which opened in 1883. The new depot was built because of the relocation of the main line through San Jose and opened on December 30, 1935. The depot was designed in the Italian Renaissance Revival style by Southern Pacific architect John H. Christie. (Caltrain.)

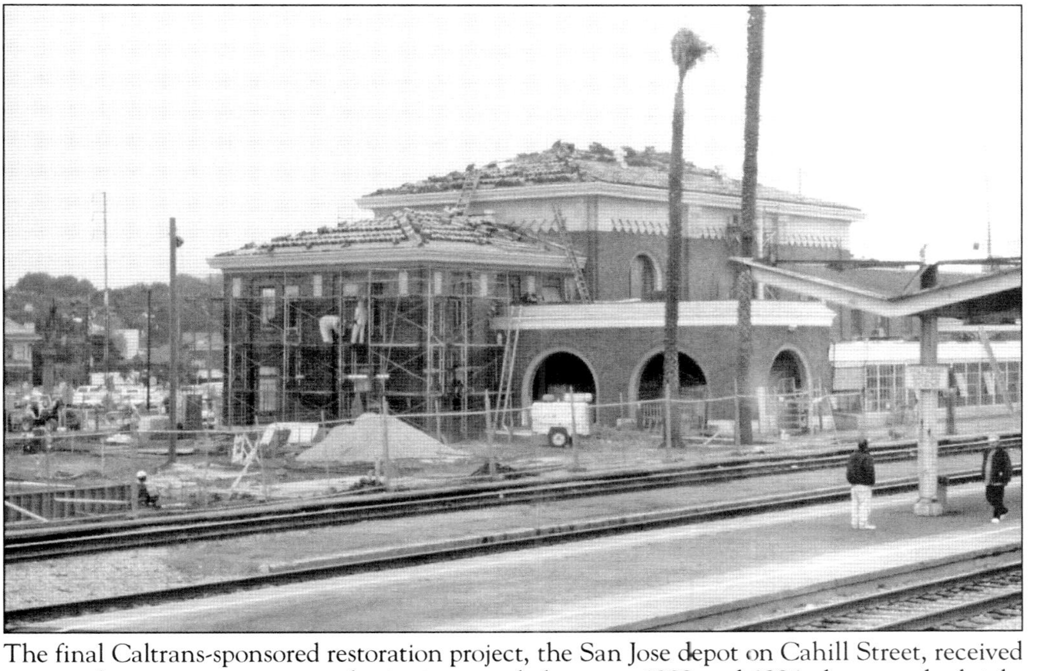

The final Caltrans-sponsored restoration project, the San Jose depot on Cahill Street, received a meticulous reconstruction and seismic upgrade between 1992 and 1994, down to the bricks and terra-cotta roof tiles. This is the view of the rear of the terminal, taken from the platform area. (Caltrain.)

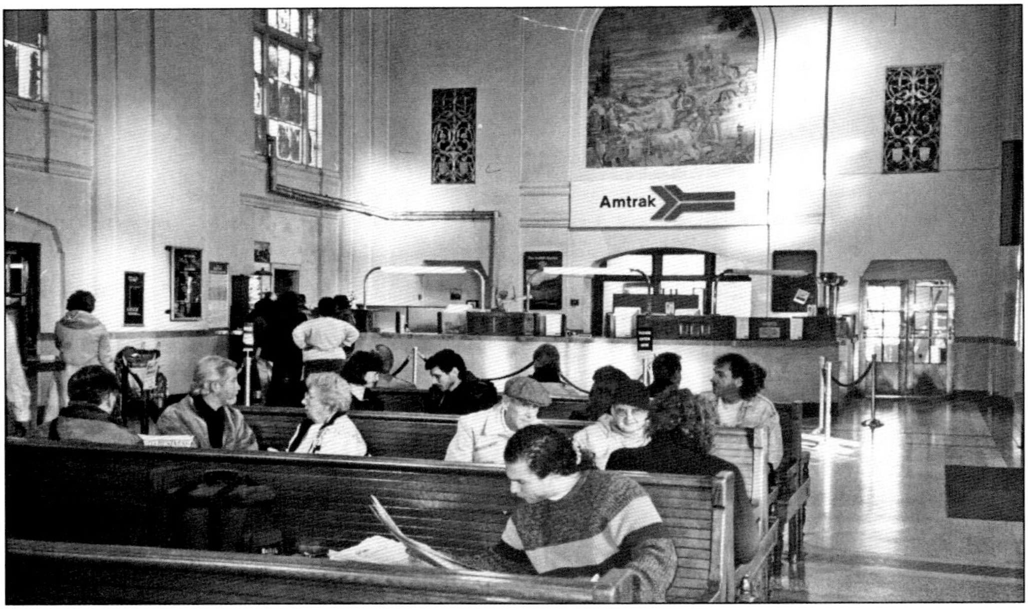


Great effort was made to achieve historical authenticity in the restoration. Test after test of color samples was required to match the original Caenstone walls of the waiting room. Paint had to be removed from the windows, and the interior needed cleaning. The restoration and seismic upgrade cost $5 million, shared among Caltrans, the Federal Transit Administration, and the Santa Clara Valley Transportation Agency. (Caltrain.)

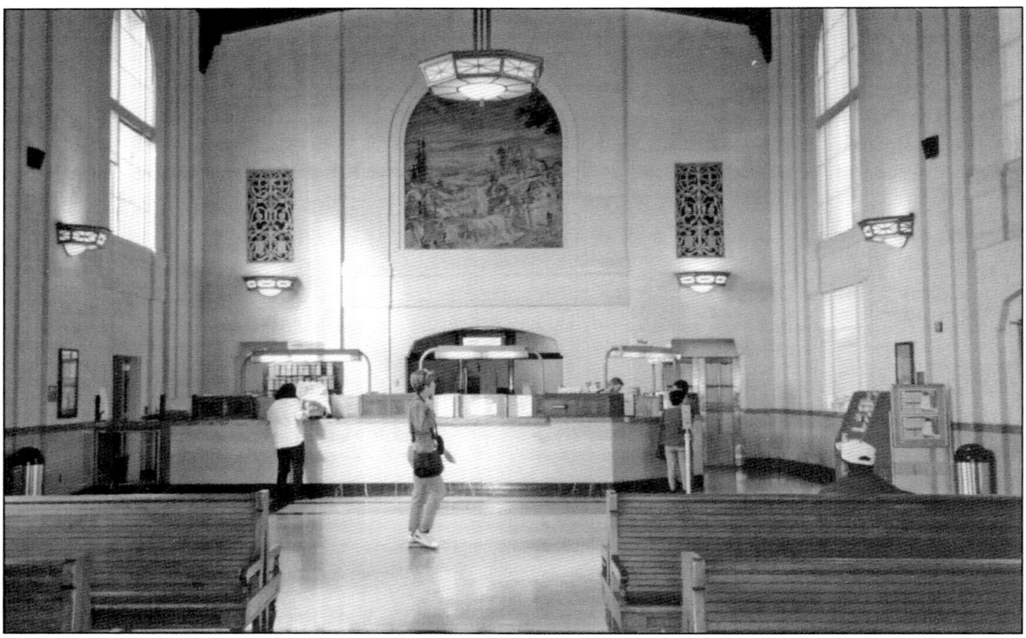

The beautiful features of the depot shone brighter, among them the marble and terrazzo floor and three enormous Art Deco–style chandeliers. Behind the ticket counter, the mural by artist John MacQuarrie was cleaned and restored. The early Santa Clara Valley scene depicted presents a wedding party arriving in the foreground, with a train crossing the panorama behind it. (Reg McGovern.)

After the 1994 renovation, the Cahill Street depot was renamed "San Jose Diridon" in 1994 in honor of then-Santa Clara County supervisor Rod Diridon, a charter member of the Peninsula Corridor Joint Powers Board. Diridon's role in transportation is included in the Way to San Jose exhibit in the waiting room. A few years later, additional work was done on the platforms, where canopies had considerable rust and deterioration, as seen in these before and after views. In addition to Caltrain's commute and weekend trains, Amtrak's *Coast Starlight*, the *Capitol Corridor*, and the *Altamont Commuter Express* trains, originating in Stockton, use the five platforms. (Right, Greg Welker; below, Caltrain.)

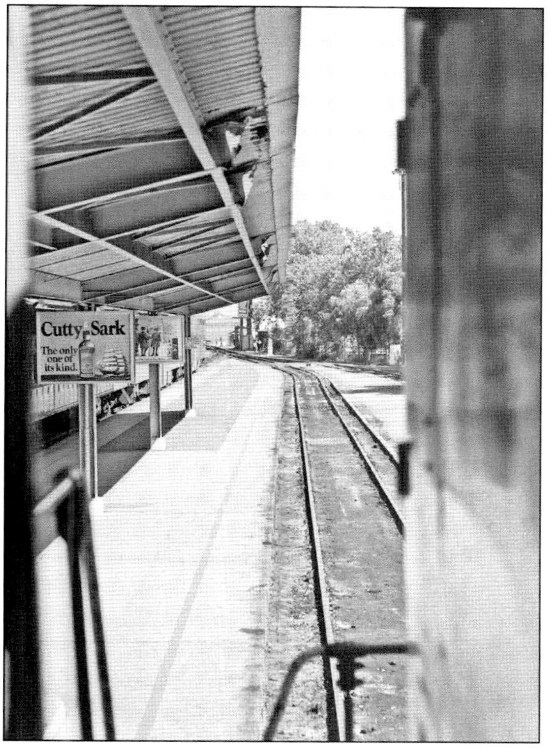


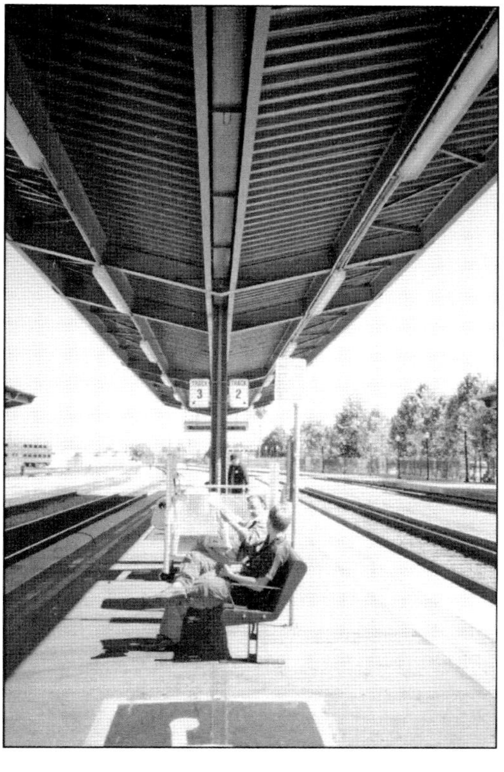